BASIC TEXTS IN COUNSELLING AND PSYCHOTHERAPY

Series Editor: Stephen Frosh

This series introduces readers to the theory and practice of counselling and psychotherapy across a wide range of topic areas. The books appeal to anyone wishing to use counselling and psychotherapeutic skills and are particularly relevant to workers in health, education, social work and related settings. The books are unusual in being rooted in psychodynamic and systemic ideas, yet being written at an accessible, readable and introductory level. Each text offers theoretical background and guidance for practice, with creative use of clinical examples.

Published

Jenny Altschuler
WORKING WITH CHRONIC ILLNESS

Bill Barnes, Sheila Ernst and Keith Hyde
AN INTRODUCTION TO GROUPWORK

Stephen Briggs
WORKING WITH ADOLESCENTS AND YOUNG ADULTS 2nd Edition

Alex Coren
SHORT-TERM PSYCHOTHERAPY

Emilia Dowling and Gill Gorell Barnes
WORKING WITH CHILDREN AND PARENTS THROUGH SEPARATION AND DIVORCE

Loretta Franklin
AN INTRODUCTION TO WORKPLACE COUNSELLING

Gill Gorell Barnes
FAMILY THERAPY IN CHANGING TIMES 2nd Edition

Fran Hedges
AN INTRODUCTION TO SYSTEMATIC THERAPY WITH INDIVIDUALS

Sally Hedges
COUNSELLING ADULTS WITH LEARNING DISABILITIES

Ravi Rana
COUNSELLING STUDENTS

Tricia Scott
INTEGRATIVE PSYCHOTHERAPY IN HEALTHCARE

Geraldine Shipton
WORKING WITH EATING DISORDERS

Laurence Spurling
AN INTRODUCTION TO PSYCHODYNAMIC COUNSELLING

Paul Terry
COUNSELLING AND PSYCHOTHERAPY WITH OLDER PEOPLE

Jan Wiener and Mannie Sher
COUNSELLING AND PSYCHOTHERAPY IN PRIMARY HEALTH CARE

Shula Wilson
DISABILITY, COUNSELLING AND PSYCHOTHERAPY

Steven Walker
CULTURALLY COMPETENT THERAPY

Invitation to authors

The Series Editor welcomes proposals for new books within the Basic Texts in Counselling and Psychotherapy series. These should be sent to Stephen Frosh at the School of Psychology, Birkbeck College, Malet Street, London, WC1E 7HX (email s.frosh@bbk.ac.uk)

Basic Texts in Counselling and Psychotherapy
Series Standing Order ISBN 0-333-69330-2

(outside North America only)

You can receive future titles in this series as they are published by placing a standing order. Please contact your bookseller or, in the case of difficulty, write to us at the address below with your name and address, the title of the series and the ISBN quoted above.

Customer Services Department, Macmillan Distribution Ltd,

Houndmills, Basingstoke, Hampshire RG21 6XS, England

WORKING WITH ADOLESCENTS AND YOUNG ADULTS

A CONTEMPORARY PSYCHODYNAMIC APPROACH

STEPHEN BRIGGS

First published 2008 by
PALGRAVE MACMILLAN

Palgrave Macmillan in the UK is an imprint of Macmillan Publishers Limited, registered in England, company number 785998, of Houndmills, Basingstoke, Hampshire RG21 6XS.

Palgrave Macmillan in the US is a division of St Martin's Press LLC, 175 Fifth Avenue, New York, NY 10010.

Palgrave Macmillan is the global academic imprint of the above companies and has companies and representatives throughout the world.

Palgrave® and Macmillan® are registered trademarks in the United States, the United Kingdom, Europe and other countries.

ISBN-13: 978-0-230-55141-1
ISBN-10: 0-230-55141-6

This book is printed on paper suitable for recycling and made from fully managed and sustained forest sources. Logging, pulping and manufacturing processes are expected to conform to the environmental regulations of the country of origin.

A catalogue record for this book is available from the British Library.

A catalog record for this book is available from the Library of Congress.

10   9   8   7   6   5   4   3   2   1

17 16 15 14 13 12 11 10 09 08

Printed and bound in China

CONTENTS

FOREWORD

In the last 50 years adolescence has forced its way into the consciousness of Western society, provoking anxiety, excitement and envy by turns in the older generation. While many of these reactions say more about the adults than the adolescents themselves, any serious student of adolescence can see that many of our young people are in deep trouble. This is witnessed by the increase in male adolescent suicides, or of young drug addicts, of the record levels of delinquency and violence in which young people are both perpetrators and victims.

Some of the tasks of adolescence captured by Stephen Briggs in Chapter 9 on leaving home – becoming a parent, becoming a student, becoming a worker, becoming a sexual partner – are now much more difficult in a world which is so complex and so rapidly changing. Young people do not have the bedrock of adult certainty to challenge and accommodate to, since most adults are themselves having to cope with such different circumstances from the situation of their own adolescence. For example, most jobs that young people are starting did not exist in their parents' generation and the jobs their parents had have disappeared. Gone are the days of following in the footsteps of parents. Thus the notion of a role model cannot be anything like as concrete as it once was. All the different aspects of becoming an adult require of young people a much deeper working through, of the tasks of adolescence in the context of parents – so vital for the support of young people – who find it much harder to contain them. In other words, it is very hard to help young people through a process which is so bewildering and anxiety-provoking for the adults themselves.

The challenge for professionals trying to help young people in trouble is clear. Society is slowly recognising that something needs to be done, but often professionals are thrust into tasks of helping young people only to find themselves faced with situations which are hard to understand and therefore hard to find ways of being constructive.

In order to deal with this, Stephen Briggs has produced a rather unique guidebook. The reader will find here a wealth of information on young people and how to go about trying to help them. His psychodynamic approach allows the reader a way of describing and understanding adolescents' deepest fears and conflicts. What he then does is to show how these fears interact with the complexities of the external lives of young people. How do they form a new, more adult identity? Briggs sees adolescent identity as being formed out of relationships – it is for him an interpersonal identity. He plots through adolescent development how their sense of subjectivity gradually changes, including the complexity of being part of a multi-ethnic society, which he explores through the experiences of teenagers from different ethnic backgrounds. The need to find ways of managing this particular task, especially now, must be one of the most important of all.

The question of parenting and working with adolescents and their impact on institutions takes us back to the problem that professionals have in working with adolescents. Young people can get 'under our skin', and we find ourselves full of and often paralysed by the very feelings which the young people cannot deal with. Briggs shows how this can be understood as the imparting of feeling – the projection – into those who are trying to care for them. Often these experiences are unpleasant and alarming as well as frustrating, but when we can understand the process then at least the struggle can be seen as relevant and helpful in our attempts to come alongside young people and help them find their lost hope and courage.

Adolescence is an odyssey which requires courage and a capacity to face loneliness, and many cannot manage this alone. In *Working with Adolescents*, Stephen Briggs helps readers help young people to resume this journey when they have lost their way, or given up altogether. It will sustain professionals in their efforts to struggle with the young people they are trying to help.

Robin Anderson
Member of the British Psychoanalytic Society
Consultant Psychiatrist
Former Chair of the Adolescent Department, Tavistock Clinic

ACKNOWLEDGEMENTS

The source of this book is the experience of working with adolescents and their families in the Adolescent Department of the Tavistock Clinic, and, over the years, many teachers, colleagues and students have provided me with rich opportunities for thinking about working with young people; among those to whom I am most grateful are Robin Anderson, Anna Dartington, Joanne Silove, Elizabeth Oliver Bellasis, Gianna Williams, Helene Dubinsky, Louise Lyon, Margot Waddell, Deirdre Moylan, Alessandra Lemma, Liz Webb, Jeannie Milligan, Andrew Cooper and Marion Bower. I am also grateful for the enriching experiences of discussing, particularly problems of suicidality, with John T. Maltsberger, Mark Goldblatt and Reinhard Lindner. The opportunities provided through the University of East London, initially in the psychosocial studies group and latterly in social work and the Centre for Social Work Research, have been invaluable for exploring the meeting points between psychoanalytic and social theories and the policy implications. This has also at the heart of the collaboration with my co-editor, Lynn Froggett, on the *Journal of Social Work Practice*.

I am grateful, too, to Stephen Frosh and to Catherine Gray, both of whom have helped me with their support and always acute editorial comments. I wish to acknowledge the many young people I have worked with, and who formed the basis for the case examples used in the book. All case material is disguised and fictionalised in order to preserve confidentiality and anonymity.

Finally, everyone in my family has played a huge part in supporting, including discussing the development of the book, generating ideas and opinions and always sustaining me.

INTRODUCTION TO THE SECOND EDITION

For this second edition of *Working with Adolescents,* the aim has been to update the text to ensure its contemporary relevance. This is a complex process, since the impact of thinking about how adolescence changes in different eras often has a very contradictory impact; sometimes it seems that everything has changed, sometimes it seems that it is just as it always was. This is a particular trick of adolescence, and a window into feeling adolescent. The complaint of the shepherd in Shakespeare's *The Winter's Tale*:

> I would there were no age between ten and three-and-twenty, or that youth would sleep out the rest, for there is nothing in the between but getting wenches with child, wronging the ancientry, stealing, fighting.
>
> (Shakespeare, 1611/1996)

shows that three central pillars of adolescence – sex, aggression and opposing authority – have been part and parcel of adolescence for centuries. On the other hand some things do change and are different. This is true for the time that has elapsed since writing the first edition of this book.

In the first edition I pointed out some emerging trends – for adolescence to last longer, for it to be more characterised by diversity, certainly more than was usually allowed for by earlier theories of adolescence. Changes in society had brought into question the meaning of identity; identity needs conceptualising now as more plural, elusive and complex; given the history of the term 'identity', it seemed preferable to work more now with the idea of 'subjectivity' or in a developmental sense, 'subjectivation' (or 'becoming a subject'). These trends that were proposed in the first edition have persisted, and then work of updating the text for the second edition has included – often – making what was perhaps tentative in the first edition more substantive in the second, together with gathering and demonstrating the relevant evidence. Thus the first edition seems now to have selected some fruitful lines.

There is now no mistaking the fact that, particularly concerning the transition to adulthood, a major rethink of traditional theorising is required, within which some more relevant models of identity forming need describing and explicating; this includes the way that contemporary contexts impact on the inner worlds of young people and the particular internal resources they need to undertake the developmental stresses of adolescence. Alongside this, there are distinct differences in the way that society – through the media and policymaking – views adolescence and its problems, and there are significant differences in the context of providing professional services. I will briefly outline how these issues have influenced the revisions I have made to this book.

Firstly, there has been an intensification of the anxieties experienced by society about adolescence. This is demonstrated through social policy and media attention to new forms of 'folk devils', including the manifestations of drug and alcohol misuse, 'hoodies', gangs, violence against others – including knife and gun crime – depression, self-harm and suicidality. Concern about adolescent development has been evidenced by research in the UK, reporting that time trends show an increase in adolescent mental health difficulties (Collishaw et al., 2004), by surveys that indicate high rates of depression and self-harm, for example the *Truth Hurts* inquiry (Brophy, 2006). As I write this introduction, there is a current focus in the media on gangs, particularly where drugs and violence are involved. Anxiety about contemporary adolescence is not confined to the UK. For example, in two visits to Italy, I encountered, firstly, agonised media attention for a young woman, who had been anorexic and then committed suicide in Rome, and, secondly, profound reaction to football crowd violence which had resulted in the death of a policeman. In this discourse, therefore, there is a strong statement that adolescent mental health is worsening, demonstrating some new kinds of problems and thus requiring new approaches to engage adolescents in helping professional services. It is also part of this discourse to link more closely the images of adolescent difficulties with mental health, and thus to put the problems in the lap of mental health services.

Alongside this, and running somewhat counter to this approach, is the evidence that adolescent experiences are profoundly affected by changing socio-economic contexts, which generate new psychological tasks and which reorganise the process and aims of adolescent development. The clearest marker for this is the lengthening of the transition to adulthood, a feature already apparent and commented upon in the first edition of this book, but substantiated since then in the emergence of theoretical discussions that recognise these changes and seek to make sense of them. These include the debate about whether there needs to be recognised a new phase of development – emerging adulthood – or, alternatively, whether greater responsibilities should be accorded to adolescents.[1] This debate is founded on the recognition that the uniquely late twentieth century and early twenty-first century organisation of the period of adolescence separates – in time-biological growth (puberty) from psychological maturity. This creates hazards and opportunities. Delaying the transition to taking up adult responsibilities can generate frustrations – which may be expressed in anti-social behaviour – and also provides opportunities for gathering skills needed in globalised and technically sophisticated adult work contexts, and in generating the inner resources needed for an uncertain and often confusing adulthood, characterised not by stability and continuity, but by turbulence, change and loss.

Further, discussions particularly focusing on the transition to adulthood have shown that class – or social and cultural capital, to use the more current terminology – has a great deal to do with whether an adolescent difficulty is likely to prove an enduring sign of psychosocial problems. When looking at the rates of disturbance and difficulty in adolescence, it is necessary to look at the liquid in the glass from two directions: it is both half full and half empty; some adolescents encounter profound and potentially socially excluding problems; others manage the personal and societal turbulence, maintain satisfying, close relatedness to others and begin working lives, supported by educational achievements.

In this context, the need for professionals is not simply that of taking in new information about adolescents today, but rather it includes understanding how professional intervention can be organised and delivered, based on an integrated understanding of the meaning of adolescence, and generating approaches to professional service delivery, in a range of health, social care and educational settings, that make sense in these contexts. In that work with adolescents requires distinctive skills, and that adolescent issues continue into the third decade, the development of discrete, specialised, multidisciplinary adolescent services that relate to the entire adolescent age range are urgently needed, both in the UK and worldwide (Patel et al., 2007). From a British perspective, the prescriptive, outcome-led and symptom-predominant approach to clinical services in risk aversive organisational cultures undermines the best way to help adolescents, which is through linking the psychological and social aspects of understanding (a psychosocial approach). Adolescence is a developmental period, albeit one in which the changes recently experienced have led to realignment of the key processes involved in aspects of development.

One of the key tensions for professionals in working with adolescents lies in recognising and assessing the extent or seriousness of a problem and weighing this against the individual's capacity for growth through development. This can lead to polarised views about the need for intervention or whether to allow time for development to take place. Getting involved in this process has the inevitable consequence of taking on some anxiety. The anxieties about adolescent troubles, and the kinds of destructive and self-destructive behaviours they can perpetrate, can lead to professionals feeling extreme emotional pressure when making these judgements. Becoming risk averse, or applying criteria for assessing pathologies that are more suited to adults, reduces options, and the capacity to notice opportunities for development is inevitably the first casualty. On the other hand, not intervening with sufficient vigour can leave an adolescent on course for adult mental health difficulties. These difficulties of assessment judgement are made more difficult when adults (including professionals) become estranged from understanding adolescence, or being alienated, or envious of adolescence, or frightened about presenting a professional authority, which is confident but also curious, and not omnipotent. Some prescribed treatments, and also some prescriptions about the difficulties of engaging adolescents, short-circuit the emotional experience of engaging with adolescence, which is the foundation for any work with young people. The approach discussed here aims to provide the knowledge for working openly and in an integrated way and also to help generate professional confidence.

For this edition, in view of the importance of the longer transition into adulthood and for professionals to recognise the importance of taking an adolescent-centred perspectives for the over-18s, I have retitled the book 'Working with Adolescents and Young Adults'. I have substantially rewritten Chapter 1 in order to fully explore the current debates and emerging knowledge about adolescent development in contemporary contexts, with particular emphasis placed on the two distinct phases of adolescence; the experience of and adjustment to puberty and the long transition to adulthood. Adolescent problems are discussed in detail in Chapters 6 and 7, including some new or extended discussions of depression, self-harm, body-image disturbance, gender identity, obesity, anti-social behaviour, including violence and drug and alcohol misuse. In Chapter 9, the process of entering adulthood is cast with the emphasis on 'becoming more adult', reflecting the later and less definite way that young adults leave home; how young adults take up different aspects of adulthood – through education, work, becoming a sexual partner and parenthood. The structure of the first edition has been retained, and Chapter 2 retains the emphasis on the process of adolescence, including the individual adolescent's experience of ownership of the adult sexual body, becoming more separate from parental figures, developing capacities for intimacy; in other words 'becoming a subject'. Some parts of the following chapters have been revised: Chapter 3 is an exploration of ethnicity and subjectivity, and in the second edition, takes note of the impact of recent political issues on ethnic identity; Chapter 4, 'Parenting Adolescents', takes into account the new context in which parenting may extend, partly at least, into the third decade; Chapter 5 addresses some of the key current organisational dynamics for working with adolescents, in the contexts of what has been described as a global crisis for adolescent services (Patel et al., 2007) and increasing risk-aversiveness (and hence defensiveness) in organisations; Chapter 8 includes some recent research and theory about suicidality. From a theoretical perspective, I have paid particular attention to the new theorising of contemporary adolescence from the perspective of social theory, gathering this together in Chapter 1 but using it wherever seems appropriate, to illustrate and advance the discussion. I have also made use of some recent theoretical developments from psychoanalysis, particularly regarding narcissism, and this particularly seems to fit the current contexts and offers understanding of why some adolescents seem to be able to turn away from destructive behaviour, in ways that an adult would be unlikely to manage. I have added to the case examples used to illustrate the discussion and, hopefully, generate the sense of what it actually means to work in this way.

The overall aim of the book, as I have said, is to enable professionals working therapeutically with adolescents to provide contemporarily relevant help, which integrates social and psychological perspectives and which provides the basis for engaging with and making sense of the profound emotional experiences of working with adolescents. The aim is therefore to appeal to a wide range of professionals, including those who are new to the field and also those who, though experienced and perhaps well-trained, have a need now to develop understanding of working with adolescents.

Adolescence is a momentous time. The changes that take place and the experiences of getting to know oneself and others, while developing a sense of a complex identity and place in the world, bring anxieties, vulnerabilities, opportunities and much to think about. Also, professionals working with adolescents and young adults have a lot to think about, and it is hoped that this book will stimulate thinking as well as provide guidance in the exacting but rewarding endeavour of working with young people.

CONTEMPORARY ADOLESCENCE: STILL THE 'AGE BETWEEN'?

Contemporary adolescence is organised now around two distinct phases. The transition from childhood to early adolescence, through the impact of puberty, is a period of intense growth and far-reaching changes – physically, cognitively, emotionally. This is followed by a long transition into adulthood, which, though inclusive of diverse 'pathways', is usually extended, lasting approximately for a decade from mid/late teens until the mid-twenties. Primarily affected by social changes, this long transition to adulthood severely tests traditional thinking about the adolescent process, particularly the central concept of identity formation. Upheavals in the social world and the changing contexts for young people mean that a new sense of turbulence has become apparent, evidenced by concerns about increasing adolescent mental health problems and the emergence of new kinds of problems.

This chapter elaborates on emerging new ways of characterising adolescence and explores the meaning of the two distinct 'phases' of development. This leads to an evaluative discussion about the limits of some traditional theories and provides some newer ways of orienting to adolescence from a psychosocial perspective. Linking with this are considerations about ways of working therapeutically with young people in difficulties. Bion's theory of container-contained is applied to thinking about ways in which anxieties of contemporary adolescence can be understood and addressed.

From the 'age between' to a central life stage

In the middle decades of the twentieth century, adolescence – though recognised as an important period for growth and development, and often a troublesome one for adolescents and those in contact with them – was treated as a kind of passing phase. Derek Miller (1969), one of the founders of the Tavistock Clinic's Adolescent Department,[1] described adolescence as 'the age between', a relatively short period of transition between childhood and adulthood, characterised by rapid changes and growth and playing a very significant role in the maturation of the individual. The 'age between' was divided into three stages: early adolescence, organised by the experience of puberty; mid-adolescence, when there may be a short period of opposition to authority, 'lasting 6 months or so', following which the adolescent entered late adolescence, left school and became 'adult'. In late adolescence, the preoccupation was with 'trying out' the inner resources that had been developed over childhood as the adolescent entered adult society.

The idea of the 'age between' positions adolescence as a transient state, preoccupied with leaving one age – childhood – and entering another – adulthood. The space in the 'age between' is therefore filled by loss and expectation, which intermingle to generate the particular tensions and turbulence of adolescence. The period in which Miller wrote – the 1960s – was a fertile period for theorising adolescence, but – almost imperceptibly initially, and then unavoidably obviously – changes in the context for and experiences of adolescence have become so great that a yawning gap now exists between these early theorisations and the actual experience of adolescents today. Despite some reports to the contrary,[2] the beginning of adolescence has changed very little in the past 50 years, in that puberty starts at around the same time and extends over the same period of 4–5 years (between the ages of 10 and 15); the period of transition to adulthood has lengthened significantly. Gluckman and Hanson (2006) show that the age at which adolescent to adult transitions are completed – using marriage and parenthood as indicators – is as late as 29/30 today, against 23/24 in the middle of the twentieth century.[3] Whereas, to use Miller's work again as an example, adolescence was thought to end with the teenage years, contemporary views consider adolescence as extending to the mid or even late twenties. There is evidence that adolescents today who complete the transition to adulthood by the end of the teenage years are disadvantaged and at risk of social exclusion (Jones, 2006). The length of adolescence is one key factor that suggests that the idea of the 'age between' inadequately conveys the meaning of contemporary adolescence; a period lasting for a span of 15–20 years is impossibly long to stay 'between'.

Along with the extension in time, the adolescent process is thought of as increasingly complex; this is accompanied by some fierce debates. Firstly, there has been controversy over whether the early adolescent period is inevitably turbulent and characterised by conflict between adolescents and their parents. Secondly, it has been asserted that the problems of adolescence are getting worse and the mental health of young people is deteriorating. Thirdly, it has been disputed whether the problems of adolescence are 'cured' by the passing of time, or whether interventions are required to prevent the onset of psychosocial difficulties that endure into adulthood. These debates are indicative of the changing nature of adolescence and initiate the need to reconceptualise based on the emergence of greater knowledge – from different sources – about both the early adolescent experiences of puberty and the later sojourn in the long period of role transition to adulthood. We can begin to explore these issues through a case example:

Case example: turbulence or transition?

Maria requested a therapeutic consultation when she was 21, because feeling depressed and having a lack of self-confidence in herself increasingly troubled her. In her consultation, Maria was very tearful and said that she felt 'stupid' for being so easily moved to tears. She felt she should be stronger, but that she is 'pathetic'. She said she is very close to her parents, especially her mother, with whom 'she could talk about almost anything'. Her mixed-race parents got on OK too, though they had had some difficulties when she was younger, when they had argued a lot about her older stepbrother, mother's son.

Maria said her adolescence had not been particularly difficult or traumatic. There had been very little conflict between her and her parents. She had got on well at school, had progressed to university, continuing to live at home, and was nearing the end of her course. She had many friends, enjoyed a 'going out' lifestyle and had boyfriends. One of these had been serious for a time, but though she is still keen on him, he wants 'some space'. Now, in comparison with her teens she is 'very up and down', and she described within herself feeling 'wobbly, not at all solid'. She felt others around her were more secure and more confident. Her brother in particular 'made her feel stupid'. He and his friends could talk about things – like chaos theory and complexity – but she felt she had nothing to say. She wished she could talk like them. She felt she ought to be more independent, especially that she ought to be more separate from her mother, but she did not like being alone and did not know what she wanted to do in the future.

Maria's situation illustrates some of the key features that need to be taken into account when thinking about contemporary adolescence.

She lives in a mixed-race reconstituted family and lives at home while going to university. She is asking for therapeutic help at the age of 21, when, in traditional terms, she would be considered 'adult' rather than 'adolescent'. She is depressed, uncertain as to why, and she comments on the closeness and openness of her relationship with her mother and her lack of conflict in her teens.

Maria's is one narrative about adolescence, and one of the crucial features of contemporary adolescence – and thinking about adolescence – is that there is considerable diversity. It is misleading to think, still, about a single normative experience of adolescence. Thus the case example introduces – but cannot inclusively represent – some key issues.

Consistent with the idea of the 'age between' was the view that, though inevitably turbulent, the adolescent's need and drive towards development led to the resolution of the problems of adolescence. Time was the cure:

> Whilst this is a time of turbulence, disturbance and struggle, often of inner uncertainties and chaos, the adolescent's growing discovery of his [sic] own sexually maturing body and physical strength, alongside his developing mind and intellect, usually enables him to move from dependence to independence.
>
> (Wise, 2000, p. 7)

Ruggiero (2006, p. 550) describes how thinking about adolescence has veered between 'a historical opposition between "sitting on the fence" (A. Freud, Winnicott, Meltzer) and being more interventionist (prevalent today)'. In 'sitting on the fence', there is faith in development trusting 'to the vis medicatrix naturae (healing power of time)'.

The more interventionist approach focuses on the way that adolescent difficulties transform into adult psychosocial disorders, for which a preventive, interventionist approach with adolescents is needed. Yet this is not simply a debate about whether either view – intervention or trusting to nature – is 'correct', for lying beneath the surface is a conflict about whether the emotional impact of adolescence can be tolerated, or not, by others in contact with adolescents. The non-interventionists seem, today, to have a touching faith in development, which is perhaps contrary to the evidence that difficulties first occurring at adolescence persist into adulthood. Contained in the non-interventionist approach, though, is a greater willingness and capacity to tolerate adolescence, not to be made unduly anxious by it, nor 'phased' by the intense emotional impact adolescents can exert on anyone close to them. The intervention-ists, on the other hand, are preoccupied with identifying risks. Two approaches towards risks are available: they can be either modified, through thought, or avoided, through risk aversion. This distinction is important for the delivery of services to adolescents, as we shall see later (Chapter 5).

The view that intervention is necessary is particularly influenced by recent epidemiological studies that show that most adult disorders begin in adolescence, between the ages of 12 and 24,[4] though often these are not detected until adulthood. Between one in four and one in five adolescents have a recognisable mental disorder in any year (Patel et al., 2007). Of course this fact can be looked at from two directions. The vast majority of adolescents (four in every five) do not have mental ill health. It is not true, therefore, that all adolescents fit the stereotype of being unstable (Graham, 2004). It is important to recognise that some adolescents succeed in negotiating adolescence: understanding why and in what circumstances is possible once this is accepted. On the other hand, a significant minority of adolescents have a recognisable mental disorder, and this implies that the risks and hazards, to which adolescents can be exposed, leave them vulnerable to the development of psychosocial disorders, which peak during the adolescent years. Suicide, self-harm, substance misuse, offending behaviour, depression and eating disorders are among the risks. Rather than growing out of these problems, if untreated, they can persist into adulthood and have detrimental effects on adult functioning (Smith and Rutter, 1995; Graham, 1986; Achenbach, 1998; Patel et al., 2007; Toumburou et al., 2007).

> The mental health of young people is enormously vulnerable because of the many, diverse challenges they face in adolescence and also because of a propensity to engage in at-risk behaviour. Some young people are also exposed to harmful circumstances which affect their mental health … Singly or more usually in combination, these at-risk behaviours and adverse circumstances increase the vulnerability of young people to psychosocial disorders.
>
> (Baruch, 2001, p. 3)

From this perspective, adolescence is a highly vulnerable period, which requires intervention; just allowing maturation to take place would neglect the opportunities for intervening to reduce risks and at worst condemn the adolescent to long-term problems. Moreover, mental health problems have implications for other aspects of adolescent development, including education achievements, substance use and abuse, violence and reproductive and sexual health (Patel et al., 2007).

We can apply these different views to our case example. Maria's depression, her tearfulness and her feelings of low self-worth – as she puts it, feeling 'pathetic' and 'stupid' – seem central to her difficulties. The causes, however, are not clear. Do they indicate longer-term problems arising out of adolescent difficulties? Or are they responses to the immediate process of change and transition she is encountering? Is she, in other words, still in a process of change and development? Is her 'identity' still being formed?

Some adolescents find that the social transitions expected of them are overwhelming. Both the transition into adolescence from childhood, which requires experiencing the powerful changes of puberty and, usually, changing schools and the late, long transition into adulthood create conditions of uncertainty and change. Maria can be identified as someone who is experiencing anxiety about the late adolescent transition, but who, in reporting that her teenage years were not particularly full of conflict, seems to fit with the view that

> There is little evidence to support the notion of wide ranging conflict between the generations. … findings from research are unequivocal. Serious conflict between parents and adolescents is true only of a small minority of families, which should bring some comfort to those parents who contemplate the onset of adolescence with trepidation.
>
> (Coleman and Hendry, 1999, p. 80)

Some adolescents, it is argued, make a smooth transition through adolescence, while others have a more stressful and turbulent experience. Parents and teenagers, like Maria and her mother, can remain connected to each other rather than becoming estranged. They can spend as much time together in adolescence as in earlier childhood, and although adolescents spend less time in total in the family, there can be a compensating sense of increased communication between them. Since adolescence is often thought of as synonymous with turbulence, it can come as a surprise that some accounts of adolescence refer to the continuity of relationships between parents and adolescents, the absence of communication breakdown with parents, the absence of symptoms of psychological distress and difficulty in relation to peers and adults (Coleman and Hendry,

1999, p. 209). Turmoil may be located in a minority of adolescents, a highly significant minority from the point of professional practice, since these are more likely to be the adolescents who are encountered by professionals.

These accounts caution against a normative approach to adolescence in which turmoil is assumed to be universal. In fact turmoil may be thought of as denoting a particular social construction of adolescence, and therefore an adult-centred approach (Roche and Tucker, 1997). As Van Heeswyk points out, the 'stormy' view of adolescence 'is the theory that underpins the commercial exploitation of young people' (1997, p. 29), who are characteristically represented as 'inherently deviant or deficient' or, more specifically,

> presented as either actively deviant or passively at risk and sometimes as both simultaneously. In general young men are more likely to be presented as actively deviant, especially in aggressive forms and especially if they are working class and/or black. Young women are more likely to be constructed as passively at risk.
>
> (Griffin, 1997, p. 18)

From this perspective, it is not just individual differences that determine whether adolescence is turbulent or proceeds in a smooth transition to adulthood, but the social context, in which some groups are more vulnerable than others, especially in terms of race, gender, class and sexuality. The contextual differences of individuals – and the availability of resources, primarily in the form of reliable and trustworthy relationships with adults – are extremely significant in whether adolescents succeed in working through the impacts of adolescence or succumb to stressful experiences, with a consequent risk to long-term mental health. The capacity within relationships between parents and adolescents to manage conflicts, understand emotionality and have adaptive strategies for resolving difficulties when they arise is fundamental; these relationships are founded on a bedrock of stability throughout childhood and reflect the integral nature of qualities of negotiability and trust on both sides. When there are problems in the parent–adolescent relationship, these can be sorely tested by the intensity of emotionality in adolescence – again this is likely to be experienced on both sides. This is experienced in different ways during adolescence, and to take this discussion further, it is necessary to think separately about the two distinct phases of contemporary adolescence.

The impact of puberty

It is widely accepted that the growth and change initiated by puberty heralds the start of adolescence. Psychoanalytic thinking about adolescence has developed some detailed accounts of the impact of the bodily changes of puberty. Melanie Klein (1922) wrote of 'the tempestuous uprush of instincts arising at puberty' (p. 56). Peter Blos (1962, 1967) discussed the eruption of infantile feelings as the pubertal adolescent experienced a crisis of separating from childhood ways of relating to parents. Now, faced with the emergence of an adult body, the adolescent identifies with the same-sex parent, and with emergent adult sexual and parenting potentiality. That is, s/he may, with this body, one day become a mother or father. Traditionally, the perspective these theories take is triangular, or Oedipal.[5] Powerful passions are stirred up and revived in the adolescent, including desire for and competition with parents. The passions of infancy and early childhood take place, in adolescence, in a context in which the new physical capacities of the adolescent make such wishes potentially realisable. Taking the boy's relationship with the father, Anderson discusses the shift in power from childhood to adolescence as relative to the parent, and as potentially destabilising:

> It is the very balance of a relatively weak child and relatively strong parents which, whatever the impulses and anxieties is a background bedrock of reality which allows for a sense of safety. In adolescence the situation is extremely different. The boy is suddenly quite strong, and with more cognitive capacity, and he could kill his father if he did not prevent himself, and yet the impulse is just as strong.
>
> (Anderson, 1999, p. xvii)

The emergence, or revival, of these passionately felt emotions unbalance relationships with parents, forcing a reorganisation or renegotiation of these relationships. Depending on the perspective, psychoanalytic accounts focus on separating, identifying and the loss of childhood relationships. These accounts also emphasise the importance of anxiety, feeling vulnerable and, through the increase in physical and cognitive capacity, an emergent sense of power. This is especially thought of as the power to act, which in both sexual and aggressive aspects can feel both liberating and frightening. These terms – anxiety, vulnerability and power – are very important ones in thinking about adolescence.

Thus, central psychoanalytic ideas about early adolescence – that it is a turbulent time, which places tremendous stress on the adolescent – contrast diametrically the idea of smooth transition, which usually emanates from a more academic psychology or sociology. Perhaps these differences represent incompatible approaches – Van Heeswyk (1997, p. 29) suggests that psychoanalysts have had more fun! From this perspective, which locates turbulence in a small but vulnerable section of adolescents, emerges the accusation that psychoanalytic theories have generalised, mistakenly, from the pathological. On the other hand, those accounts which describe smooth transitions are often based on self-report rather than contemporary clinical accounts and may tend to emphasise 'coping' rather than feeling overwhelmed. Many accounts point out that the miserable, abject and difficult aspects of adolescence are 'forgotten' by adults (Jacobs, 1990; Griffin, 1997; Sayers, 1991). These disowned aspects of having a more turbulent time of it in adolescence are then projected back on to adolescents by adults, who do not wish to know about the feelings they themselves experienced in adolescence.

Jacobs (1990) discusses how memories of adolescence tend to be split between idealisation of moments of success, achievement and energy, and those which are abject and miserable. He thinks that early adolescence embodies the latter and late adolescence the former:

Early adolescence ... is 'a time of awkwardness, of disproportions, of frightening sexual maturation, of pimples, and of new and untried feelings. Nothing is set. Nothing is solid. Everything is in flux and change'. The aim with early adolescence, is to get past it and then, not to look back. In contrast, late adolescence is idealised, especially as future experiences include disappointments and frustrations.

Sayers (1991) interviewed adults who had either 'forgotten' their adolescence or who recalled it as a nightmare. She quotes Andre Green:

We outgrow adolescence with the idea of having lived through an exalting moment that we will never forget, but, in reality, sometimes when we look back we realize we had a narrow escape.

(Green, 1992)

Whether, for example, Maria has been more affected by puberty than she recalls and whether she is putting the misery of her earlier

adolescence out of mind can only be discovered by further exploration with her. She does say that she feels wobbly, not solid inside,
and that compared with others, such as her brother, she questions
the strength of her own mind and the capacity to commit herself to
expressing her own thoughts. She does express the idea that she is
uncertain in her identity.

Our understanding of puberty has been changed by recent studies
of the changes in the brain.[6] Neuroscientific developments open up
the possibility of bringing together several hitherto disparate strands.
According to these studies, the turmoil of the pubertal years and the
impulsiveness of some adolescent behaviour may have a neural cause.
This evidence claims that later development – in the period of puberty
particularly, but continuing through adolescence – of the brain affects,
among other things, the cognitive controls needed for mature behaviour; these are therefore underdeveloped in adolescence. Changes
to the brain at puberty have an effect on cognition, affect regulation,
learning and memory; the brain shows 'greater neural plasticity'
(Patton and Viner, 2007, p. 1132). Stressful experiences during puberty
can affect brain development adversely, increasing vulnerability to
psychopathologies; enrichment of the social and learning environments may be able to reverse the effects of early adverse experiences.
It is possible that greater neural plasticity thus provides what Blos
(1967) has described as 'a second chance' in development in early
adolescence.

Adding emerging knowledge about brain development to the
picture we have of puberty enables new alignments to be considered. Maturity increases the capacity to control behaviour – and the
adolescent requires a 'facilitating environment' while these changes
take effect: time is one 'cure', having stable and understanding
relationships with parents is another. On the other hand, adverse
contexts increase the potential for stressful experience leading to
lasting disorders; intervention is necessary when there is adversity,
in order to reduce the potential for enduring problems taking root
in early adolescence. This also demonstrates the need to connect
internal, biological and psychological and external – social – aspects
of experience.

Psychosocial perspectives on adolescence

Adolescence is a psychosocial concept. In societies where there is an
early rather than extended transition to adulthood, the social contribution in many cultures is usually in the form of a ritualised passage

into adulthood. In extended adolescence the interaction between the social context and psychological development is more complex. One of the unique differences in the way that adolescence has been organised since the mid-twentieth century, in the developed world, is that 'the development of reproductive capacity and sexual activity precede role transitions into parenthood and marriage by more than a decade' (Patton and Viner, 2007, pp. 1131–2). This produces what Gluckman and Hanson (2006) call a mismatch of biological and psychological transitions. This 'mismatch' has been theorised as important for development, a problem that infantilises young people (Graham, 2004) and provokes risks and opportunities.

Erikson's concept of the 'psychosocial moratorium' theorised the new organisation of adolescence, developing the idea of a 'playful' space for the consolidation of identity in the time gap between the development of biological maturity and taking up adult roles. In the psychosocial moratorium, the adolescent aims to suspend commitment and to explore the possibilities available in society in the quest for identity. For Erikson, identity was essential for psychic survival, for 'there is no feeling of being alive without a sense of identity' (Erikson, 1968, p. 129). Developing an identity means separating from others, becoming an individual and gaining a sense of self and other. The adolescent has to distinguish between self and others through formulating answers to the questions 'who am I and who am I like? And also who am I not?'

Though considered playful, in the sense of not being committed, the moratorium generated considerable pressure and intensity. The adolescent can be in a pained state and 'is apt to suffer more deeply than he ever did before or ever will again from a confusion of roles' (Erikson, 1968, p. 167). Under these tensions, there are conflicting pressures either to regress or to attempt to 'foreclose' on suspending commitment or the exploration of desires. Anxieties can lead to actions, the development of patterns of delinquency or promiscuity, which can become fixed as anti-social or self-destructive patterns of relating and behaving. All of these have the impact of restricting the quest for identity, the test of which is the commitment to and engagement with intimacy; 'only an attempt to engage in intimate fellowship and competition or in sexual intimacy fully reveals the latent weakness of identity' (Erikson, 1968, p. 167). The capacity of the individual to become involved and remain true to the self demonstrates whether the identity, which has been forged in the moratorium, will stand the test of application to the real-life tasks of adulthood.

Erikson's work on identity underpins contemporary thinking about adolescence. On the other hand, this model of adolescence is restrictive and probably outmoded by the emergence of more recent ways of thinking about relationships. Erikson has been criticised specifically for focusing on individualism, autonomy and achievement through his antipathy towards collectives (Sayers, 1991) rather than paying attention to the importance of relationships (Noam, 1999), and thus being predominantly 'masculine' and diminishing femininity in his approach.[7] The essential mechanism of a 'fit' or 'misfit' between the individual and the culture, which varies from time and place, is a flexible and adaptable one. However, the conceptualisation of identity as the outcome is far too solid and unitary for the experience of modernity, which is characterised by unpredictability and uncertainty. In other words, Erikson had a rather stable view of societies. Even as he was conceiving 'Identity, Youth and Crisis', Emery and Trist were formulating ideas about turbulent systems, in which 'dynamic properties arise not simply from the field itself. The "ground" is in motion', and this leads to increasing uncertainty (1969, p. 249). In modernity, all that is solid melts into air.

Identity crisis

At this point, we can return to Maria's predicament. She is facing an uncertain future, not knowing what she wants to do. In terms of her identity, she feels wobbly and unable to make commitments. She is close to her mother, but the process of separating from her and finding her own mind has probably not taken place. She finds she cannot join in discussions and thus feels ill-equipped to enter social relationships. It is probable that she has not been able to work out her rivalry with her brother, and his with her. The context of this is an uncertain future in a complex society. Appropriately, she says that she cannot talk about chaos theory and complexity!

It is possible when working with adolescents to notice 'Eriksonian' identity conflicts and struggles, as adolescents seek direction and aim to test commitments. They may also pull back from commitment, appropriately, because it feels too early, or 'foreclosing'. They may communicate a sense of being in flux. On the other hand, it is often the case that the withdrawal into an identity-forming moratorium indicates a defensive withdrawal from relationships, and the idealisation of the past, indicating a difficulty in undertaking internally the process of mourning that is needed in order to relinquish childhood.

Isolation and lack of engagement

Bill, an 18-year-old, maintains that he cannot commit himself to knowing what path to take in his life because he has no way of knowing what he wants to do, or what would be best for him. He proposes this as an existential dilemma that, since the aim of life is death, there is little point in choosing any particular form of engagement. This stance means that he pulls back from relationships and spends very long periods of time on his own. Yet behind this rationalisation lies a very painful predicament in which he feels he has to cover up a sense of failure. He sees himself as very bright and yet he has the greatest difficulty in applying himself to his studies. Rather than engage with frustrations, he withdraws to 'start over again', saying he needs 'time out'. On one occasion he failed an exam and was completely devastated. He felt it was all downhill from childhood, in which he idealised himself as a little boy Bill who was 'good at everything'. He felt he could still 'do anything' and he compared himself with David Beckham, who had simply had a lucky break. Idealisation of the past was supported by his grandiosities. His fear that he was 'losing it' constituted a crisis of loss and a fear of loss of control.

Distress in intimacy

Kirsty, also 18, has a boyfriend, and the relationship has become fairly serious. At first she hoped it would be more successful than her previous relationships, which had been very short-lived, but eventually the relationship began to fall apart in mutual recriminations and hurt. Kirsty felt unable to be with her boyfriend without feeling extremely pained, jealous, suspicious and furious, and was also quite incapable of spending any time apart from him without experiencing intense loneliness. In an overwhelmed and distressed state, she stopped seeing him and said she wanted a life without commitment, where she felt free. Kirsty oscillated between feeling overwhelmed when involved and lonely when withdrawing from others.

In both these examples the 'identity crisis' is centrally about a difficulty encountered in making and sustaining emotional contact with others. In slightly different ways, both Bill and Kirsty experience a need to withdraw from contact with others through difficulties in regulating or managing the emotional impact of contact. In both cases there is a sense of loss involved in the experience of engagement, and both withdraw from attempting to manage intense feelings to idealisations of states where this is not felt to be so urgent. Both experience a loss of control through engagement, through becoming overwhelmed by the emotions that are thus generated.

Identity and transition today: turbulence and risks

One way of thinking about the qualitative psychosocial changes for young people since Erikson formulated his ideas about identity is to adapt Roberts's (1995) well-used metaphor of train and car journeys. Roberts suggests that adolescence used to be like a train journey. The route is predictable and the destination prearranged. It is possible to travel together with others and develop a sense of cohesion, community and camaraderie with other passengers, who share the same route and aim for the destination. Though there are possibilities of changing route, these can only be made at planned stops.

In contrast, contemporary adolescence is more like a car journey. There is an appearance of freedom and autonomy over the journey compared with trains, and a sense of control over the choice of routes and destination through the individual driver constantly making a series of individual decisions. There is much less of a collective sense of travelling together in a car, though 'virtual contact' can be maintained with others through radio, stereo, mobile phone and even an on-board Internet connection.

The train journey is rather like Erikson's model of identity, where the journey provides the 'moratorium'. The predictability of the train journey is replaced by the confusing image of the car journey, which provides a semblance or illusion of control and independence, but unequal opportunities (some start the car journey in a Porsche!), and greater responsibility for decision-making and isolation from others. In the car journey the problem is about joining with others as well as separating from them. Additionally the car journey confronts the driver with a set of unpredictable risks.

The first wave of adolescence in the mid-twentieth century, the rise in teenage spending power and the spread of rock music, with images and language of unconventionality, was strongly supported by and transmitted through media (Martin, 1981). The second wave of adolescence in the late twentieth and early twenty-first centuries is characterised by globalisation, consumerism and the invasion of 'space' by increasing numbers and intensities of images and increasing fragmentation. Frosh (1991) characterises this as 'This babble – the constant speech of mass media and computer, all different, all distorted – produces a set of competing discourses that are experienced subjectively as mysterious and confusing, but yet are constitutive of our consciousness of the world' (p. 58) and which lead to 'incomprehension and misrecognition', so that the 'fragmentation of the cultural environment becomes a buzzing and booming confusion in the head' (p. 188). For adolescents, this 'babble' has taken form in generating new communication methods, which have radical impacts on friendship networks and intimacy. MSN, My Space and Facebook lead twenty-first century virtual peer networks into new ways of being with and separate from others; it is possible to amass great numbers of 'friends', feel in contact with others and never be alone. Of course the risks of these virtual social networks are well documented and generate a 'moral panic' in the media.

The effects of change through globalisation and technological advances are to blur the distinction between adolescence and adulthood, through creating a context for adulthood which is distinctly 'adolescent', with an 'upside' which provides a sense of excitement and the thrill of new possibilities, alongside a questioning or deconstruction of old certainties. In this lie great possibilities for rethinking relationships, for overthrowing old prejudices and for 'individualisation', subjectively or objectively feeling free of the old constraining structures of thought and action. On the 'downside' there is an exposure to the fragmentation of the cultural environment and to new risks. Consistency and stability of relationships are central to the potential for fragmentation. In the absence of a bedrock of certainty and predictability, anxiety and a fear of loss of control are heightened. There is in this sense an encounter with loss – loss of a sense of a centre and of a past in which there are certainties of tradition. Whether excitement and thrill or a sense of loss and a fear of loss of control are uppermost, these are essential reactions to the changes of modernity and mirror the movement from latency to adolescence. The loss of the 'bedrock' of certainty means that everyone is in the process of 'leaving home', or – to mix the developmental analogy – it is not only God who ceases to exist, but also latency, the intermission of certainty, reliability and predictability, which are sidelined to the periphery of 'anorak' activities such as collecting stamps and pricing antiques.

Adolescents do not simply have to deal with the problem of leaving childhood certainties and dependencies but they also have to gain a way of relating to adult postmodern society. This means encountering turbulence in the sociocultural context and the fluctuating, shifting, rapidly changing and uncertain adult world. It means moving into an adult world, which is extremely diverse and definable in many different ways.

Two themes which emerge from this analysis and which are extremely important for contemporary adolescence are, firstly, the experience of loss and the importance and difficulty of mourning, and secondly fear of loss of control. The anxieties and defences that are brought about by both these issues are important to a consideration of adolescent identity development and in particular to the forms of feeling that flow from contemporary conditions.

Late adolescence and emerging adulthood

There has been considerable new thinking and discussion about the impact of late modernity and postmodernity on adolescence. Much of this emanates from the individualisation in risk society theory (Beck, 1992). The diversity of adolescent experiences precludes a normative or monolithic approach to identity, such as Erikson's. Post-traditional identity is characterised as more open, fluid, complex and questioning of traditions (Johannsson, 2007). It is more differentiated and inclusive of a number of identifications; it is reflexive, and changes over time in a 'continuous project of self' (Thomson et al., 2004). It is influenced by and makes use of the vast flow of information through, predominantly, the Internet. There is a choice between keeping in touch with new information, or becoming marginalised outside reflexive society (Johannsson, 2007, p. 105).

The individualised, calculative approach to information and risks has changed the way that identity is theorised. Though refined, debated and critiqued, the approach is central to contemporary thinking about identity. A central debate is the relationship between structures and individual agency. There are those, for example Arnett (2000, 2004), who propose a new life stage of emerging adulthood.

Arnett's (2004) thesis is that throughout their twenties, young people make increasing commitments to more stable partnerships, and adult identity through preferred occupational pathways. They typically do not regard themselves as adults, but as on the *threshold* of making long-term commitments. Around the mid-twenties, there is a reduction in the amount of time young people are engaged in drinking, using drugs, delinquency (Arnett, 2000). Arnett posed the question, 'what does it mean to make the transition from adolescence to adulthood?' and, using survey data, found that the criteria used by his young adult respondents were essentially individualistic:

- Accepting responsibility for oneself
- Making independent decisions
- Becoming financially independent
- Standing alone as a self-sufficient person

These individualised, abstract, even moral criteria replace (for these American respondents) the traditional concrete or actual events that signify rites of passage from adolescence to adulthood, the traditional markers of transition: finishing full-time education, beginning full-time work and marriage. These, Arnett suggests, are seen as 'irrelevant to the attainment of adult status'. However, Arnett's respondents also identified criteria for adulthood that promoted mature relatedness, including developing greater concern for others and avoiding behaviour that might harm others. Tensions between more narcissistic and more relational objectives are indicative of the potential conflicts in risk societies. The biographies of young people studied by Thomson et al. (2004) showed that alongside the individualised 'continuous project of self' there were also ideas about maturity expressed in more relational terms, developing, through this, the idea of thinking about the needs of others. Thus the tension of identity involves the reflexive, narcissistic 'what's in it for me?' (Johannsson, 2007, p. 105) and the interdependent 'you have to think of someone else now' (Thomson et al., 2004, p. 224).

There is recognition that increasing inequalities and social exclusion indicate the problematic side to individualisation. Agency is in fact limited by structures and leads to biographies grounded in different backgrounds of class, place, gender and ethnicity. Identity depends on and is conditioned by the biographical history of the individual – what has taken place before. It is wrought within a complex matrix, made up of social capital, 'the personal, financial, social and cultural resources to which the growing individual has access, and by the social and institutional contexts through which the individual moves' (Bynner, 2005, p. 379).

Self-esteem, resilience and a sense of competence are necessary for young people to negotiate their way through this matrix. These concepts are summarising categories containing complex interpersonal and intrapsychic experiences and dynamics, as we shall discuss (Chapter 2). However, if we accept them for now as a starting point, it follows that they are interrelated. Experiences of competence may encourage investments in a particular area of activity, and this encourages self-esteem. There occur critical moments which form turning points in an individual's life course that involve retrospective self-definition (Thomson et al., 2004). These then form trajectories or pathways in which '… the effective exercise of agency in both creating and responding to new opportunities. There can be "stagnant" or "damaged" transitions; there can also be repaired and progressive transitions' (Bynner, 2005, p. 379).

A particular field for these experiences is education, in a context where skills needed for employment increasingly require the acquisition of higher levels of educational qualifications and society is invested in a discourse in which educational attainment is at the centre. Young people can experience competence, enhancing a particular aspect of identity, through educational success, or alternatively a sense of failure, exclusion and loss of esteem through not achieving. Clinical experiences of working with adolescents show that it is very difficult to not buy into the educational route to adulthood; not only do they feel they have failed, but also that they are left behind and isolated as more 'successful' peers go on to university. The case example of Bill, above, is one example where failing an exam was experienced as catastrophic.

Social exclusion is often the experience of those who take 'fast track' routes to adulthood, which do not include post-secondary education; these young people leave education at or before the minimum leaving age, have no longer a 'working class' job market available and are subject to early family formation, teenage pregnancy, and offending or drug and alcohol misuse. On the other hand, 'slow track' transitions involve a longer period of semi-independent living whilst undertaking education, deferring financial independence, full-time employment and family formation and dependence on parental support.

Thus adolescence is 'a window of risk' (Furlong and Cartmel, 1997) when viewed from the perspective of changing social contexts. Social exclusion, through 'fast track' transitions to adulthood and 'slow track' extensions to adolescence and emerging adulthood, increase the potential for damage to identity and mental health. Individualisation promotes the idea of individual responsibility for life events, an 'epistemological fallacy' according to Furlong and Cartmel (1997), who add that 'As individuals are made to feel more responsible for life-events, uncertainty and risk have taken their toll on young people's mental health' (Furlong and Cartmel, 1997, p. 9).

The view that adolescent mental health is deteriorating in contemporary conditions is supported by recent research (Collishaw et al., 2004) but media attention for increased levels of depression, self-harm, offending and so on tends to separate the evidence for mental health disorders from understanding of the causes and meaning which is to be found in the nature of the experiences of growing up, becoming more adult in contemporary societal contexts. These discussions about the worsening of adolescent mental health also lose sight of the moments in individual biographies when possibilities for growth and development, rather than destructive or self-destructive ways of relating, can be turned to and grasped. 'Agency' can be available within the constraints and opportunities of individual, interpersonal and social contexts.

Narcissism, negotiability, fragmentation and containment

Tensions between growing up in an individualised risk society and developing relational capacities and aims are reflected in the recent development of psychoanalytic thinking about adolescence. Particularly, the concept of narcissism[8] has been revisited in order to understand the ways that development and growth can take place within unfavourable contexts that buck the trend, so to speak, of the emergence of more destructive and self-destructive ways of relating. Waddell (2006) points out that it 'is the swiftness with which what seem to be deeply entrenched narcissistic structures may be modified or modulated in response to even quite small internal or external change' (p. 23). Alternatively, the opposite route can be taken – more intensive narcissistic states can be equally rapidly be taken up with consequent increases in problematic behaviours. Often these changes – in one direction or another – occur around changes towards tolerating being more separate or dependent (Flynn and Skogstad, 2006).

Case example

Kathryn, 18, came for assessment for therapy in a very distressed state; she was depressed, self-harming and had recently taken an overdose. She talked about always being depressed; the quality of her presentation and discussion of her background promoted the idea that she was very deeply involved with self-destructive ways of relating. Whenever she felt alone, or threatened with being on her own, she would get into a tearful rage which could escalate to the point that she would self-harm. However, she made a good contact in her once weekly therapy, and after a few weeks reported a seemingly small incident in which, feeling desperately alone and abandoned, and about to fly into one of her wild tearful rages she managed to stop, and sat down to have a coffee in a café. Strangely, she reported, as though she had for the first time discovered this, she didn't mind being on her own; it was actually quite pleasant.

Kathryn's allowing herself to be on her own for this moment allowed her a new possibility, one she had not suspected, but which gave her a momentary sense of a new competence, one which she could report back to her therapy and build upon it. Her new competence is about bringing within her range of options something that previously she felt terrorised her. Her experience was linked with a sense that she felt a connection to her therapy, which provided her a sense of containment and an opportunity to discover a more negotiable side of herself. The role of containment is central to therapeutic work with adolescents of all ages, and this will be illustrated using a case example of someone in the midst of the process of extended adolescence, or 'emerging adulthood', in which he demonstrated some destructive and self-destructive behaviour.

Case example

Howard, at 21, was in his last year at university when he was referred for psychotherapy. He arrived about thirty minutes late for the first appointment, and came into the consulting room tightly clutching a piece of paper, which I saw was his appointment letter. Looking tense, he sat down without taking off his coat and apologised for being late, in a way which suggested he was making a great effort to be off hand, or 'cool'. He had an air of self-deprecation, which continued when he told me he really did not know why he was here. His doctor had suggested he came, because he kept 'going mad when he got drunk'. He said he did not think he was a priority – as many other people might have more need of counselling.

He then told me something of himself, his family and his earlier adolescence. His teens, he said, had not been particularly 'turbulent', though his mother had been ill and father was away at work a great deal. His older brother and sister had been much more in need of parental attention, and he had 'got on with it' completing his schooling, taking a 'gap year' to 'get away from it all' and then going to University. Now, however, he was in constant conflict with his mother, who he felt favoured his siblings, and his father was 'as useless as a hole in the head'. This description could have been applied to himself, for when he described what it meant to 'go mad when he got drunk', he told me about times, which he subsequently could not remember, in which he became violent towards others and put himself at risk, in ways which suggested he was not able to think about protecting himself.

Young people, like anyone else can be very anxious at the prospect of having a therapeutic consultation, and this seemed to be prominent in the way he started this meeting. He was palpably anxious, and his lateness and tension, the way he clutched the letter communicated this. He was trying on the surface to be 'cool', and keep himself 'buttoned up', as he sat with his coat wrapped round him, as though forming a protective skin,[9] but intense emotion was near the surface. In his first contact in therapy, Howard's need for containment of his anxieties is to the forefront.

The container–contained relationship

Bion's ideas about the relationship between the container and contained occupy a very central place in current psychoanalytic thinking. Bion (1962) described a process which begins in early infancy when the infant, expels or projects emotions which are too powerful, intense or unknown, into the mother.[10] If the mother is receptive to the infant's states of mind, and feels the infant's feelings in herself, it is possible that the infant's states of mind and feelings, can be tolerated and known by the mother, and that some sense can then be made of them. Feelings that were too powerful for the infant to hold within her/himself can be thus made tolerable. This 'contains' the emotions and the mother acts as a 'container' for them. The mother's state of mind in this process of containment, which Bion (1962) called 'reverie', constitutes openness to emotional communications of these kinds. That is, the mother's mind is not predetermining of the meaning of the infant's communications and needs, but some space is available for uncertainty and ambiguity in communications, and for new ways of thinking about meaning.

Britton (1998) emphasises the aspect of Bion's theory in which the container–contained relationship enables precursors of thought to be transformed from 'nearly sensory-somatic' qualities into 'something more mental'. Bion called the 'nearly sensory-somatic' as beta-elements and the 'something more mental' as alpha-elements. The beta, or precursors of thought, leaves the mind to enter the realms of somatic, perceptual or action. Britton gives the example of an adult analysand, Miss A, who literally expelled unwanted thoughts down the lavatory. '*There were days when she did this so often that she broke the mechanism*' (1998, p. 19). Britton's patient remembered in her adolescence traumatically going to an air raid shelter with her mother and being caught between wishing to escape a suffocating experience in the shelter and her fear of bombs falling in the street.

> Her conflict was intense and apparently irresolvable. She collapsed in the doorway, retaining consciousness but becoming paralysed, mute and entirely without bodily sensations. … It was this state of anaesthesia that had been used by her internal voice as a threat

ever after, compelling her to perform compulsively her irrational activities – 'If you don't do this you will get the feelings'. The feelings she dreaded were actually the experience of having no feelings.

(p. 20)

Faced with the predicament of being stuck at the threshold, where both inside and outside felt intolerably dangerous, Miss A sought 'sanctuary and meaning' in her analysis. She tried to find, in other words, a place that was safe and where, once she was inside it, she could gain coherence of her thoughts. Communication takes place through the projection of feelings, unconsciously, as well as through direct verbal communication. It is through the mother/therapist being receptive to the unconscious communications – projections – that the infant/patient has the opportunity of being understood, and of gaining self-understanding and coherence.

If we return now to Howard, there are two points that can be considered about his identity in relation to his need for contain-ment. Firstly, the experience he describes of 'going mad' happens in a way that he does not consciously understand. He does not appear to know which intense emotions drive this behaviour, and when he has such an incident, it is experienced as a rupture to his sense of continuity and coherence. His identity is that he is subject to these rupturing passages, and the sense of having a continuous identity is threatened, but restored through getting to know these processes, in emotional contact with someone else, who performs the function of containing through availability and receptivity. Identity formation occurs within these relationships rather than as a solitary pursuit.

At the beginning of the therapeutic consultation, Howard was unsure whether he would be 'held in mind'. He says he is not a priority. He conveys in his anxiety that he has to work very hard to contain himself, taking a very tight grip on his paper, wrapping his coat round him and trying to keep emotions in check by play-ing them down, dismissing them, trying, as it were to make them smaller. This communicates a thought that 'grown ups' do not need to be looked after in this way, but rather, they aim to do it for them-selves; he wants to be, and to be seen to be a 'grown up'.

Being held in mind, and not being held in mind

Adolescent anxieties about starting therapy include feeling unsure how it will help, or even will it take place. A fragile sense of newly formed and hard-won independence may feel easily crushed. It is

important to distinguish between the fragility of adolescent independence and a more deeply seated sense of not being 'held in
mind', which has led to patterns of relating to others based on a need
for self-sufficiency because there is no expectation of being helped.
For Howard, both anxieties about his performance in therapy and a
deeper lack of containment were present in varying degree.

Having a sense of being kept in mind provides the opportunity
to reflect on emotional experiences. Having a notion that someone
takes in one's thoughts and predicaments and takes them seriously
enables communication of inner states to take place. For example:

Case example

*A youth worker is aware that a 17-year-old, Jack, is in difficulties follow-
ing a traumatic loss. She asks Jack if he would like to talk about himself,
but Jack declines, saying talking will only make it worse. The youth worker
says OK, but adds that it seems that it must be bad, then. Some time later
she sees Jack is still in the same state of mind and again asks him if he wants
to talk about it. He again declines but seems to hesitate as though he would
like to talk, if only he could. Some time later, the youth worker meets Jack
by chance, and this time he begins the conversation and says that he really
would like to talk about it, if possible, because he is very troubled by his
thoughts, but he will be nervous about talking to someone.*

The youth worker's attention for this young person, over a period
of time conveys to Jack that he is kept in mind. Jack has to struggle
with the idea he has that talking may increase the difficulty rather
than easing it. Britton (1998) describes the experience of an absence
of containment as leading to a particular state of mind in which
there is reduced hope or faith in the possibility of communicating to
others about states of mind:

> If a mother fails to absorb the infant's projective identification and
> resists any attempt by the child to know her mind, she gives the
> child a picture of a world that does not want to know it and does
> not want to be known'.
>
> (1998, p. 23)

He goes on to describe two different relationships based on the
failure of the container–contained relationship. The first is akin
to the adolescent fear that the newly achieved independence will
be overtaken and lost in contact with adults. There is a 'fear of

being taken in and then destroyed, of one's nature being taken in by another's devouring curiosity and consumed in the process, of oneself being comprehended and nullified during the process' (p. 25). Alternatively there is a fear that the containing person will deny access, entry and acceptance. These represent a fear of loss of identity and fear of loss of agency.

Containing transition and turbulence in adolescence

Positive experiences of relationships between adolescents and parents involve the capacity to engage, on both sides, in intense negotiations, and the capacity to adapt to the process of adolescence through restructuring relationships (Coleman and Hendry, 1999). Thus, at a family level, adolescence is not conflict free, nor is there absence of potential emotional conflict, but if changes are engaged with and negotiated the quality of turbulence is transformed.

Containment addresses potential turbulence. Waddell (1998) points out that the re-emergence of conflicts in adolescence 'tests the quality of early containment and internalisation' (p. 128). The adolescent has to make use of the resources that have been provided in infancy and early childhood to understand, make sense of and contain the impact of anxiety, conflict, ambiguity and uncertainty of internal change in adolescence. The adolescent, in other words, draws on the experiences of being contained in infancy and early childhood. Moreover, as well as drawing on past experiences of parenting, the adolescent make demands of parents in the present context. These demands may be severe, or intense.

Through the need for containment, the adolescent's quest for identity is undertaken in close relationship with others. If the parent and the adolescent can tolerate experiences of uncertainty, anxiety, change, ambiguity, as well as oscillations of feeling, the quality of turbulence is transformed. The mental flexibility required by these processes is extremely significant.

If we now return to the case discussed earlier, Howard, and consider his adolescence, Howard suggested that the transition through his teens contrasted with the turbulence and dilemmas of the present. Through his teens Howard focused on a structure – study at school and University – and a strategy – to 'get away from it all'. Now he is uncertain what to do, or what route to take. He has to make decisions. This is like switching from a train journey to a car, to return to Roberts' metaphor. Howard now feels uncertain about the future. His conflicting feelings about his parents – in his current relationships with them, and in his mind – his representations of them, are pushed into the forefront.

It is possible that the smoother 'transition' through his teens has given an illusion of a journey towards adulthood, but one in which the problems have been shelved rather than resolved. In trying to 'get away from it all' he took flight – understandably, perhaps – from a difficult situation in the family, but he is now left with an unsatisfactory, even dangerous internal situation. In his need to draw on internal resources to make decisions for the future, he has become aware of the difficulty this internal situation presents, and this has made thinking about himself unbearable. As soon as he thinks, he drowns her thoughts (literally, given the role of alcohol in his difficulties). In this way he is still 'getting away from it all'.

Between us, Howard and I need to find a way in which he can use therapy to think his own thoughts and bear the emotional discomfort. But through the lack within of a flexible, containing aspect of himself, the discomfort of his own thoughts is burdensome. He wishes to put the burden into me, in the manner of a container–contained relationship. His communication to me is that he wishes me to take in these overwhelming thoughts. When I try to return these in tolerable form, Howard complains that I 'make him think'. He was disturbed by trying to hold his own feelings, and by feelings of depression and loss. Discomfort and depression were the consequences for Howard of engaging with what Anderson and Dartington (1998) call the 'adolescent process':

> If the adolescent is to successfully achieve adulthood, he [sic] must re-negotiate every aspect of his relationship with himself, and with his external and internal objects in a new context – this activity is what we often refer to as the adolescent process. It is like a review of the life that has been lived so far. … all adolescents have to deal with the experience of being out of balance to some extent. Indeed it seems to be those young people who have the inner strength and resources to bear to continue the experience of being naturally out of balance, as well as an environment which can support this, who can achieve the best adjustment in adult life.
>
> (1998, p. 3)

There is an echo of Erikson's thinking of the relationship between the individual and society in this formulation of the adolescent process, but with the difference that the emphasis is placed on the process of engagement with relationships, both internal and external. There is an emphasis, in other words, on what happens when the adolescent is in contact with others, and how the processes of containing emotionality leads to the claiming or reclaiming of individuality. The process of seeking identity has to take place through and within relatedness with others.

Summary

The upheavals of puberty and the long transition to adulthood have created new conditions and contexts for adolescence. The separation of the period of biological maturation from the period of role transition to adulthood is central to understanding adolescence in contemporary societies. This situation generates diverse views which either lament the lack of responsibilities given to adolescents (and young adults) or see it as providing an opportunity for the development of more open, reflexive identities. All the recent social evidence adds to the picture that the quality of the adolescent transition to adulthood is diverse, largely affected by stratification and exclusion (Bynner, 2005).

Recent psychosocial approaches to understanding biographies of young people emphasise the tension between individualised and relational aspects of identity. The renewed interest in narcissism in adolescence, from a psychoanalytic perspective helps to orientate to this tension. It has recently been discussed, variously, that in considering adolescence it is necessary to

- take account of threshold states in late adolescence/early adulthood (Arnett), which represent development and aspiration still in progress or transition rather than final destinations being reached
- explore the quality of transitions; whether they are creative or stagnant (Bynner) and the impact of these on identity, or subjectivity (see chapter 2)
- recognise there is often an absence or confusion of structure, pressing time limits or deadlines (e.g. exam time tables) alongside an apparently endless process (e.g. becoming qualified enough, financially independent etc)
- be aware of the potential for development, emotionally, psychologically, cognitively, and this instils fluidity even where the trends for an individual appear stuck and (self)destructive

- be aware of the emotional impact of internal and external change on a sense of stability, and the propensity for this to stimulate fear of fragmentation. This indicates the importance of containment in therapeutic work in turbulent conditions
- conversely be aware that an experience of competence in a particular field can trigger hope and a new means of experiencing self more hopefully.

2

BECOMING A SUBJECT IN ADOLESCENCE

In this chapter, the aim is to look closely at what it means to experience being adolescent in contemporary contexts. It focuses on experiences of developing identity through both separating from parental figures, becoming more independent and also experiencing dependency on and intimacy with others. Thus, there is a focus on ways in which adolescents acquire and relate to an emerging adult sexual body and on the qualities of relationships that they form. As was shown in Chapter 1, recent thinking has changed the way the adolescent process is understood, particularly with regard to the deepening and increasingly complex link between the internal and social worlds.

This chapter applies these recent ideas about adolescence, especially those which emphasise the development of subjectivity, to understanding adolescent development. Firstly, there is an exploration, through the discussion of case examples, of ways of thinking about the process of separation from parental figures and the world of childhood. This is followed by a focus on ways in which adolescents experience the impact of bodily changes and their development of attitudes to love and sexuality. Running through both these discussions is an appreciation of how increasing awareness of internal experiences provides a foundation for emerging adolescent subjectivity, which is understood as consisting of 'becoming a subject' through both individualisation and relatedness. Thus, tensions between developing separateness and independence, on the one hand, and dependency and intimacy, on the other hand, in the process of becoming more adult are related to recent thinking about narcissism in adolescence. This chapter is based on complex theoretical ideas, and the aim is to explain these clearly, in conjunction with case examples.

Processes of separating in adolescence

Adolescent subjectivity is developed in a climate of internal and social change. Newness and loss pervade these experiences and the adolescent is constantly in a process of evaluating and re-evaluating the meaning of moments of change and experiences of transition. Anxiety and a fluctuating sense of the meaning and implications of experience are to the forefront. The complexities of relatedness to others – adults in all kinds of roles and peers – are particularly subject to momentary fluctuations, as the adolescent subject experiences herself or himself in different ways in relation to others, and also in making sense of self and the world. Thus, there is a constant reworking of experiences relating to newness, opportunities, loss, a sense of agency, success and failure, repetitions, feeling stuck or moving on and changing. In contemporary conditions, there is no one way of conceptualising this process, but instead it is important to take into account a number of key vertices. These include, firstly, the more linear growth towards autonomy, individuation and separateness, as the position of being a child in the family is left behind; secondly, shifts between states of mind in relatedness to oneself and others; thirdly, the role of self-esteem and narcissism; and fourthly, relatedness within power relations. These four conceptions of the meaning of adolescent development can be explored through, initially, discussing a case example. This example takes an apparently unremarkable passage from a therapy session, but one which contains a 'critical moment' in the transition to adulthood.

Case example

Martin, now 19, has been in therapy for a year. His therapy will end when he leaves for University, to a city in a different part of the country. He was anxious about the ending of his therapy, and about leaving home. He began one session by telling me he had a dream that he had failed his exams. It was just like last year.

He very rarely talked about dreams and was in fact very anxious when unconscious aspects of himself 'slipped' into his sessions. I tried to ask him for some more details about the dream, but he did not want to talk about it, and I felt that if I pursued the subject he would close up. He said that his mother had wished him luck with his exams; but he knew she did not mean it, because she really did not want him to go to University and leave home. He sounded aggrieved. I said that he had started the session feeling anxious and that he seemed to feel he had a lot to handle at the moment, including different ways of looking at how to think about leaving home and therapy.

We did talk then about his dream, in which he spoke again about feeling he was in the same situation as last year, and that after a year's therapy, nothing was different. I said it was true that his dream referred to failing exams, and that he felt drawn to similarities with last year, but that it was also possible to think about some differences between then and now. He asked what I meant, and I said that he seems, for example, much more aware of his feelings now, though this awareness puts an additional pressure and burden upon him. He was thoughtful for a moment and then said that he did feel he was different and that he is more aware of his failings. I paused, wondering whether to draw attention to the implicit idea that feelings are synonymous with failings. In fact I said that he did seem to be worried that in the future he would fail in his attempts to manage this burden, of bearing his own feelings himself, after his therapy ended.

*There was a pause and he seemed tense. He said he was going to change the subject. He wanted to **know** what would happen in the future. Will he be able to still come to see me? He said he wanted to prepare himself.*

This example of Martin is taken at a point at which he is facing separation from his therapy, and from being a child, living at home to being a student, living away from home. This change is upon him; it is urgent, cannot be avoided or put off and is preoccupying. It necessitates a change in relationships – leaving school, home and therapy – and also a change in the way he sees himself, through his change of role. These experiences can be explored now in terms of three aspects of this process: separation-individuation, oscillation between different states of mind, or 'positions', and the development of subjectivity, within power relations.

Separation-individuation

Martin is in a phase of change in which the movement towards greater independence leaves him feeling anxious, and in this state, more infantile feelings are pressing upon him. He is in a dilemma about leaving or staying, wanting to leave and wanting to stay. This relates to the model of separation-individuation which Blos (1962, 1967) applied to adolescence. The adolescent, like the toddler in early childhood, 'hatches' into a separate individual. This explains the contradictory states of mind that can be observed in toddlers, who wish sometimes to be with the mother, while at other times they wish to assert independence and autonomy. Adolescence provides a 'second chance' in development because the eruption of infantile feelings and the developmental importance of regression repeat the 'toddler' dynamics of separation-individuation. Adolescents move out of a childhood immersion in the family, in the same way that toddlers 'hatch from the symbiotic membrane to become an individual toddler', so that infantile ties to the parents and dependencies on the family are shed. Adolescence is thus marked by both disengagement from the internalised relationships of childhood and engagement – or re-engagement – with infantile wishes, desires and relationships through the impact of the loosening of the relatively predictable world of latency.[1]

Oscillation between different states of mind

Within the therapeutic session, Martin's anxieties produce two different configurations of relatedness. In the first of these states of mind, he struggles with the impact inside himself of the fears and pains of separating. In this mode he reports on a dream, which symbolises his experiences, he talks about his anxieties and locates within himself the responsibility for managing his feelings of becoming more separate. He is thoughtful, and struggles with difficult issues and experiences. In his second mode, when his anxiety about bearing his own feelings becomes oppressive and overwhelming, he calls upon others, who are then invested with responsibilities for the feelings he has about separation. His emotional experiences become more defined as actions from someone towards him, rather than as emerging from within himself. In this second mode of relating, there is a blurring of boundaries between self and others, turbulence and need, together with anxieties which have a more persecutory quality. Thus Martin is somewhat precariously poised between two ways of relating.

Bion (1963) discussed the way that new experiences and the forming of new thoughts about self and others have the effect of making the kind of shift between different ways of relating described in Martin's case. Bion's thinking developed Klein's views of the paranoid schizoid and depressive positions,[2] and he supplied the notation PS <-> D to indicate the two-way nature of this oscillation. Just as being overwhelmed by depressive anxiety, pain, guilt and separateness may trigger a return to PS, so a lessening of persecutory anxiety, an increased awareness of the needs of the other and a greater contact with reality can initiate a move towards D. The oscillation between positions occurs throughout life and is very important in adolescence, because the experiences of newness and change produce this movement between paranoid schizoid and depressive positions. From an adult point of view, adolescents move between times when they are more negotiable (more D) and times when they are more difficult, demanding, 'unreasonable' etc. (more PS). It is also important to this conceptualisation that the movement is between fields, or states of mind, rather than as progression and regression, or stages of development.

Self-esteem, competence and failure

Thirdly, a central part of the intersubjective field in the passage from Martin's therapy session is the discussion of fear of failure and repetitions of previous experiences. It seemed important that this was understood to be an expression of the fragility of Martin's self-esteem rather than a more destructive wish to defeat his therapy and avoid the pains of separating and growing apart from his family. In working with adolescents, the difference between these two aspects of narcissism is hard to identify and be sure of. The recent elaboration of the theory of narcissism in relation to adolescence (Waddell, 2006; Flynn and Skogstad, 2006; Anastopoulos, 2006) emphasises, on the one hand, the essential vulnerability of adolescent development and the need for bolstering of fragile self-esteem when faced with 'intolerable uncertainties' and thus to 'restore a fragile self-conception … serving as a defence against feelings of isolation and possibly of smallness and humiliation' (Waddell, 2006, p. 24). On the other hand lie trends for more destructive, repetitive behaviour – destructive narcissism – which adolescents turn to face when under pressure to develop in stressful internal and external contexts. The trend towards (self)destructive narcissism may become entrenched, or alternatively, can be turned away from.

In taking up and promoting positively with Martin that there is growth and development since last year, rather than agreeing with his own gloomy self-prognosis, I am in effect recognising, holding and presenting to Martin the capacity for development and growth, and the evidence for it, while he is assuaged by self doubts. This makes it possible to name his fear of failing in the task of bearing his own feelings when he leaves home, a fear that earlier Martin located in his mother, saying that she did not wish him to leave home. This may or may not have been true, or partially true, in fact, but holds a projective truth in this session. Naming the fear also shifts the focus towards an emotional state and away from a 'fact'.

The tension between narcissism in the sense of constituting a belief in oneself and a store of self-esteem, and that which signifies a retreat from relatedness with others has a special meaning in adolescence when the capacity for mature relatedness is emergent and located within a complex configuration of internal and external factors. It forms, as Waddell describes, a distinctive 'adolescent organisation' and thus has to be differentiated from adult narcissistic characteristics and behaviours in terms of what might be inferred about the implications of these for the individual.

Through the concept of narcissism it is possible to understand something of the precariousness of self-esteem in adolescents, as they develop, and also to provide some depth for the meaning of self-esteem, which can seem rather wooden when used sociologically. This 'field' for adolescent development is inclusive of self-esteeming, self-criticising and self-destroying aspects, thoughts and intentions.

Power, vulnerability and subject relations

A fourth approach to the material in Martin's case focuses on the idea that he is involved in an emotional field in which there is a sense of power and vulnerability. This comes to the centre of the discussions between us when he becomes preoccupied with 'knowing', through changing the subject. He introduced his own preoccupation of wanting to know from me about the future, and this had the effect of producing a discontinuity in the session. In order to accomplish this manoeuvre, he first of all has to position me as 'knowing' something, which he can then contest. His assertion aims to wrest some power and/or knowledge from me, by challenging me to tell him what will happen; that is, what I have in mind for him, and specifically will I continue to see him. In doing so he finds a way, however uncomfortably for both of us, of asserting himself and attending to his needs, so that for a moment the conflict inside him between being independent and being dependent is resolved, as he says, by changing the subject. Thus I have to relate directly to this predicament.

The intersection of issues of achieving greater independence, shifting between different states of mind and power and vulnerability can be further explored through another case example:

Case example

Lizzie, who is 17 and approaching A levels, complains about being at school. She says she has lost all interest in studying and can't wait to leave.

She says she is bored and wants to work and earn money. She experiences her peers as immature and says she is much happier in the company of older people. She spends much of her time in therapy talking about boyfriends, who are always much older than she is. She says that she expects older boy-friends to be able to look after her better than boyfriends of her own age. In these relationships an initial enthusiasm with extravagant hopes is quickly turned to bitter disappointment and disillusionment, when she feels her boyfriend has let her down. Unperturbed, and defiant, she continues to search for another, who will not disappoint her.

Lizzie seems caught up in a repetitive pattern in her relationships in which her boredom with school and her own age peers, together with seeking a solution through acquiring an older boyfriend, indicates a difficulty she has in her development. There is a paradoxical wish for independence and being looked after in a childlike way. There is, it seems, conflict and anxiety around independence and separateness. Her repeated pattern of relationships show her cling-ing both to childhood wishes to be looked after by a parent figure, and a defence against feeling separate. Here it is possible to detect that her identity is not developed in the sense that she cannot yet bear the uncertainties and pains of mutuality in relatedness, for which the capacity to be separate is a prerequisite to obtaining the kind of robust self-esteem on which these relationships rest. Instead she deploys a narcissistic pattern of relating which reflects her as yet limited capacities, and which is to an extent self destructive and denying of the need to face the pains of becoming separate. Her relationships repeat Oedipal[3] conflicts and desire. Whenever Lizzie becomes more aware of the intensity of her wish to avoid feeling separate and alone, she becomes intensely anxious and then she clings more tenaciously to her defensive and repetitive patterns. In effect she turns to a more paranoid schizoid way of relating, in which an idealised relationship is felt to solve her problems and obviate the need to develop a sense of separateness within herself.

In this predicament she is driven to achieve a powerful position, with regard to the difficulties she feels she faces in her internal world and her intersubjective relations, and thus to avoid the intense feelings of vulnerability that she would feel through ordinary dependency on others. But because she is unaware (and terrified) of the unconscious processes that drive her, she is intensely subject to these forces, rather than being able to modify their intensity through reflection.

Kennedy (1998) makes a useful distinction between being 'sub-ject to' and 'subject of' the forces and experiences with which the individual is in contact, both from within and without. Being 'subject to' acknowledges the process of being on the receiving end of internal and external forces, with a consequent limitation of agency. Being 'subject of' implies the capacity to appropriate the forces acting on and in the subject – to state for oneself. The movement from being 'subject to' to being 'subject of' is undertaken through an inward reflective process, which takes account and appropriates the experience.

Becoming a subject in adolescence is closely linked with experiences of separation, and through reflection on experience, being able to take into account aspects of oneself, and one's situation in the social world. Cahn (1998) has applied these ideas to adolescence. He has conceptualised adolescence as being primarily concerned with 'subjectivation' (becoming a subject). This is taken to mean the process where the adolescent confers meaning to intrapsychic and intersubjective experiences of change. Cahn's view of 'subjectivation' is that the individual adolescent is involved in an internal struggle and a social process in becoming-a-subject, leading to a sense of self in the world (individual identity) and holding a sense of truth(s). Alternatively, the process may be unfulfilling and may 'lure him/her into a closed ideology or delusion, alienating or imprisoning him/her and distorting his/her world' (Cahn, 1998, p. 159). Thus the adolescent develops characteristic ways of relating to new experiences, primarily in relationships. There may be adolescents who tend to relate newness back to the familiar or already known, while others are open to the unknown. Preference for the familiar and known leads to repetitive or mechanical ways of relating, while, at the other extreme, a privileging of newness over the familiar can lead to a manic search for excitement. Between these two extremes are oscillating moments of openness and closure. Subjectivity is not 'hatched' (as Blos described), but it, rather elusively, comes into focus and then recedes; or it focuses on one aspect before another takes precedence. Kennedy (2000) argues that the sense of becoming a subject is experienced around times of opening up and closing down, of being present and absent, and appearing and disappearing. Adolescents are thus involved in an uncertain and essentially anxious process, of discovering moments of 'being themselves', in the course of developing their sense of their own subjectivity. When they are, or feel themselves to be, 'subject to' experiences from within or outside; that is, from the social world, there results a sense of inauthenticity and frustration.

Case example

Joseph is agonised by his relationships with his peers in a sixth form college. He feels he is rather stuck in a role he took up, as being at the centre of decision making in his group. He found that if he felt he wished to relate to others in a less powerful way, he was not listened to or taken seriously. As a consequence he began to feel very frustrated with his peers, and misunderstood by them.

Joseph does not talk much about his home life to his friends. He tries to protect himself from having to discuss a background he finds alternatively painful and humiliating. His father is frequently depressed, and Joseph is very intolerant of his depression. He complains with intense frustration that his father does not do anything to help himself. Thus he cannot bear his father's states of mind, which probably are, in fact, quite provocative.

Joseph was initially quite unaware that he could not tolerate depression or depressive feelings in himself, and that his father mirrored for him his own difficulty in tolerating depressed feelings and vulnerability. Whenever he was involved in the kind of relating in which depressive feelings emerged, he withdrew from the relationship, with a critical thought that he, and others, ought to 'pull themselves together'. In his therapy, he began to become aware of and tolerate his depressed feelings and vulnerability. This led him to feel more sympathetic to his father and to also engage with his peers in discussions of an emotional nature. He could, for example, let them comment on his emotional states without feeling attacked.

Joseph's situation illustrates how reflection upon and containment of unbearable aspects of the self increase the possibilities of separating from parental figures and generating greater internal independence. Joseph was 'subject to' being like his father internally, and his fear of depressed feelings led him to compensate through taking up powerful roles with his friends. Through reflection in his therapy he was able to get to know these aspects of himself and gradually to feel less terrorised by them. This introduced a more depressive field in which toleration of his own feelings was accompanied by greater sympathy for his father and greater flexibility in his relationships with his peers.

Then, instead of having to adopt powerful, knowing positions with them, he was more able to enter the to-and-fro of discussion about himself and others and could be more open about himself, his emotional life and his background, selectively, with others. Powerfulness based on avoidance and denial of vulnerability was transformed into power/knowledge based on reflection on inner states, leading to more flexibility in his subject positions. He did not have to be the powerful leader all the time. He thus became more 'subject of' than 'subject to', and an identity based on but separate from his childhood began to emerge.

The perspective of subject relations is recent and it has not been applied extensively to adolescence, nor is there a coherently developed infantile model of subject relations, to which professionals working with adolescents can refer. One account is provided by Urwin (1998). She discusses how an infant's subjectivity is located in 'social practices which occur frequently and regularly in particular infants' lives, such as feeding, bathing and other care taking operations, greetings and farewells, certain forms of regularised play and games and so on' (p. 282). The prioritising of social practices cuts across the individual – context dichotomy, and raises the question as to where individuals are 'positioned' in a particular discourse. Secondly, Urwin creates a central place in her thinking for the ubiquity of power relations, which, following Foucault, she claims 'are integral to the production and reproduction of discourses' (p. 284). Power is relative and depends on positioning within discourses, so that individuals are not statically once and for all powerful or powerless. Power relations 'interpenetrate the reproduction of subjectivity throughout children's development' (p. 285). Urwin claims that these developments do not in any way replace the emphasis on emotionality and unconscious processes that are central to psychoanalytic thinking, but rather they provide a framework for thinking about another domain – subjectivity – within a psychoanalytic discourse.[4]

Urwin applies this model to infant development. The one-year-old, in his glorious and majestic omnipotence, entertains an illusion of control while also is increasingly aware of dependency on adults. Adults can intervene to reposition the baby in more 'adult' directions, while the baby's discovery of separation is experienced as annihilating. A new relation between baby and mother emerges, in which the assertion of more adult and powerful positioning is brought about through the suppression of more dependent positions. The tension between two conflicting wishes – to be independent and to be dependent – leads to the infant oscillating between the two, so that gaining one implies a loss of the other.

In my own experience I recall observing an infant, Samantha, who (at 17 months, 13 days) was 'playing with some shoes. She selected a pair of her mother's and put one foot into one of these shoes, looking serious, concentrating. She stopped, took her foot out, and ran down the corridor. She ran back with a packet of baby wipes, calling out 'mummy' (Briggs, 1997).

Samantha tries out, quite literally, what it feels like to be in mummy's shoes, but a baby self who needs a mummy reasserts itself, and she urgently aims to put mother in role, and herself in a dependent baby position rather than grown-up mummy role. She oscillated between taking a powerful position but abandoned this when her need for a mother became predominant. It can be inferred that anxiety – a fear of loss of mother and her position of being mothered – lay in between her movement from one position to another.

Adolescents, in this model, position themselves more or less powerfully, depending on the way that vulnerabilities are felt within the self. Those adolescents – like Lizzie and Joseph – who become stuck in a kind of powerful position, betray difficulties in relating to dependency, vulnerability and loss internally, and narcissistic type defences are then deployed. Joseph's development was freed up when he could tolerate his own vulnerability, and he could then move between different subject positions, intrapsychically and intersubjectively. Martin experienced a moment, when he demanded knowledge from me, when he was engaged in the conflict between power and vulnerability, and this followed naming of his fear of being alone with the burden of his feelings. Assertiveness took place in a moment in which he was aware of his fragility. Urwin concludes that '*we are produced as capable of assertive action, yet also fragile and acutely vulnerable*' (p. 321). Lizzie shows that defending against the fear of vulnerability and the search for relatively powerful positions can lead to repetitious and conservative behaviour, and this avoids knowing about – becoming subject of – the nature and meaning of specific anxieties about being more separate and thus more 'grown up'.

Relating to the body: puberty and the emergence of adult love and sexuality

Central to becoming-a-subject in adolescence is the assimilation or appropriation of the images of and relationships to the bodily changes of puberty. Internal conflict stems from the way this process of ownership is accomplished and the difficulties that are encountered. Laufer and Laufer (1984) discuss the way that conflict revolves around the 'ownership of the body' (p. 38):

> One important issue is whether the adolescent can emotionally experience his [sic] mature body as belonging to himself or reacts as if his body still belonged to his mother, who first cared for it.
>
> (ibid., p. 39)

Cahn (1998) and Ladame (2008) discuss subjectivation as constituting a process of protecting the adolescent from the risks of alienation – being a stranger in her or his own body and mind – that are active while the impact of puberty is taking place. Before subjectivation is achieved, the experience of not knowing oneself means that internal reality cannot be known nor can the adolescent have control of it – she or he is 'subject to' whatever is changing within, beyond her or his control.

There are many traditional and recent views about the appropriation by the adolescent of her or his maturing body, and the consequent emergence of sexual and loving subjectivity. Recognising the diversity of adolescence, it is important to allow for different ways in which subjectivation can take place, and these constitute different pathways through adolescence. Here three of these 'routes' will be explored – appropriating the power of infantile phantasy, taking an aesthetic route and entering into sexual discourses.

Appropriating the power of infantile phantasy

In the classical view, puberty springs upon the adolescent, from the quiescence of latency, breaking down *'an internal system of civilisation; a structure of defences whereby law and order and sublimations have been established to some extent'* (Hoxter, 1964, p. 14). This leads to an awareness of power, either as an intense process to which one is subject, or as an infiltration of powerfulness into the subject, so that there is an awareness that physical and mental power is available and can be used. Thus the adolescent has the physical means to put infantile phantasies into practice. *'He* [sic] *can really attack, destroy, rob, murder or commit suicide, and he can really have sexual experiences of a heterosexual or homosexual kind'* (Hoxter, 1964, p. 13).

Recapitulation of the Oedipal conflicts of early childhood has long been considered an essential aspect of the turbulence of adolescence, for boys and girls (Jones, 1922; Waddell, 1998). The intense anxieties produced by the intense desires breaking through and breaching the defences of latency lead to either a wish to deny sexuality or to act.

The process of accepting the bodily changes may become fraught. The adolescent oscillates between states of mind in which she or he more wishes to be – or identify with – being a child to her or his parents and times when she or he wishes to move forward to being *like* the parents. To progress requires recognition of the developmental nature of past hurts, such as being excluded from the parental relationship and indeed for the range of humiliations, pains and narcissistic wounds experienced in childhood. This involves allow-ing for not having a perfect childhood or even the childhood that one wished to have.

The recent development of our understanding of the proc-ess of maturation of the brain during adolescence maps on to this route towards appropriation of the power of infantile phan-tasy. Generating the capacity to control cognitively the increasing strength of the body and mind, and making sense of these internal experiences, is a cumulative process that takes place alongside the changes in the body.

Taking the aesthetic route

The vividness of the aesthetic encounter in adolescence may be pro-found, almost as Sacks (1986) describes the impact of a heightened sense of smell in transforming everyday experiences. Rose Tremain in 'The way I found her' begins her story and her character's first awareness of puberty with an aesthetic encounter:

> I once thought beauty was something found only in old paintings. It never really occurred to me that ordinary people could be beau-tiful, here and now. And then I saw – that day in July – that they could be and that my mother was one of them.

This awakening with its new view of the world will have implica-tions that will be worked out and worked through in the course of the story. It is arresting that this narrative – albeit fictional – shows adolescence emerging through an encounter with beauty.[5] Perhaps this avoids in a quasi – intellectual way the problem of aggression and sexuality. The aesthetic encounter is a way of awakening to adult sexuality, and the potential for adult love.

Case example

A young man I saw for a therapeutic consultation, Stan, told me he did not get on with his girlfriend; they argued and they seemed not to have similar interests. He then looked at me directly and said, 'I do love her though', as though to make a clear point; that it was not his girlfriend that was the problem, in his perspective, but rather his problem in loving.

Anna Dartington used to ask adolescents as they talked about their entangled and troublesome relationships, 'but do you love him/her?' and I think thus acknowledged for the adolescents that an adult was prepared to take their loves seriously. Using Urwin's model of emergent power relations, it could be said that this is a way of promoting a more powerful, adult position in the adolescent. On the other hand, taking the adolescent's wish to love seriously involves acknowledging both the complexity of the emotion, the oscillations between love and hate, and the potential violence in the adolescent's awakening to this quality of experience. Lewis Little, the hero of Tremain's novel, became entangled in a state of murderousness and guilt:

> In the night, after beginning to read Crime and Punishment I had a dream about Raskolnikov and I woke up sweating. I didn't know whether, in the nightmare, I'd been Raskolnikov or his intended victim, Alena Ivanovna. For a moment it seemed to me as if everything in my attic room was yellow and I felt suffocated and sick.
>
> (p. 110)

These nightmares and the confusion of roles – murderer or victim – appear as the flipside of the aesthetic conflict. The emphasis here is on the disturbing impact of new emotional experiences, and with Bion's idea of 'catastrophic change'. Catastrophic change refers to the view that 'all development brings in its train the threat of catastrophe to the mind' (Hinshelwood, 1989), which is ultimately its annihilation or breakdown. The violence of the explosiveness of catastrophic change proposes that the aesthetic conflict is being subject to the impact of violence within, which degrades the 'beautiful' object.

For Bion, catastrophic change occurred in the little oscillations between the paranoid schizoid and the depressive positions. A movement towards loving involves anxieties and pains about the other person and about being separate. When concern and guilt feel intolerable, the anxiety about annihilation in the paranoid schizoid position is re-experienced. It is impossible, Bion wrote, to 'escape the odium inseparable from the mind, refuge is sure to be sought in mindlessness, sexualisation, acting out, and degrees of stupor' (Bion, 1970, p. 126). Perhaps stupor refers to the adolescent's propensity to sleep in! The 'odium' of the mind, or, as Kristeva (1982) refers, to a similar kind of notion 'abjection', that is located very close to the body and to love.

The idea of catastrophic change at puberty was expressed succinctly by a 13-year-old boy, who said that *though he was growing it was not a problem for him, but he had two friends who did have problems, because for one of them his bones were growing faster than his muscles and ligaments, and with the other friend it was the other way round; his muscles were growing faster than his bones. One of them was very stiff and the other was very floppy.* This disaster – located projectively in his friends – also indicated that two qualities that had been in synchrony with each other until puberty were now violently opposed to each other, an acute problem for the container–contained relationship.

Engaging with sexual discourses

Traditionally, thinking about adolescence has emphasised the development, through puberty, of adult sexuality and its impact on the individual. This does not take into account the multiplicities and diversities which prevail in contemporary contexts and the complex ways in which adolescents have to engage with current themes, or discourses, about sexuality. A 'discourse', as Foucault discussed the term, refers to 'the way in which meanings cohere around an assumed central proposition, which gives them their value and significance' (Hollway and Jefferson, 2000, p. 14).[6] Foucault pointed out that sex had been 'put into discourses' which regulated the development of the individual, and the species:

> [sex] was at the pivot of two axes which developed the entire political technology of life. On the one hand it was tied to the discipline of the body; the harnessing, intensification and distribution of forces, the adjustment and economy of energies. On the other hand it was applied to the regulation of populations ... sex was the means of access both to the life of the body and the life of the species'.
>
> (1979, p. 145)

Though seemingly at odds with psychoanalytic accounts of sexuality, Foucault's work, in fact, contextualises and provides an underpinning philosophical standpoint for contemporary thinking.[7] Foucault provides a way of thinking about different discourses of sexuality, and his conceptualisations take into account the multiplicity of contemporary sexual discourses. Contemporary discourses include the 'promiscuous discourse', which holds that 'sex with many partners can be both pleasurable and harmless' (Hollway, 1989), alongside a discourse, post AIDS, of the fear of the damaging effects of sex, especially male homosexual sex. There is a discourse about 'heterosexual erotic love', which is a specific cultural product (Chodorow, 1995, p. 91). Dominant 'discourses' can exclude those of other cultures, and, though gay sexuality has increased its status, becoming more visible and tolerated in some sections of society, this is still a 'deeply stigmatised identity' (Edwards, 1997).

Sexual discourses are diverse, and they are also ubiquitous. For adolescents the ubiquity of discourses of sex mean that it 'penetrates and controls everyday pleasure', it 'incites and intensifies' and is 'produced' by talk (including media – talk and images) about sexuality (Foucault, 1979). It is indeed extremely difficult for adolescents to turn away from such dominance, and to still find an identity. Being a 'nerd' may be an oppositional and derogated alternative 'discourse' for a contemporary adolescent, but it contests or resists the mainstream of pervasive sexuality, rather than arising in isolation to it.

Since sexual discourses are all pervasive, the body becomes the focus – or 'site' – for the experiencing of self and society and a preoccupation with issues of control, integrity and autonomy. The body is suffused with potential meaning through intersubjective experiences. Just making contact with others has this effect. Additionally, developing an identity is inevitably connected with developing a bodily identity, and subjectivity must be thought of as emerging from a mind/body unity, rather than from a split between the two. Bodily and emotional unity may be demonstrated through the embodiment of emotionality. For example, words we use – being affected, upset, touched, moved, shocked, alarmed etc. – indicate this unity and embodiment of experience.[8] Mental processes can symbolise these embodied experiences.

The working upon bodily experience, transforming it or symbolising it connects with both an old tradition in psychoanalysis, which was central to Freud's early work, and a current psychosocial viewpoint. The body is a 'theatre' (McDougall 1986) and states of body – for example, being held – can be transferred through symbolism, dreaming and phantasising, into states of mind. This has a particular relevance for thinking about eating disorders and other problems relating to the body image (see Chapter 7). Bion's development of the mind on the model of the digestive system makes parallel physical and mental states. 'It is important', he wrote, when discussing the transformation of 'beta elements' into 'alpha' 'to distinguish between memories and undigested facts'. Alpha function in this analogy is the stomach, the storehouse, in which experiences are transformed into thoughts, memories and symbolic representation. 'Beta elements are stored but differ from alpha elements in that they are not so much memories as undigested facts' (Bion, 1962, pp. 6–7).

Bion's model of the mind can be applied to the continual transformation of self in situated contexts, when the raw experiences of self are subject to processes of reflection.

Through engagement in sociocultural and interpersonal contact, the body is in constant transformation through experience, so that there is 'a continuous stream of affect between the everyday social environment and the ways in which people might come to subjectively experience their bodies to feel who they are' (Buytendijk, 1974, p. 174).

Adolescents are particularly affected by these processes. The experience of puberty has a tremendous and turbulent impact in social situations, demonstrating tension between the containment of bodily experience, through reflection, attempting to control turbulence,[9] and managing what is happening internally, the fluidity of experiences.[10] The interaction of internal and social factors in producing experiences of the body during adolescence has been a focus of recent studies. Prendergast (1995), discussing girl's experiences of menstruation, suggests that 'experience of bodily shock, fragmentation and disorder accompanies menstrual experience in the West' (p. 210). The 'body is in the mind', in a preoccupying sense, so that the adolescent is constantly involved in managing, controlling or containing experiences. In some circumstances, the adolescent defensively distances from bodily experiences and objectifies the body or dissociates from it. Awareness of emerging adult embodiment is developed as much through social relations – especially school peers – and through the containing capacity of the mother, as through 'identification' with parents. Sayers' (1991) reports of accounts of girls reaching puberty show mothers to be either dismissing of the girl's emotional experience (that is how it is remembered) or objectifying of 'it' in the way they discuss menstruation and sexuality. Thus it is the context in which emerging adult sexuality is contained, which is the most powerful factor in adolescent engagement with sexual discourses.

How internal factors and social experiences of parents, families and peers produce understanding of ways of 'doing' gender has been the focus of recent discussions for boys (Frosh et al., 2002), and girls and boys in schools (Prendergast and Forrest, 1997). Johannsson (2007) gathers together 'doing gender' for both boys and girls. Gendered identities are seen to be relational and plural, contextual, performative and potentially fragile; how individual girls and boys develop engagement with sexual – and gendered – discourses can be explored here through case examples, where the aim is to focus on the meaning and implications for the individuals concerned of the interplay of internal and social experiences.

Case example

Satya, who was 18 when she began therapy, provides an example of a young woman whose experiences of and at puberty underpinned her anxieties about her development. An aspect of her experience of puberty was illustrated by a dream. 'She was in a lift in which she regularly travels. On this occasion it travelled as usual, floor by floor, until it reached the 12th floor. Then it took off, exploding upwards and she was fearful both that it would not stop and that it would crash to earth'. The understanding we came to share about this dream was that each floor represented a year of her life; the 12th floor related to the onset of puberty, which began when she was 11. After puberty, the gradual progress, floor by floor, or year by year, was replaced with a violent explosiveness. Satya's experience of the transition from childhood to adolescence was then explosive, fearful and catastrophic.

The impact of puberty and early adolescence was complicated by Satya's sexual experiences at this time. Her guilt about her rather precocious sexuality turned into an attempt to make sure others did not notice and she assumed a rather excessively child-like appearance. In her looks and in her clothes, she seemed more like a young girl than a young woman. She portrayed the adult world as monstrous, and she talked about not being able to find a path to join the worlds in which adults lived. She knew she had to go into the adult world, but she was terrified of it. She wanted to have a boyfriend but she was terrified of closeness. She had a sense of not being integrated in her body, which was represented in dreams of houses which had 'bits' stuck on randomly, and haphazardly rather than planned or integrated development. She felt herself to be missing an important part of herself, which she thought of as bodily, and which felt dirty and ugly, but which she could not describe in words.

For Satya, adult sexual bodies had become abject and contaminated. Kristeva (1982) in developing the idea of abjection, controversially perhaps, represented female sexuality as an uncontainable flow, as characterised by menstrual blood. The abject includes food and bodily incorporation, abjection towards bodily waste, the horror of the corpse and towards sexual difference. As a descriptive category, the abject does capture something of the awfulness and degradation of the way some adolescents experience the body. In groups, the most debased, despised feelings and thoughts can be projected into others, and this makes life especially miserable when the others in the group return these feelings, and others, in taunts or verbal and physical assaults.[11]

As well as recapitulating early infantile and Oedipal development, for girls the experience of puberty *'introduces its own fundamental changes and challenges to physical and psychological integrity'* (Plaut and Hutchinson, 1986, p. 418). In this view, male and female experiences of puberty are seen to be qualitatively different, and that for the girl especially there is a fundamental or new experience to account for at puberty. The impact of puberty then needs to be taken seriously as a transforming experience, and as having meaning in its own right. There has been considerable recent understanding of 'how romantic and sexual desires are formed during adolescence, when there is a coming together of childhood, culture and pubertal development' (Chodorow, 1995, p. 102). Particularly through exploring the experiences of peers, friendships, education, and parents, studies have shown how girls' subjectivity can be bodily focussed and subject to intense peer scrutiny. It is now commonplace that girls' identities are relational, with capacities for intimacy and emotionality. These identities may of course be a source for exerting pressures to achieve relative to other girls and also boys. The inclusion of educational attainment as an identifier can produce 'classroom superiority'[12] to boys (Johannsson, 2007). For girls, educational achievement has taken on a particular emphasis and thus 'being happy cannot be separated from good academic performance' (Walkerdine et al., 2001, p. 136). Sexuality as well as happiness gyrates around the centrality of the educational attainment discourse, generating meaning, self-esteem and developmental crises.

Emergent masculinity

The essential background to understanding young masculinities is the idea expressed in the dichotomy between emotional, relational girls and 'doing', acting boys. Sayers (1991) expressed this view when she suggested that while young women seem to maintain relatedness with others – even if disappointed in the quality of the relationships – young men find it difficult to maintain this kind of contact and become divided internally (Sayers, 1991). The diversity of male experiences of puberty and early adolescence, and the plurality of masculinities has been shown to consist of boys' capacities to relate differently depending on the context at the time. Frosh et al. (2002) showed that boys are capable of emotional and deep articulacy in contexts where these potentialities are recognised – especially in mixed gender groups and talking to adults, and more likely to express 'hegemonic' masculinities in same sex groups. Hegemonic masculinities privilege sporting and physical prowess and downgrades 'softer qualities such as educational achievements. It is in these circumstances that homophobia arises as a definition of a non-acceptable identity within hegemonic masculinity. The difficulty of 'coming out' in strongly homophobic hegemonic masculine cultures creates particular tensions around gay sexuality in adolescence. Hawton and Rodham (2006, p. 81) found that young people (boys and girls) with worries about homosexual orientation were highly associated with suicidal ideation and behaviour.[13] The tensions and anxieties about sexual orientation is probably explained by fears surrounding peer and parent response. This oppressive social context does not facilitate containment of the 'normal' bisexuality of early adolescence (Blos, 1967).

For boys caught up with hegemonic masculinity, the lure of girlfriends provides opportunities for the legitimisation through these relationships of less 'macho' ways of relating. Being with a girlfriend can provide opportunities for expression of more tender and emotional characteristics. However, when boys' development is subject to difficulties, their subjectivity can become stuck, often within hegemonic masculinity, as the following case examples illustrate.

Case example

One boy, Jerry, 11, experienced puberty as exciting and dangerous. His discussions were interspersed with talk of power kites that 'go high' and of having a 'six inch knife'. He was preoccupied with size and power and risk. He told me his kite might not be the biggest one but it still might pull him off the ground.

Jerry had difficulty in maintaining contact in relationships and the manic excitement and violence of his feelings at puberty threatened to split him off further from others and thus from the possibility of having these feelings modulated through containment. The vicissitudes of bodily experiences at puberty can lead to abject experiences.

Case example

Harry, 17, told me that his life had changed twice in adolescence. He portrayed himself as having a rather miserable childhood. He started his therapy as a rather insubstantial figure, wrapped usually in a bulky jacket and baseball cap. He spoke in a low monotone and complained of sleeplessness, and depression.

Interactions at home were very thinly described and he could not with any substance talk about the kind of child he had been. He was not really able to describe satisfying times with his parents, or convey a sense of being able to call on them when he was in difficulties. This rather abject picture of himself was redeemed when he found, quite by chance when he was 12, a sudden and surprising ability to play golf. Indeed he was so good that he obtained sponsorship at a national level. When he was 15, he found, almost as suddenly, that his skills stopped developing. He lost his sponsorship and his hopes of being a sports star.

After the loss of his hopes of sporting stardom, Harry could not find new routes to satisfaction within himself. He seemed to have few resources inside himself to draw on and mourn the loss of narcissistic gratification he had invested in the ideal of becoming a star. It seemed important that the discovery of the sporting ability arose out of a childhood, which seemed not to be nourishing. Harry's hope of becoming a sporting star complies with hegemonic masculinity, valuing 'doing', physicality. In Harry's case, the common fantasy in adolescence of becoming a star was made all the more poignant and tantalising by the fact that it nearly became attainable – he found a talent in himself and got within touching distance of it. The loss of his sporting aspirations was painful and difficult to mourn, leaving him empty of hope or aspiration and suggestive of the idea that when there is such an emphasis on activity, 'doing', masculinity can seem an empty or fragile concept (Frosh et al., 2002). On the other hand Harry's suddenly acquired sporting ability had the effect of lifting him above the misery of his internal world, and the limitations of his relationships. Sayers (1991) illustrates the way adolescents idolise others, mainly male sporting or music stars. Blos (1984) approved hero worship and idolisation, and the cult of poster personality, which adorns teenage bedrooms. Sayers (1991, p. 117), with a wealth of self-reports, show that the heroes and idols of adolescence are long remembered. Harry, though, was taking himself as hero. His sudden emergence of a physical prowess following puberty brought a sense of power and achievement, triumphing briefly over his miserable childhood. The hope for sporting success was harnessed as a means of saving himself from his inner world. It had the effect of making it seem unnecessary to undertake the emotional work of adolescence. In this sense, it was stuck on to his identity like Satya stuck adulthood on to her body. Harry wished to turn himself into an idol and in losing this possibility, lost his 'ideal'. Hanna Segal (1995) considers the difference between idealisation and ideal, pointing out that idealisation is narcissistic, in the paranoid schizoid position, while having ideals can be depressive:

> Idealisation is a distortion of realities and a dangerous stance, since it is invariably accompanied by splitting and projection – idealising

oneself and one's ideas or groups at the expense of paranoid attitudes to others. Having ideals is very different; it is not pathological
to hope for a better future; for instance for peace and to strive for it,
whilst recognising how hard it is to attain, and that the opposition
to it comes not only from others but also has its roots in ourselves.

(1995, p. 204)

Summary

- This chapter has explored the meaning of subjectivity in adolescence, the process in which adolescents have diverse experiences
  of bodily changes and separation from familiar ways of relating
  as a child.
- While traditional views of separating are uni-directional, recent
  thinking suggests that the conceptualisation of movements
  between positions provides a more flexible and adaptable way
  of looking at adolescent development. The movement between
  paranoid schizoid and depressive positions and the taking up
  of subject positions within different contexts of power and vulnerability are two ways in which understanding of adolescent
  development is deepened.
- Adolescents may experience both powerful and vulnerable
  aspects of themselves. The case examples show adolescents strug-
  gling within these dimensions to make sense of change, separating and their relationships with others. Change is experienced in
  complex ways and has deep emotional impact.
- A very important consideration in adolescent development is the
  embodiment of change. The changes of puberty and the engagement with having a mature body lead to engagement with adult
  sexuality and love. Adolescents take diverse 'routes' to establishing gendered identity, including appropriating the power of
  infantile phantasies, encountering the aesthetic and entering into
  sexual discourses.
- Adolescent development needs to be considered as taking place
  through the interplay of internal and social processes, including
  the construction of gender. Childhood, pubertal development
  and culture interact to create different meanings for male and
  female adolescents in the appropriation of maturity.

3

ETHNICITY AND IDENTITY IN ADOLESCENCE

One of the important ways in which a unitary sense of identity formation in adolescence has been severely disturbed is through the impact of the diversity of ethnic identities. This chapter explores the impact of ethnicities on identity construction in adolescence, through developing and applying the discussion of subjectivity and identity in Chapter 2. How these considerations affect thinking about therapeutic work is discussed and illustrated with case examples.

Across cultural boundaries

Ethnic identity formation in adolescence involves both social and internal processes:

> the point of confluence of economic, political, cultural and psychic processes ... where multiple subject positions are juxtaposed, contested, proclaimed or disavowed.
>
> (Brah, 1996, p. 208)

Thus it is important, following the discussion in Chapter 2, to consider the specific meanings of 'becoming-a-subject' that emerge for adolescents in cross-cultural, multicultural and different cultural contexts. Subjectivation protects the adolescent from vulnerabilities that arise from being 'subject to' internal and social forces during the period in which the adolescent in an intense internal struggle of ownership of the body, mind and desires. Vulnerabilities and the struggles of subjectivation are more complex and intense in contested or conflictual areas, leaving more potentially beyond the individual's control. If the process may be unfulfilling and may 'lure him/her into a closed ideology or delusion, alienating or imprisoning him/her and distorting his/her world' (Cahn, 1998, p. 159). Involvement in the struggle to find and establish identity in terms of ethnicity involves the adolescent, especially the minority ethnic adolescent, in difficult and exacting processes of developing cohesiveness, a sense of self, within complex and divisive contexts. How sociocultural practices become produced and reproduced as individual development and identity is central to understanding these processes. Professionals working with adolescents from a range of cultures have to be sensitive to and understanding of different nuances of meaning, and multiple, plural contexts. This has been shown to be important in therapeutic work, though this kind of work still requires much more detailed exploration (Bains, 2001).

Case example

Pavan, an Indian woman of 18, told me on her first meeting with me, that she had asked to come to the clinic because she had heard it was a 'good place'. She came, she said, from an extended family in which her grandparents and her father's sister and her family lived in the same household as her parents and siblings.

Pavan said she was doing A levels, and she was worried about them, as she had no confidence in her work and she needed her A levels to be able to leave home. In fact her work had been going down hill for some time. She said she was very anxious about her schoolwork, and felt urgently that some help was needed. In a despondent, pessimistic way she asked me how long she would have to come to therapy for it to make a difference. She thought it would take years for her therapy to help her, and she did not have that long – her A levels were in a matter of months. When I asked her about cultural issues, in the context of her starting therapy, she very definitely said no, cultural issues were not important to her, and added that 'all her friends are white'.

Pavan's response to the question of culture created ambiguity. She seemed to convey that she is quite comfortable in white company, and it may be thought of as a way of reassuring me, a white man, that she had no problem with me. On the other hand, if taken literally, it may mean there are problems with same culture friends. Talking about culture directly seems to make her anxious, and this is an important consideration at the beginning of a therapeutic relationship, when the adolescent may already feel anxious and vulnerable. The adolescent may respond in a compliant way to thinking directly about this issue, and the topic may have been raised many times at school and in other contexts. Pavan does seem to be quite protective of me from the beginning. She was very descriptive about her family structure and explained to me, to put me in the picture. Perhaps she expects me to misunderstand her situation; perhaps she thinks the only model of a family in my mind is of a nuclear family. At the same time as being descriptive, she denied the close family connections a name – she does not assert, for example, that she lives in an Indian family. As the discussion continued, the wish to leave home and to get away from her culture appeared to be very linked. The discussion of leaving home suggested a cultural issue was important, since this is not usually an uncontested option for a young woman in an Indian family.

There are pressures on ethnic minority adolescents to assimilate to another culture. The experience of starting therapy is a cross-cultural experience for a young woman like Pavan, and her initial contact with me constitutes an accommodation to other cultures, the culture of psychotherapy, and the culture of the clinic. Often, 'psychotherapy is perceived as a type of treatment that has its roots firmly planted in the host culture' (Bains, 2001, p. 68). Pavan's accommodation was accompanied by her awareness of a problem in herself and within her family, which has led to her starting therapy. She may have a very wide range of feelings and thoughts about this, and like many adolescents who refer themselves, starting therapy may be undertaken with a doubtful or ambiguous relationship with her family in mind. The quality of Pavan's early communications, that is, the way she talks about her family, suggests that a boundary (between siblings and cousins) is blurred. She seems to be under an imperative to get away from home, and given this she appears to be reassuring herself that she has found a 'good place', which will help. She is thus in a vulnerable position between two cultures in which communications are tinged with ambiguity and multiple meanings.

Two possibilities thus emerge very early in this therapy; firstly, that Pavan has an anxious approach to meeting a white man in a therapist's role, in a new culture and, expecting not to be understood, she is fearful and thus tries to reassure, and protect. The second possibility is that there is a problem within her family, which she needs to get away from, and that this seems to mean making a move across cultures, away from her own, and potentially rejecting her own. Rejection of her family and culture, together with an idealisation of English culture and the 'good' place of the clinic may also be Pavan's attempts to deal with her difficulties, and these attempts also place her in a vulnerable position. Thus, in terms of her identity,

Pavan is developing within a context in which the potential loss of her identity as an Indian woman is accompanied by anxiety about acceptance across a cultural boundary. Like many young people from ethnic minority backgrounds, she starts therapy when there is 'a deepening and widening divide between themselves and family members, mainly parents' (Bains, 2001, p. 66).

Tolerating and not tolerating difference

Identity is constructed around issues of sameness and difference, within power relations. 'Every identity is founded on an exclusion and, in that sense, is an "effect of power". There must be something which is external to an identity' (Hall, 2000, p. 234). Ethnic identity is formed in a context of racism, so that the experience of negative experiences in social contact has a dynamic effect on process of assimilation and acculturation, which are internalised. Racism is, of course, a powerfully destructive experience, which is extremely hurtful to victims and also denying of their status as individuals, as subjects. It occurs in a paranoid–schizoid field, in which unwanted or unbearable aspects of the self are split off and put into others (Rustin, 1991) in order to avoid an experience of difference and to sustain a distorted sense of superior power. Racism in these terms lies deeply configured in the unconscious, and racist dynamics are extremely early, primitive and infantile. For example, Tan (1993) points out that extreme violence and hatred are central to racism, and that they are used to aim at obliterating difference. He adds that 'difference serves as a constant reminder of the painful early experience of impending loss of the "good breast" which for some infants is unbearable' (p. 33).

The racist subject aims to construct a divided world in which sameness and difference are equated with goodness and badness, and in which the 'bad' is located outside, as an enemy or demonised other.

The idea that unbearable or intolerable experiences of separation are a motive force in racism connects with the adolescent preoccupation with separation from internal parental figures. The process of forming identity, of sorting the 'me' from the 'not me' and differentiating, therefore, sameness and difference, are to the forefront of adolescent experiences. Tolerating difference, and thus moving from a paranoid schizoid into a depressive field, occurs in the process of flux, in which the adolescent characteristically develops. In adolescence, attempts to be open to difference and moments of closure can follow each other quite rapidly, movement in one direction or another, being triggered by what might seem to be a small event.

Back (1997) provides an example in which friendships between two white British and a Vietnamese young man briefly flourish, and then breakdown under the impact of difference being too difficult to tolerate. The painfulness that results is substantial. When the Vietnamese man was asked by a new youth club worker how to spell his name – Tanyi – one of the white friends, Cliff, answered 'just write it Tony'. Back points out that Anglicisation of names is accommodated by Vietnamese youth on the grounds that the whites could not pronounce their names properly. But on this occasion, and within the rather precarious nature of their friendship, Cliff exerts dominance and his resentment of difference is communicated. Tanyi stopped seeing the other boys and stopped going to the youth club. Though white young men justified the absence of Vietnamese young men from the youth club with the view that 'they just like to keep themselves to themselves', Tanyi told a youth worker that he had stopped attending because of the racist 'verbals' he suffered, and that he did not 'want them to use me as something to play with'. Thus Tanyi expressed the impact of the projective processes to which he was subjected, that he was scapegoated within this group, and he was objectified as a 'toy'. Within the power relationship between Cliff and Tanyi, negative experiences of cross-cultural contact are projected into Tanyi, who withdraws into a same cultural network.

This example shows the potential fluidity of group formation and its precariousness. It also illustrates in microcosm how contact across cultures can tenuously be made, and then the power with which the negative attributions and the powerful assertions of sameness – on the basis of agreeing with the dominant – lead to withdrawal. The more threatened an individual, family and culture, the more the withdrawal leads to organisation based on sameness. This has a protective function for the oppressed individual, family and culture, but it also occurs in a persecutory field in which negative experiences are taken in, or internalised, to become part of identity (Bains, 2001).

If we return to Pavan's case, the complexities of negative experiences, in the context of making contact with a new, different culture, and with a white therapist are evident. The sense of badness within, and her protective approach to me, may indicate a problem within her family, a way of dealing with anticipated experiences of not being understood and an expectation of negative experience. 'The overarching context is not simply multicultural, but one which contains cultural hierarchies, dominant ideologies as well as cultural and political struggle. The individual's psyche cannot escape these issues, it reflects them and is obliged to constantly find ways to resolve and survive them' (Lowe, 2001). In the therapeutic encounter, it is extremely difficult to be clear in which domain the meaning of experiences such as these belong. Bains emphasises that:

> It should be noted that when dealing with the psychological effects of social processes (i.e. racism) it is extremely difficult to differentiate between whether a defence is dysfunctional (e.g. a result of underlying conflicts) or functional (e.g. appropriate) or both. However, perceived experiences of racism do require the attention from the therapist and appropriate intervention when necessary to engage the young person in the therapeutic process.
>
> (Bains, 2001, p. 68)

Cultural identity and hybridity

Adolescents seeking therapy are often involved in a 'deepening and wider divide between themselves and family members, mainly parents' (Bains, 2001, p. 66). Thus therapists and other professional workers become involved in complex patterns of individual and cultural change, and an encounter, in 'juxtaposed, contested, proclaimed or disavowed' dimensions with the meaning of 'multicultural' or cross-cultural connections and change.

Thus therapists and other professionals are working now from positions in which everyone – professionals, institutions, adolescents, their families and networks – is involved in pluralistic cultural contexts. In the background, is the contradictory, even paradoxical, experience of 'globalisation', which makes everything the same, and, pulling in the opposite direction, increases diversity, so that there is no longer a monolithic, binary difference absolute sameness and absolute difference, but 'every concept or meaning is inscribed in a chain or in a system within which it refers to the other, to other concepts (meanings) by means of the systematic play of differences. … Meaning here has no origin or final destination, cannot be finally fixed, is always in process, "positional" along a spectrum' (Hall, 2000, p. 216).

The contradictory presence of increasing sameness and new forms of difference is most vividly seen in the problems and possibilities of muticulturalism. Hall makes this contradictory state of multiculturalism clear. On the one hand there are transitional elements which appear to open up a new notion of multicultural identity, while at the same time there are new racisms which 'are abroad everywhere and gaining ground' (p. 238). He points out that the celebration of the anniversary of the arrival of the 'Windrush' occurred at the same time as the Macpherson Inquiry report into the death of Stephen Lawrence – a juxtaposition that is 'deeply paradigmatic of the contradictory state of British multiculturalism'.

Multicultural relationships and intersubjectivities contain deeply contradictory states. It is, on the one hand, situated in a context of white dominance, where anyone else is other (black) and in which the ascription, black, marks a sign of resistance. They are subject to the invasive projections of racism and, more subtly, objectification, as stereotypical representatives – Hall's (1988) 'the violent avenger' is one kind of projected image of black youth, which persists in the attribution of violent deviance, not only to African Caribbean young men, but, more recently, also to the Asian gang (Alexander, 2000). 'Celebratory multiculturalism', for example, highly valuing ethnic food, objectifies and disguises the experiences of contested, racist intersubjective encounters (Parker, 2000). Particularly in the realm of the body, sport and sexuality, the projection of the 'hyper-physicality' of the black body produces a 'celebratory' image, which masks denigratory undertones. In these encounters 'the shadow of the Other falls upon the Self' (Bhabha, 1990).

As well as these risks and hazards, there are new opportunities in multicultural contexts. Young people are influenced by those who 'speak a new language of hybridity and diaspora, neither torn between two cultures nor simply one or the other, but complex dynamic fusions' (Bhattacharyya and Gabriel, 1997). The consciousness of these self-definitions stand for the adoption of the need that, in diasporic conditions, 'people are often obliged to adopt shifting, multiple or hyphenated positions of identification. … Even where the more traditionally orientated sections (of society) are concerned the principle of heterogeneity continues to be strongly operative' (Hall, 2000). Hall gives typological examples of 'hybridisation':

the black teenager who is a dance-hall DJ, plays jungle music but supports Manchester United, or the Muslim student who wears baggy, hip-hop, street style jeans but is never absent from Friday prayers.

But, he also adds that 'hybridity' does not describe an individual, 'who can be contrasted as fully formed subjects with "traditionals" and "moderns"'. Within the process of 'hyphenation' or 'hybridisation' there are possibilities for transformation, which make a distinction between 'traditional' and 'modern' inadequate in that they produce fixed, inaccurate stereotypes. Hall refers to Homi Bhabha's discussion of the 'ambiguous, anxious moment of transition' as 'not simply appropriation or adaptation, it is a process through which cultures are required to revise their own systems of reference, norms and values by departing from their habitual or 'inbred' rules of transformation. Ambivalence and antagonism accompany any act of cultural translation because negotiating with the 'difference of the other' reveals the radical insufficiency of our own systems of meaning and signification' (Bhabha, 1997).

Adolescents face their own quests for identity within two overlapping processes, in which individual and cultural identity are both decentred. The ethnic minority adolescent's struggle is subject to adaptation and assimilation to and within a 'host' culture. The host adolescent, because of dominance, has more choice. Relinquishing a position of centredness, with all the privileges it seems to confer, is based more on depressive qualities of being able and willing to accept and tolerate difference, without foreclosing in negative, racist or celebratory multiculturalism. In practical terms, therapeutic work with adolescents from minority ethnic backgrounds involves the therapist in complex ways of making sense of the individual within her/his culture, and the relationship between the adolescent and her/himself.

Case example

Azma, 18, an Egyptian woman, came to therapy feeling depressed and unable to study or participate in class, where she became intransigently silent. She began her therapy energetically, striking up a good rapport and feeling understanding of and relief from her depression. She began to be able to study again and to speak in class. Not speaking became a major theme, for as well as not speaking in class, she told me she did not speak to her father. During this silence I would try to say what I felt may be the current meaning of her silence, and she would from time to time indicate her agreement or otherwise by turning her head either towards me, or away from me. She did, verbally, indicate agreement that she was worried about keeping or losing control. As she began to be more articulate, she exerted control by insisting on choosing what she would talk about and refusing to entertain discussion of any other subject; that is, she would not respond to me if I used anything other than the exact words she had used.

In these circumstances, a working theory is extremely useful. Britton (1998) in his work on 'triangular space' has developed a way of thinking about the problem of difference, through discussion of situations where it seems difficult for someone to accept a different perspective. The capacity for tolerating different perspectives arises from the early relationship between the infant and the parents.

> If the link between the parents perceived in love and hate can be tolerated in the child's mind it provides the child with a prototype for an object relationship of a third kind in which he or she is a witness and not a participant. A third position then comes into existence from which object relationships can be observed. Given this we can also envisage being observed. This provides us with a capacity for seeing ourselves in interaction with others and for entertaining another point of view whilst retaining our own – for observing ourselves whilst being ourselves. I call the mental freedom provided by this process triangular space.
>
> (1998, p. 42)

The problem for those patients in analysis who could not tolerate the third position is that the idea of another point of view is overwhelming, and threatens obliteration of the self. Any approach to a different perspective is usually met with withdrawal or violence. Britton suggests that technically at this point the only way to proceed is to demonstrate understanding of the patient's point of view, by putting it into words. This calms the patient, and provides a sense of understanding, but not collusion or agreement. The need for agreement, Britton argues, becomes insistent when disagreement needs to be annihilated. He proposes a 'general rule',

> the need for agreement is inversely proportional to the expectation of understanding. When expectation of understanding is high, difference of opinion is tolerable; when expectation of understanding is fairly high, difference is fairly tolerable; when there is no expectation of understanding, the need for agreement is absolute.
>
> (p. 57)

In this way Britton links the capacity for tolerance of difference with the experience of containment, so that the capacity to tolerate different perspectives marks a freedom or flexibility internally, in which agreement is not felt to be imperative. The greater degree of internal freedom implies greater separateness and a capacity to relinquish control of the other. If we add to this the context of adolescent identity formation, the capacity to occupy the 'third position' facilitates the capacity to move between subject positions. The acceptance of links between other people, and within others' minds mirrors the movement between different subject positions.

The problem of difference between Azma and me can be stated in external or social terms. Whereas she was Egyptian, Muslim, female and adolescent, I am White British, male, adult and my upbringing was Christian. In the relationship with her I also came to hold, or contain, the problems that were so difficult to discuss, that affected her in her family and school. The intensity of her silence and need for me to agree with her increased as she obtained greater freedom in her family and school.

How is it possible to account for these experiences of Azma in her therapy? Her silence seemed on one level to have the quality of repetition, so that her father, her tutor and I at different times experienced this silence. It also seemed to be the case that when the silence became located in her therapy, that she became freer in her other, external situations, her family and school. It is true her silence was a furious one, though this did not explain why she was furious. She was able to stay in therapy and listen to my thoughts as she was silent, occasionally indicating agreement, and when I spoke about her need to be in control, and her fear of it, she spoke in agreement. But there seemed to be something very important missing. I could say to her 'look, there's silence here, like there was silence at school and at home, and we can try and think together about this'; yet this was not possible, until, indirectly, she brought material which expressed her position in cultural terms that more openness was possible.

She talked to me over a number of sessions about two groups of school friends. One group was focused on homework, the other on parties and going out. She is a member of the homework group, but she would also like to be in the party group. On one occasion she told me that at lunchtime she went to sit with the party group. Then she saw that there was only one member of the homework group, and she felt awful that she had left this girl on her own. To compound her misery the girls in the party group asked her, rather rejectingly, what she was doing joining them. She said she would not to do that again.

It seems very clear that the homework and party groups represent two aspects of herself, or two identifications she would like to have. She does not mention the ethnicity of the members of the two groups, but she seems to convey that the homework group is mainly Asian, or Muslim. Two more significant features occur to me. Firstly, there is the sense of a part of herself who feels left and abandoned (like the girl in the homework group) and second, she has the utmost difficulty moving between the two positions represented by the two groups.

Azma demonstrates a difficulty in moving between subject positions through her extremely constrained way of relating to me in her therapy. There was tremendous difficulty in discussing some apparently straightforward issues, particularly with regard to descriptive issues about the impact of her cultural background on her life within her family, at school and in her therapy. Azma's therapy became extremely important to her and became for her the means whereby she had been able to become more successful in the cross-cultural domain of school. When she was more confident in speaking in her therapy, she spoke about how she was constrained severely by her parents in where she could go and whom she could see, and that her parents would not countenance dating. Ultimately she expected that a marriage would be arranged for her, but that she did not think about it much. The forbidden external – dating – was mirrored by the way she dealt with her own feelings about sex and sexuality by *not* thinking.

Azma became increasingly aware of belonging to her parents' culture, but feeling able to negotiate within that sphere, and alongside this, she became more confident and less agonised in her peer relationships. Though she often had a feeling of being misunderstood, and she dreaded abandonment and rejection, she did develop a new kind of relation with her self, which was both rooted in her parents' culture, and different from her parents.

Strong cultural ties

Azma felt that she was able to reach a point in which she could have a sense of relating both within her family and across the cultural boundary. These positions were continuously changing, and agonised. In the reflective way in which she looked at herself in own culture, she felt able to draw on its strengths. Azma was able to get hold of a sense of belonging, in a strong culture.

Parekh (1991) points to the strong ties of an ethnic nature in Asian and Afro-Caribbean communities which are,

> ethnic in nature, that is, physically distinguishable, bonded by social ties arising out of shared customs, language and practice of inter-marriage- and having their distinct history, collective memories, geographical origins, views of life and modes of social organisation.

But also, at the same time, there is a sense of turbulence:

Great changes are afoot within ethnic communities and every family has become a terrain of subdued or explosive struggles. In every family, husband and wife, parents and children, brothers and sisters are having to re-negotiate and re-define their patterns of relationship in a manner that takes account both of traditional values and those characteristic of their adopted country. Different families reach their own inherently tentative conclusions.

(Hall, 2000, pp. 220–1)

The idea of a strong culture, and maintaining a place within it, that is identifying with it or feeling a sense of belonging with it, is helpful to adolescents. Though the ground is in motion in terms of the changes within families, the capacity to think about and relate to a culture, which is substantial, but also alive and changing, is distinctly advantageous. Parekh indicates the robustness of having traditions, facing change and becoming different.

Recent contexts, particularly post 9/11, illustrate the tensions and new alignments within strong culture, amidst new racisms. A current focus on Muslim experiences and the pre-eminence in this discourse of the close interrelationship between religion, culture and family as markers of identity, has necessitated both rethinking and revisions of multiculturalism. One strand of this is the recognition that, as described in one recent study of Muslim youth, 'religion featured as a higher context marker, or guiding principle, than culture and was even used to contest cultural practice' (Malik et al., 2007, p. 43). 'Faith sensitive' services have thus been developed to recognise and enable response to the vulnerabilities experienced by many young Muslims. A second strand is the retreat from holding complexities and ambivalences, halting and reconstituting the quest for 'hybridity'. Thus contexts are both more conflicted and simplified – in the 'with us or against us' paradigm, creating new paradoxes. Post 9/11, Azma, for example, found herself able to worry about the potential effects of war on her parents' homeland, to condemn both war and terrorism and to find a clear voice. In contrast she said her parents were confused and frightened, not knowing where to stand.

Thus, this provides a new angle on the view that adolescents are affected by attacks on their culture through the negative experiences of racism, and this can bring about closer attachments with family and other same culture contacts as a protective withdrawal under the persecutory conditions of racism. Secondly, the family's history and experience of migration affect adolescents, especially if the circumstances are traumatic. There is loss in every transition and migration. Eisenbruch (1990) has referred to the idea of 'cultural bereavement' when there is disruption through migration. Bains (2001) points out that the reason for migration and feelings of loss, stretching over generations affects adolescents, within their families. Concretely this may be experienced by the absence of especially the father returning to the home country. She also evidences the way that loss of home is reinforced by disillusion in the new country, reinforced by experiences of racism. Sometimes, adolescents become adrift from their families, and an acute sense of not belonging ensues.

Nowhere is this more clearly experienced than in the current crisis over asylum seeking young people, who are frequently trapped between a traumatic past in a home country from which they have either fled or been forced to leave and a 'Kafkaeque world of Asylum and Immigration Law' (Simpson, 2005, p. 270). The complex physical, political and emotional needs of young people are beginning to be closely described. 'Whenever the home is lost', Papadopolous (2002, p. 24) writes, 'all the organizing and containing functions break wide open and there is a possibility of disintegration'. Simpson's account of a 16-year-old asylum-seeking young woman vividly illustrates the mental pain and also the pull towards complete fragmentation that corrosively undermines subjectivity. The concreteness of the loss of a home, meaning 'the physical and metaphorical meanings of containment' (Papadopoulos, 2002, p. 24), vividly highlights the connection between identity and the need to belong.

A sense of belonging

Becoming stuck or frozen without a sense of belonging is most likely to cause serious difficulties. Noam (1999) has argued that a sense of belonging is an important component of adolescent development, and one which stands to some extent opposed to the 'task' of developing a coherent, integrated identity; 'to yearn for belonging is to be able to risk relationship and loss' (p. 61). If this yearning is exaggerated then masochism, loss of self and an easily exploited social conformity result. Rather than achieving an integrated and solitary identity, the need is *the capacity to belong to multiple worlds, to live with them and to be able to travel between them*' (p. 60) through maintaining contact with these worlds, rather than feeling excluded from them. Noam gives an example of a 19/20-year-old in therapy following a serious suicidal attempt.

Rosa did not fit in with her family, nor did she fit in at college. She attempted to develop intimate relationships but this led to a series of brief sexual relationships which left her feeling vulnerable and hateful towards herself. As a child in her family and as a student, Rosa felt she was between two worlds and belonged to neither. She decided to travel, with the purpose of setting up events for the college's alumni association, and Noam understood that with this plan she became a worker, maintaining her connections with both the college and her family. Through rearranging the context in which she lived, Rosa shifted her subject position. Noam discusses the implications for therapy;

'I remember the dramatic moment when she came to my office with flowers to announce that she was leaving for an indefinite amount of time, maybe even forever'. But Rosa was clear that she would stay in touch and her case should not be considered 'closed'. Noam agreed that it was important to allow this, because 'part of the need to belong is to continue to belong during separations' (p. 60), despite the administrative and audit anxieties this created in the organisation, an apt example of the conflict working with adolescents places on organisational norms.

Noam sees adolescents like Rosa as 'seeking contexts of affirmation' in order to take up subject positions which 'rearrange the context' in which they live (p. 60). This is in turn predicated on the history of insecure attachments that adolescents seeking therapy bring, and the impact on adolescent development of these histories.

Hall (2000) refers to Habermas, writing of political intersubjectivity, saying 'From a normative point of view the integrity of the individual legal person cannot be guaranteed without protecting the inter-subjectively shared experiences and life contexts in which the person has been socialized and formed his or her identity. The identity of the individual is interwoven with collective identities and can be stabilized only in a cultural network that cannot be appropriated as private property, any more than the mother tongue itself can. Hence the individual remains the bearer of "rights to cultural membership"'(Habermas, 1994).

This speaks to the priority of an unalienable cultural belonging, cuts through the dichotomy of individual-collective (Hall, 2000, p. 231), and it is particularly interesting in that it addresses the problem of sharing. The bedrock of identity in a culture, language and the 'intersubjectively shared experiences and life-contexts', is a precondition for sharing across cultures. This is a position which is fairly close to the view Stern (1985) puts forward about the infant's capacity to intersubjectively share mental states, which is that the infant needs to experience the 'attuned' mother paying attention to the infant's communicative rhythms. Without this there is foreclosure, and communication with others, including across cultures, excludes difference. This, in terms of adolescent identity and subjectivity is extremely important, that a shift between subject positions is predicated on a 'secure base' or an experience of containment. This can be put very simply. Difference is not tolerable without enough sameness. A sense of sameness, or identification, begins to be developed in early infancy, and is not only about the taking in by another of the emotions that are too difficult to bear within oneself, but is predicated on the way the parent/container returns these experiences. Often this is thought of as mirroring, a reflecting back of 'sameness' but it is more subtle than this. The 'mirroring' process includes an element of difference through differentiation of self and other, in qualities that are bearable. This requires a great sensitivity. Sameness and difference are not things, or just polarised opposites (though they can be), they are 'positional along a spectrum' and in dynamic relation with each other. The importance and subtleties of understanding the meaning of what is projected, and what can be fed back mean that therapists have to work very hard within a reflective psycho-social space when working with issues of ethnic identity with adolescents. It means tolerating and thinking about meaning in a context that is ambiguous, painful and often precarious, even fragile. It is very important to have space for the meanings that emerge from the sociocultural space because

psychotherapy undertaken with young adults ... suggests that cross-cultural factors may have a significant effect in the development of self-autonomy, the formation of a self-identity and the acceptance of a sexual self.

(Bains, 2001, p. 73)

Summary

- In this chapter ethnic identity formation in adolescence is explored. Ethnic identity makes a significant contribution to overall identity formation and subjectivity.
- The space in which ethnic identity develops is subject to forces that operate across sociocultural and psychic domains, creating a complex, ambiguous context for therapeutic work with adolescents.
- Negative experiences – racism – are very significant for identity formation in adolescence, and minority ethnic adolescents are

involved in precarious processes of engaging at a cross-cultural level. Withdrawal into same culture groups may be a consequence of experiencing racism. Adolescents have to face considerable difficulties in trying to negotiate and survive these experiences.

- White adolescents who cannot tolerate the experience of difference defend against this by splitting and projecting in order to maintain the semblance (delusion) of a powerful oppressive sameness. The psychic roots of racism are very deep and infantile. They are closely connected with inability to face the loss of separation, and thus are very active in adolescence.
- There are risks and hazards and opportunities in multicultural contacts. The discussion of 'hybridity' focuses on one of these ambiguous possibilities, in the context of individuals and cultures being in agonised flux.
- Case examples illustrate the qualities, difficulties, ambiguities and fragilities of therblapeutic contact with adolescents. The importance of containment, mirroring, a sense of belonging, and the capacity to take into account meaning at a sociocultural level are important in facilitating therapeutic work.

4

PARENTING ADOLESCENTS

This chapter explores the roles of parents with adolescents. This is a very broad undertaking, since, as we have seen, the period of adolescence is extended in contemporary societies. The long period of adolescence places different demands on parents, at different times. Initially, as the child experiences puberty space has to be made for this new factor, allowing the child to become adolescent. Parenting a 13-year-old is very different from parenting a 19-year-old, or a 24-year-old. The 24-year-old nonetheless may be living at home and be partly dependent on parents financially. Young people, usually after around 18, may live away from home and still retain a relationship with parents, in which they are dependent, in varying degrees, financially or emotionally.

In a recent UK survey (Collishaw et al., 2004), parents recorded that their adolescent children, across all social backgrounds, have higher levels of emotional difficulties and conduct problems than in the past.[1] Changes in broad societal trends and in family dynamics are suggested as the most likely causes of these increased levels of difficulties (p. 1360). Anxieties, supported by research about worsening mental health in adolescence, focus on the question of parenting adolescents. These have two particular emphases. Firstly, there is concern that changing societal patterns of families for adolescents, including rising divorce rates, single and step-parent families, dual-earner households and the greater use of day care facilities, contributes to worsening adolescent mental health. Secondly, it is suggested that, within families, emotional and conduct difficulties are increasing through parenting practices and through worsening of relationships between parents and adolescents. Professional practice experience tends to support these views, though inevitably this takes a snapshot of adolescents with problems. Disrupted and conflictual relationships are undoubtedly a cause of adolescent difficulties, though these are mediated more successfully in some cases than others. Continuity and predictability of relationships – from infancy onwards – are also central to mental health, but it is also important to take into account the subjective experience of the child/adolescent to deal with particular difficulties; some are more resilient than others, and traumatic experiences are both objective (in the sense that anyone would be affected) and subjective (in that some are more affected than others).

One of the problems is the anxiety generated by adolescents in changing contexts – a recurring theme through the past 60 years of parent–adolescent relationships in which panics about the adolescent independence to do what parents don't like puts the adolescent beyond parent's control,[2] and this stirs up fear of lack of control. The changing nature of parental authority and the loss of traditional authorities in the changing adult world provoke anxiety, not knowing and not understanding. Changes in the structure, values and authorities in families complexify the process of parenting adolescents, and parents too can feel the ground itself is in motion in turbulent contexts. Emotional difficulties and being badly behaved are signs of turbulence.

The aim of this chapter will be to focus on the ways adolescents and their parents relate to each other in contexts of change and diversity. The emphasis in this discussion is placed on how anxiety from within and around the adolescent impacts on families, and, secondly, how the impact of loss, which arises in parent–adolescent relationships in many ways, needs to be negotiated in order that the relationship can continue to be effective and enduring. The process of mourning, in the sense of renegotiating and re-evaluating as the adolescent grows, opens up possibilities for the enrichment of the relationship, and its continuing viability. Difficulties in being able to flexibly address the changing contexts can lead to difficulties, conflicts and becoming stuck in past modes of relating. Earlier difficulties in the parent–child relationship can become crystallised as patterns on a larger scale in adolescence, along with the new factor of adolescence itself. There are though new opportunities. Thirdly, the chapter will assess the qualities that are demanded of parents throughout extended adolescence and some of the ways that problems experienced in parenting can be thought about, particularly from the perspective of offering therapeutic work to parents.

Parenting adolescents

There is some consensus, from different viewpoints, that a capacity in parents to move between the adolescent's fluctuating states of mind and positioning helps retain receptivity and communication. Coleman and Hendry (1999) show that a parental capacity to connect with the intensity of emotions in early adolescence is an important constituent of maintaining connection in relationships, as, too, is the ability to renegotiate relationships. Anderson emphasises that 'there is a fluctuation between the need to use parents as temporary recipients of projections and the ability to contain anxiety and be more independent' (1999, p. 166). Moving between different relational positions, being responsive now to the need to allow the adolescent to try to contain emotional states in herself/himself, now to the need for the parent to act as a container of unmanageable feelings, makes parenting of adolescents demanding. The difficulty of parenting lies in the intensity of feelings, which are projected on to parental figures. Anderson sums up this difficulty:

> Sometimes it feels as though all the unwanted feelings, hopelessness, incompetence, and fear on the one hand, and responsibility and worry without the power to go with it on the other, are left with the parents.
>
> (1999, p. 166)

Therefore it is important to think how certain qualities of relationship make for developmental possibilities in adolescence, and, alternatively, those which lead to developmental difficulties. It is also important to assess how the turbulence and diversity of the contemporary social context affect the relationships between adolescents and parental figures. The relationship between the adolescent and parents is a fluid emotional force field, often complicated by projective processes. It can be difficult to know, in a family, who is holding what feeling, attitude or position on behalf of whom. A critical emotion in early adolescence is anxiety, though this may be experienced, outside the family as being initially expressed by one member of a family about another. Parents can be bewildered by the onset of adolescence, and the changes in their 'children' and feel ill-equipped to get to a balanced view of this. The teenager may then be experienced as 'a teenager from hell', or a 'teen-alien'.

The overarching aim in working therapeutically with parents of adolescents is to provide a space or setting in which anxieties can be held and understood, so that parental confidence can be increased, and projections into the adolescent can be reduced. This overall aim involves some quite complicated processes. The following example traces a sense of disturbance in an adolescent's relationship with his parents, in which the pain of the situation is projected between family members.

Case example

Mrs F has approached her GP because she is worried about her son Jamie, who is now 13. She told the GP that Jamie's behaviour has deteriorated especially at school, where he is often in trouble. At a recent meeting at school with his teachers, she was told that he was at risk of suspension from school, because of his aggression towards other students, his non compliance with authority and his frequent absence at lessons. Additionally, Jamie's parents were told that it had been suspected he was involved with using drugs. Mrs F told her GP that Jamie was increasingly uncommunicative at home, and that there were frequent arguments between Jamie and his father. She felt that the problems had been gradually getting worse over the past two years and that Jamie had never really settled into his secondary school. However, she was at a loss to know what was causing these difficulties and that though worried about Jamie she 'did not know what was the matter with him' nor could she or anyone else 'get through to him'. She had a daughter two years younger than Jamie who was not causing any concern. She asked the GP if there was someone Jamie could see who might accomplish what she could not, and 'get through to him'.

At this point the GP has the problem of deciding how to proceed with Mrs F's request. She can either suggest that mother spends some time with the Practice's counsellor talking this through in some more detail (Wiener and Sher, 1998), she can agree to mother's request to refer Jamie for a therapeutic consultation or she can suggest that the family have a therapeutic consultation together. Alternatively, she could suggest that Mrs F, either alone or with Mr F and perhaps also Jamie, meet with teachers again to try to find ways of resolving these difficulties, and it may be that the school has a counsellor attached who could see Jamie. However, one missing aspect is that the GP has not seen Jamie, nor does she know how Jamie may view any of these options, especially the ones that involve him attending meetings or therapeutic consultations. More information would help, but the GP has a knife-edge decision to make, and this will depend to some extent on the way Mrs F impacts upon her. If Mrs F communicates an urgency and insistence about Jamie being seen, it may be difficult to propose alternatives without becoming embroiled in complicated discussions.

The situation has the hallmarks of a narrative about a 'folk devil' (Cohen, 1973) in the making; an uncommunicative, aggressive male adolescent, who is beyond comprehension is suspected of turning to drugs. There is worry about Jamie, and possibly worry for him, which already has spread across three institutions – the family, the school and the GP practice – and may shortly encompass a fourth – an organisation offering therapeutic consultation to adolescents and their families. Let us continue with the case.

The GP ascertains from Mrs F that Jamie knows of this meeting, and that Jamie is willing to attend a therapeutic consultation. She then refers Jamie to an adolescent therapeutic service, and an appointment is sent to Jamie. He does not attend, but shortly before the end of the hour offered for the appointment, mother telephones the service and speaks with the therapist. She says that Jamie is not willing to attend and she is worried that he will have lost his chance for help. She communicates an urgent worry, amounting to fearfulness at the lost opportunity. She says he really does need help and yet he is so stubborn about not attending. She had made it clear she would come with him and wait for him but he would still not come. After some discussion, taking into account mother's urgency, the therapist offers an appointment for them both. Mother said she thought it might work if father came too and the therapist agreed to a consultation with all three. They attended.

At this meeting, Mrs F began by reiterating her concerns about Jamie, speaking about how difficult it was to talk to Jamie and how difficult he was to understand. She spoke of his difficulties in school, and what his teachers had told her about him. As she proceeded, she asked Jamie to confirm that each of her statements was true. Jamie lowered his head and did not reply until Mrs F mentioned the allegation of drug dealing and then Jamie retorted 'I never'. The atmosphere developed into that resembling a courtroom, in which Jamie was firmly placed in the witness box, and he responded by putting the case for the defence. When asked what he thought about coming for the therapeutic consultation, Jamie said that he did not mind but he would not come on his own. He added that he thought everything was being exaggerated and there was nothing that needed to be done, but his parents, especially his mother worried a lot.

Then Mr F, with barely controlled fury, spoke of his many grievances about his son, who, he was convinced, would end up in a lot of trouble.

He said that Jamie humiliated him by not taking his advice and that he never complied with father's wishes. For example, Mr F said that he had asked Jamie to meet him at a certain place and time and when Jamie did not appear, he felt 'left high and dry'. Jamie's shoulders hunched and he turned away, looking at the floor as father was talking. Mrs F invited Mr F to tell the therapist about the time he chased Jamie out of the house and down the street. Father retorted that Mrs F should tell this story; both Mr F and Jamie seemed embarrassed. Mrs F then said she felt something had to be done, but that she had no idea what this might be; she was at her wits end, and she just hoped Jamie might open up to someone outside the situation. A feeling began to emerge, unspoken, that they felt the consultation was going to be futile. The mother added that Jamie had been a difficult child, especially when a baby, and she thought he had grown out of this before the present difficulties began. She hoped that it would not have an effect on Sharon, Jamie's sister, who was ten and who had been no trouble at all so far.

The therapist, feeling that anything she says may confirm one or more members of the family as failing, and that she could add to their worry, fury and embarrassment, is under pressure to act as judge in this courtroom atmosphere. In fact she suggests that the difficulties need careful consideration, that they all have something important to contribute to discussing how to improve the situation between them, and asks the parents to meet with her again. Jamie is offered the choice of attending if he feels he wishes to, with the understanding that his presence would be welcomed, but that he may have thoughts about whether he prefers the therapist and the parents to talk in his presence or in his absence about his situation.

Jamie's position as not communicating or understandable generates anxiety in his parents, who, with increasing forcefulness, try to gain access to him, through chasing after him and focusing on requests to get him to 'open up'. Thus both parents have lost contact with appropriate boundaries.

In this family all four members of the family have adopted subjective positions, or 'stances' with which they identify, in a paranoid schizoid field. Mother is worried, but unable to find inside herself a way of making contact with Jamie, who is felt to be as much causing difficulties as being in need of understanding. Father has grievances about Jamie and expresses these aggressively – both verbally and by chasing after him. Sharon is identified as absent, and as not having difficulties. Jamie is both a victim of parental not understanding and provocative to his parents,[3] and it seemed evident that Jamie knew his behaviour would successfully 'wind up' his father. In the consultation, Jamie did not respond to his father's complaints, except to noticeably turn away from him. His expression seemed to shut father out and to increase the intensity of controlled humiliation and rage. It seemed that father and son were on collision course, and that Jamie's strategy of running away was in effect goading his father, and projecting his fury into him. From a different perspective, his relationships with his father appeared to mirror, and reverse, the relationships Jamie had at school, where he was not only thought of as not complying with authority but also of 'chasing after' other students. There is an escalating and progressively distorting picture emerging of the relationships in the family and in the wider network, in which adults are becoming 'infected' by the feelings of helplessness and a punitive wish to take control.

Anxiety and positioning in families of adolescents

Where anxiety is high, and the availability of a reflective, thoughtful containment is impaired, there is both a 'contagion' and concreteness in the projection of anxiety, originating from and/or instigated by the presence of an adolescent. In the F family, in the absence of connectedness and understanding, something which seems to focus on the difficulties of male adolescence begins to run through the family, the school and then into other institutions. Mrs F experiences anxiety passively, as brought about by Jamie's behaviour. Mr F has an identity as trying to catch and control the elusive Jamie.

The image of Mr F pursuing Jamie is an apt metaphor for 'chasing' adolescents, through the impact of anxiety that leads to a fear of losing control. This is a common dynamic and is guaranteed to bring an end to fruitful communication. Mrs F's passive not understanding is paradigmatic of a position in which all the difficulty of adolescence is located in the adolescent. This can be contrasted with adults permitting themselves to be 'used', in a reflective containing space, by the adolescent for the projection into them of emotions and states of mind that the adolescent is bothered by, in order to find meaning in what is unknown or uncertain.

Jamie's position is also paradigmatic of difficulties in communication in relationships between adolescents and adults, in that he projects worry and aggression into his parents, in the hope or expectation that these feelings will be taken in or that he will then no longer have to deal with them himself. In this situation the problem includes the parental feeling that Jamie is not understandable. Adolescents require parents to move between two positions; first, the position in which they are negotiable, and manage, or aim to manage, their emotional responsibilities within themselves, and expect to be negotiated with. Second, they need the parent to take in the emotionality, which they cannot manage themselves, and to think about its meaning with and for them. Different states of mind need containment over time and in different adolescents. It is hugely important that the different demands on parents – for negotiation or containment – are not muddled, since the adolescent's new developments stem from *both* the capacity to respond to times and issues which they manage emotionally within the self, *and* times when they can experience the parent's emotional availability for their most difficult or puzzling feelings. Differentiating times when the adolescent experiences greater independence through the capacity for managing her/his own states of mind from times when states of mind which require understanding of a particularly difficult or dangerous aspect of the self is an important parental function during adolescence.

The absence or constriction of the 'negotiable' side of things is indicative of difficulties in the transition from childhood to adolescence, and, socially, from primary to secondary school. The anxiety that is thus mobilised, and not contained, becomes contagious and distortable and is highly likely to escalate.

Changing families

Processes of accelerating social change have created new diversities, and amongst the most significant of these are a new range of family structures, models and cultural values. These new models of families emerge tentatively and provisionally. Differences of languages, histories, and customs create newness, change and complex levels of conflict between tradition and newness. Increased individualisation, reduced relational bonds and the later age for becoming a parent have all impacted on family experiences. Changing patterns of authority in adult society realigns authority within families. For example the prevalent educational discourse involves parents as well as adolescents (and younger children) in a target driven exam culture, in which parental authority may be entwined with the exam success, or failure, of children. For example, there is an increase in families headed by a lone parent, and an increasing number of adolescents have lived in a family in which change in parenting relationship has taken place. More children are born outside marriage, and 'conventional notions of marriage are being replaced by more fluid relationship structures'

(Coleman and Hendry, 1999, p. 87). Dartington (1998) points out there are at least three categories of single parents, who derive their positions from bereavement, divorce and being single and that these positions have different meanings for the parent. Adolescents will therefore experience different family structures, and also, in some cases, during childhood and adolescence they will have experience of more than one family structure. Families may separate and reconstitute, so that both the loss of a family relationship and the arrival of new family members will take place. The birth of babies and new partners and their children are both in this category of new arrivals. Thus in thinking about adolescents' experiences of families, it is not sufficient to be aware of structure and structural changes, but also to understand something of the quality of the context, and the changes. Is there a painful or unthinkable loss? What kinds of conflicts are alive in the family? Is it possible that there are benefits and opportunities brought by changes? Are emotional experiences of change, and loss, processed in the family, to some extent at least?

In these conditions, there is no centre or solidity; instead of a reliable and predictable model of a 'family' there is unpredictability and 'risk'. The family in the mind and the family in social reality may be quite different entities. The problem for adolescents in this context is that their involvement in the individual and internal changes of adolescence has to be experienced and worked through in the context of a changing and unpredictable world. The parents and carers of adolescents have to be able to maintain a capacity to make contact with the emotionality of adolescents, to make and maintain links between the past, present and future when they themselves are in a process of turbulent change. This is demanding, and yet the task of parenting adolescence is itself demanding emotionally and mentally, since adolescents, despite perhaps protestations to the contrary, have great need of parents, who can contain the intensity of emotions and make contact in a negotiable way. In exploring relationships between parents, carers and adolescents, the themes of control and fear of loss of control, and the difficulties of mourning are to the forefront.

Families of adolescents

Changes to the family, the increase in lone parent families and the multiplicity of models of the family pose real problems for traditional theories of family relationships. As Dartington (1998) has noted, 'traditional literature is full of warnings about what happens to children who are separated from the idealised, balanced, containing couple'

(p. 14). Britton (1989) developed the idea of the 'third' position as constituting a reflective space in the mind in which there are internal connections and links. Thus if the parent can draw on this reflective capacity internally, through representations of good, helpful and sustaining relationships with others, an internal couple is in existence. In practice most parents need to draw on others in the external world to make a reflective and containing connection or link. The case illustrations in this chapter show the way that therapeutic consultation can be used as a reflective space, in order to develop the capacity for thinking about emotionality with parents and adolescents throughout the extended period of adolescence. The previous example, of Jamie and his parents, illustrated tensions and anxieties in parenting an early adolescent; the next of these case examples illustrates a young person in her mid-teens living with her single parent, father.

Case example

Simone, 16, had a restricted social existence. She was interested and motivated to succeed in her schoolwork, but she had no friends and no social life outside the home. Her rather defensive view of this isolation from peers was that she could not find anyone who was like-minded, meaning serious and academic. Simone's father had become very worried about her and came with her for therapeutic consultations.

Simone's mother had some time ago eloped and now lived abroad with her new husband. Father had a girlfriend, who stayed with them some of the time, but who did not seem very committed to the relationship. Simone's older brother, Michael was now near the end of his first year at university, living away from home most of the time. With all these absences, father and Simone felt stuck together, as she put it 'like two monkeys in a cage'. It was very difficult for either of them to think about becoming more separate from each other, and they put their hopes in the passage of time providing a solution.

Frequently, father would talk about setting a boundary between them, or about acting independently of Simone, only to become anxious and sabotage these thoughts. On one occasion he found himself with some time and went to a bookshop. He said he could have spent all day there, but then became worried about Simone and phoned her.

For her part, Simone expected and demanded open access to father, including access to his bedroom. On occasions she got into bed to 'have a cuddle'. It seemed unlikely that any sexual enactments took place, and Simone exerted terrific control over her desires and needs through intense exercise and a low calorie diet.

There was, between Simone and her father, an intolerable sense of depression and a dread of separateness, which had to be avoided. This was closely linked with problem of emotionality in this 'pair' that difficult feelings had to be quickly left behind. Father sadly and rather tragically talked about his childhood and adolescence.

He described a 'disastrous' marriage between his parents, and a mother who had been very depressed. When he spoke of his father he said he was 'sadly relieved' when he died, because he made him jump through hoops. His siblings, a brother and a sister, had had problems, and his sister had emigrated. Simone's father had spent many years after his father's death, shouldering the responsibility of the care of his depressed mother.

Father seemed to long for a relationship which might offer the possibility not just of enduring difficulty and depression, but also of sustaining a hope of repairing or transforming these experiences. His awareness of missing this kind of relationship with another person, and inside himself, appeared to free Simone from the role she had of telling him to 'pull himself together and get on with it' when he was depressed. Instead Simone began to speak of missing a 'mother who she could go shopping with', a very 'ordinary' relationship and the kind she usually shunned.

In the relationship, both Simone and her father are stuck, or frozen, in a way that seems fateful. Bollas (1991) has made a distinction between fate and destiny. The 'fated' individual is acted upon by forces to which s/he has to follow a script. In contrast 'destiny' can be made, or carved, or reached for, and involves active authorship or agency:

A person who is fated, who is fundamentally interred in an internal world of self and object relationships that endlessly repeat the same scenarios, has very little sense of a future that is at all different from the internal environment they carry around with them. The sense of fate is a feeling of despair to influence the course of one's life. A sense of destiny, however is a different state, when the person feels he is moving in a personality progression that gives him a sense of steering his course.

(Bollas, 1991, p. 41)

When Simone and her father were able to bear the painfulness of what has been missed and lost, a different position emerged, in which there were new possibilities and a greater openness. These followed from a more active engagement with internal processes (destiny) – rather than being fated to follow a repetitious and circumscribed closure.

Becoming caught up in grievances and resentments is a defence against mourning and also against awareness. These occur, often, in families with adolescents when a painful separation is involved. Parental separation, unless the parents emotionally digest the experience creates vulnerability for difficulties in development, in the triangle of mother, father, adolescent. Feeling injured can lead to grievance, revenge or, through awareness of damage, reparation. Steiner (1993) has argued that revenge 'is a complex phenomenon' in that, in taking revenge, there is an attempt to 'stand up and against those who injure us and threaten our objects' (p. 85). Thus revenge may indicate the presence of a capacity to face experience rather than evade it, through harbouring resentment and grievances. On the other hand, revenge, though illustrating an awareness of pain, is also a way of evading the overwhelming impact of damage for which no reparation seems possible.

There are problems between mothers and sons in circumstances such as the case of Simone and her father, of finding appropriate boundaries to permit separateness, and also to acknowledge that adolescent sexuality requires different boundaries than in earlier childhood. In both father–daughter and mother–son relationships, there can be a difficulty in the regulation of intimacy and distance.

Sayers (1991) gives an example of a father, in Carson McCullers novel *The Member of the Wedding*, who becomes insensitive with his daughter through feeling uncomfortable with the need to redefine the relationship between them, as his daughter reached puberty:

'Who is this great big long-legged twelve year old blunderbuss who still wants to sleep with her old papa. ... She began to have a grudge against her father and they looked at each other in a slant-eyed way' (quoted in Sayers, 1991, p. 76).

Different parents

In contexts of diversity, adolescents may have to endure, and be able to make sense of very different images of parents. The idealisation of the 1950's family, with father at work and mother in the kitchen is thus replaced by complex and contradictory images of parents. Changes in family patterns, with families in processes of repeated change and re-constitution means that adolescents are more exposed, not only to separation, loss and uncertainty, but also to different parental lifestyles and parental sexuality. In the idealised family, parental sex is firmly behind closed doors, so that at the extreme, it is invisible. Adolescents are free in these circumstances to generate the illusion that parental sex is no longer an active issue. In more turbulent contexts, parents may appear 'wacky' to their adolescents. One 15-year-old boy described the sense of embarrassment he felt when his young mother of 33 attended parents' evenings at school, dressed in short skirt and leather jacket. He said, in resignation, that she was always out, at work and with friends, that they lived on ready meals from Sainsbury's, and that he sometimes wished he 'had a mother in an apron'. *The Independent* reported this at the Reading festival:

> One woman in her forties with five nose rings and a lip stud had no qualms about dancing. ... By shaking maniacally like a dog as it leaves the sea. Then she said to her daughter of about 10 in a delightful suburban mumsy voice 'Jeanette, if you can't behave I'm taking you home and you won't see Eminem.
>
> (Steel, 28 August 2001)

The account is intended to sound 'wacky' and contrasts, journalistically, images of mothers that seem incongruent. More seriously, a young woman of 19 complained to me that '*my mother's got a new boyfriend and it's doing my head in*'. With a definite attempt at establishing her superiority she added that her mother was '*going on about her new boyfriend and her ex-husband, and it reminds me how I used to be, always having two boyfriends*'.

It seems imperative to differentiate between the 'wacky' from the destructive, and the different from the perpetration of damaging and abusive experiences. Early adolescents find it difficult to think about their parents' lives – and this is one of the differentiating, separating struggles of adolescence, to gain a sense of perspective about parents in place of childhood idealisations and distortions. This is a painful, difficult and anxious process. Adolescents dislike having to deal with the detail of parents' lives, and then to have to contain within themselves ideas about parents as they are, in their lives, with roles other than parenting. One 18-year-old found it difficult to gain a sense of herself as separate from her mother. Her mother had been very lonely and depressed when she was young and had wanted to involve her daughter in her life as a support for her. This led to the girl having to listen to the details of her mother's current relationship dilemmas. Tom's parents were in conflict because his father had had an affair. Tom – 15 – was devastated by this knowledge and felt his world had been turned upside down. His previously admired father became synonymous with betrayal, disillusion and contempt. Tom complained furiously, with unconscious humour, that it was a burden having a father who 'always screwed up'. Tom was swept from childhood idealisation of his father to intense disillusionment in a way which was too intense and too sudden for him to accommodate. He seemed to be unable within himself, to mediate the impact of this on his inner world, and the effect was traumatic. Other adolescents may, in different circumstances have adapted to this experience in different ways. These examples may be thought of as coming within a category of difficult experiences for the adolescent to digest and come to terms with. More extreme is the exposure to aspects of parental behaviour, including parental sexuality, which can be damaging, destructive and abusive.

Case example

Josie, 18, initially told me that her mother was eccentric, and that she had many problems and neglected her. The relationship had got much worse during adolescence and Josie had moved out to live with a friend's family. This produced complex and ambivalent feelings, in that Josie felt relieved not to be living with her mother but also guilty at leaving her. She had a tendency to discuss her mother in extreme terms as extremely bizarre and monstrous, or ideally anticipating Josie's needs and wishes. Josie thus talked about perfectly idealised times when she and her mother were fused together, and this included going out together, dressed alike. On the other side of this extreme split, Josie had memories of her mother leaving her at home as a small child while her mother went out to drink and party, and times when mother would return home with a sequence of boyfriends.

The unpredictability of Josie's environment, which threatened her sense of internal continuity left her with difficulties in maintaining intimate relationships and also in being separate. She idealised the times when her mother was 'in tune' with her, and also seemed to be (unconsciously) identified with her when her behaviour mirrored the way she talked about her mother. Josie had difficulties in separating from her mother internally, and from recognising difference between them, which she experienced as extremes – ideal or awful. In these circumstances, the adolescent is left with a difficult task of developing a sense of identity, which is separate from parental figures. To mourn the loss of parents and childhood that one wished one had had is a difficult emotional task, made extremely onerous by the impact of disturbance and difficulty in the parents which has been inflicted upon or projected into the adolescent. Adolescents in these circumstances may become very defended and stuck in their development, or encounter a difficult range of emotional experiences, in which hate and resentment, grievances about the parent(s) and a fear of their own emotionality strongly feature. In each case, a detailed exploration of the relationship and its meaning for the adolescent is necessary in order to facilitate the process of mourning.

Parents in pain about adolescents

The process of parenting adolescents means being in touch with a particular pain of separation, in which adolescence marks the beginning of the end of childhood. The ultimate loss of the relationship is conceptualised in the anticipation of the adolescent leaving home and of relinquishing to others the central role in the child's life. This stirs up in parents their past experiences of separation and loss. The fear of not being in control is activated in both adolescents and their parents because the process of change in adolescence is driven by inevitability. Individually and culturally, defences against this loss are also activated. In parents, the experience of separating from the adolescent can reactivate infantile feelings of the fear of loss. It is of course a function of parenting to worry about the adolescent's emerging adulthood and increased independence, and to think about this anxiety and take a perspective on it, attempting to evaluate the risks and hazards involved. In conditions of modernity many of these risks and hazards will be new and will not relate to parental sociocultural experiences.

Change occurs more quickly in the sociocultural sphere than in the internal world, which has to contend with the conservatism stemming from the internalisation of values from the parents' parents' generation. Transgenerational differences are complex. The cultural inheritance of the child is also based on the past, through internalising the parents' internal parents and their values and sociocultural worlds. Parents have internalised past values and attitudes that appropriated to past conditions. Parents may say, for example, that they draw on their experiences of parenting, which 'never did them any harm', as a way of communicating loyalty to this kind of internalisation and also of avoiding the anxiety and confusion that arises with contemporary processes of change and turbulence.[4]

Internal authority lags behind contemporary conditions, and this can be destabilising of parenting in conditions of rapid social change where the process of individualisation reduces links with established or traditional authority. Contemporary partner relationships may be conceptualised as fragile, owing to increasing diversity and also the retreat from traditional authorities, for example with regard to marriage, and, as a compensation for increased anxiety, the need for certainty and reassurance also increases. In contemporary conditions, parents' anxieties require internal reflection and, perhaps to a greater extent than in traditional cultures, there has to be more reliance on internal, or individual authority, rather than reference to external authorities. There is thus a process of individualisation within parenting, as Beck-Gernsheim discusses:

> Since individualisation also fosters a longing for the opposite world of intimacy, security and closeness, most people will continue to live within a partnership or family. But such ties are not the same as before, in their scope or in their degree of obligation and permanence. Out of many different strivings, longings, efforts and mistakes, out of successful and often unsuccessful experiments, a wider spectrum of the private is taking shape. As people make choices, negotiating and deciding the everyday details of do-it-yourself relationships, a 'normal chaos' of love, suffering and diversity is growing and developing.
>
> (Beck-Gernsheim, 1998, p. 67)

Thus parenting takes place within a complex configuration, in which the parents' internal worlds play a very central part. Parents need to make individualised decisions; which worries and concerns about an adolescent need to be borne, and which should be acted upon? This can be an anxious process because it involves parents in complex fields of ambiguity, uncertainty and newness. At the extremes, parents may try to eradicate risks for their adolescents, leading to the impossibility of achieving separation, or to treating all risks alike, leading to a 'sink or swim' approach to separateness and independence.

Parents have to face painful experiences of loss. These start from the process of separating, accepting the gathering independence of the adolescent, which then draws in the parents' own experiences, and challenging and testing the parents' own inner resources and capacities. Parents are more able to be in contact with their adolescents if they can recall, experience and reflect upon significant aspects of their own childhood and adolescent years. Simone's father had to mourn painfully his relationships with his parents and the relationships within his family, in order to find a space internally in which he could allow Simone some separateness.

Parental experiences of sociocultural change from their own childhood and adolescence to the contemporary adolescence of their sons and daughters also need to be thought about. The ways that they have been swept along within the changes of modernity also contribute to the difficulties, and sometimes enormities, of facing loss. Simply, parents may find themselves in circumstances and qualities of relationship they had not anticipated, envisaged or thought possible. They can seem a long way from where they expected to be. Parents may have to find within themselves ways of thinking about what is different, and to be able to bear the consequent anxieties and pains.

Difficulties of mourning can thus become extremely complex, and possibly resented, reviving early experiences of 'unfairness' (Young and Gibb, 1998). Grievances against their own parents, who may be felt to have given too little and inflicted losses and separations upon them as children may be stirred up. The parent has to encounter the configuration of grievance, resentment, a wish to control, and the problem of finding within a sense of perspective and reparation being imaginable and possible.

Case example

Mrs M's son, Gerry, an only child, was badly hurt in a car accident, leaving him with serious injuries. Prior to the accident, which happened when he was 17, Gerry had experienced some difficulties during his childhood and early adolescence, and there was a possibility that he was in some way partly responsible for the accident, perhaps through acting in a self-destructive way. Mrs M and Gerry's father had separated when Gerry was 13. Initially, Mrs M requested a consultation for both Gerry and herself, but Gerry did not wish to attend and Mrs M then asked for some therapeutic meetings alone.

After Gerry's accident Mrs M was overcome with guilt about her son and devoted herself to looking after him in a compulsive way. Her relationship with Gerry deteriorated and so did Gerry's mental health. Gerry was admitted to an inpatient unit. Mrs M's guilt and panic intensified and she felt she had lost her relationship with her son, and that Gerry had lost his opportunities in life. Gerry's accident and illness were crushing to Mrs M, who had been over involved in her son's life, and her expectations of Gerry had been huge.

Thus, Mrs M found herself very much alone, worried about her son and herself. She told me her dreams, one of which aptly summed up her state of mind. She said she was in a warm swimming pool, alone, but then she had to leave the swimming pool and she went into the sea where a tidal wave chased her. She had to run to keep ahead of it, which she did just, but she had to keep running. Mrs M's internal world was split between idealised, peaceful and dangerous, threatening states. She felt she had been evicted from a predictable and satisfactory world into one which was unrelenting, remorseless and dangerous. Her pain and worry about her son's accident and illness were mixed with a sense of fury with Gerry, her ex-husband, and all professionals who were involved with her son. She constantly complained to and about them for, as she saw it, the inadequate treatment provided for Gerry. In her relationship with me this represented her fury that I provided 'inadequate treatment' for her, because I could not restore her world as it had been before Gerry's accident, or, to be more accurate, how she now perceived it to have been.

Alongside this constellation Mrs M talked about a conflictual relationship with her own mother, and her grievances that her mother had been depriving when Mrs M was a child. She felt that she did not belong anywhere, and she identified with her parents' origins in Spain.

Painfully, Mrs M linked her grief for Gerry with her isolation in the swimming pool and she regretted that she had not taken up a more active position in the conflicts in her life. Instead of trying to confront conflictual and difficult issues she felt that she had passively stepped back and lived her life through Gerry. She told me another dream in which she went to a party hosted by a couple who had been together through thick and thin. She found she was there with her ex-husband and wondered why she was back with him again.

The idea of a couple going through 'thick and thin' referred to the link she had made with me in her therapy, which had endured during the most difficult time in her life, when she had felt acutely alone. In providing a reflective therapeutic space in which Mrs M could think about her emotions and states of mind, she was able to gain a sense of connectedness with others. She could come out of the swimming pool and bear turbulence. In irritatingly finding herself back with her ex-husband, Mrs M could identify her tendency to repetitively seek idealised solutions. She saw that she wished to do this in her therapeutic relationship with me, which she felt should have no ending. By addressing the limits of the relationship and the similarities between her way of relating to me as well as to others, it was possible to reflect on this and to avoid the therapeutic relationship becoming another 'warm swimming pool' or an idealistic retreat from the turbulence of lived experience.

Mourning, letting go of her control, omnipotence and idealisation lead to the possibility of facing reality and a more depressive field. Loss is experienced very deeply, and relates ultimately to the very earliest of experiences. Mrs M illustrates the quality of losses faced by contemporary parents of adolescents; the loss of not belonging through being dislocated from her parents' culture, the loss of her idealisation of her family of origin and of her nuclear family. Each of these tests the internal capacity to reflect and maintain an internal dialogue between past internalisations and current contexts. Srinath (1998) points out that 'survivors of trauma may sometimes be preoccupied with rescue phantasies or be driven by a compulsive desire to rescue others. Although this behaviour may have something genuinely reparative in it, it can also deal with the survivor's own intolerable feelings of helplessness, impotence, guilt and humiliation, via a projective identification into others of those feelings' (p. 143). This can have the flavour of parents' trying to rescue themselves from the present. This puts tremendous pressure on the therapist, who has to bear both the loss and its impact on the parent(s), to help the parent bear the pain, and to make sense of the context to which pain relates, both in its infantile and sociocultural dimensions. There is also the requirement to resist the pressure to reassure too quickly, to seek instant solutions and to 'split' into an idealised couple, which leaves the threatening, conflictual and unpleasant aspects outside.

Summary

- Parenting adolescence involves intensity of feeling, and requires the flexibility to move between the different positions adolescents take up with regard to their development. Particularly parents need to recognise and respond differently to times when adolescents are negotiable and attempting to contain experience within themselves, and times when they need to project intense feelings into a parent or a parent figure.
- Anxiety within and about adolescents can sweep through family members and networks who are involved. In the absence of a containing reflective space where the meaning of anxiety can be thought about, parents may take up defensive positions of passivity or of trying to keep or take control.
- In the context of change and diversity, parenting models are plural, and tentative, and it is important to avoid stereotypical

thinking, or putting all families within one model. The capacity to make a thoughtful reflective link internally and/or with others can form an important sense of a 'couple' when there are single or separated parents.

- 'Different' parents can create a 'field' of uncertainty and anxiety for adolescents, alongside the anxieties emanating from internal changes in adolescence. When experiences of separation and loss are not contained by parents, difficulties in mourning arise for both parents and adolescents, and these impact on development in powerful and potentially damaging ways.

- The aim of working therapeutically with parents is to provide a reflective, bounded containing space in which anxieties can be thought about. Recognition of painful experiences in the present and past provides possibilities for opening up ways of relating which enhance the qualities of parent–adolescent relationships and provide developmental opportunities.

5

CONTAINING ADOLESCENCE IN ORGANISATIONS

This chapter continues the discussion in Chapter 4 about the impact of adolescent emotionality on adults with whom they are in contact. In this chapter the focus is on those who work with adolescents in professional capacities. The chapter takes a particular perspective, that of discussing how the power of adolescent emotionality affects professionals who work with adolescents, and thus provides a context of intensity to the work. As well as needing to contend with intense emotions, the professional can make use of these to inform work and understanding. The first part of the chapter focuses on the often-intense emotional experiences of working with adolescents in organisations, illustrated through some case examples. These are then explored in relation to current organisational practices and the changing nature of organisations. Particular attention is paid in this discussion to the view that in the context of the global challenges of adolescent mental health, a crisis exists in the way that adolescent services meet the needs of young people. The chapter ends with a discussion of how engaging contact can be made with vulnerable adolescents who seek or need therapeutic help.

The emotional impact of adolescence

In Chapter 4, the example of Jamie and his parents illustrated the way that anxiety in and about adolescents can powerfully sweep through a family, and into organisations. In that example, the family, the school, the GP practice and the agency providing therapeutic work for adolescents were all impacted upon, to varying degrees by the anxiety in and around Jamie. Thus relationships between adolescents and adults are subject to three particular forces – anxiety, the projection of some emotional states under the pressure of managing intense feelings and of being 'swept along' by adolescent emotionality. Understanding the impact of adolescence on groups, in families and elsewhere, and vice versa, the impact of groups, families and organisations on adolescence means taking these processes into account.

Case example

Mrs J a teacher in an educational unit for young people who have been excluded from school (a Pupil Referral Unit) returned to work after the Easter holidays to find that a group of her 16-year-old students blocked her way into school. They then ran ahead into the classroom and locked the door, leaving Mrs J standing helplessly outside the door. Feeling more dismayed than threatened by the boys' behaviour, Mrs J waited by the door, gathering her thoughts. She pictured an escalation of the difficulty if she had to seek help from colleagues, and she was also worried about what was being done to her classroom. Was some form of destructiveness taking place in there? Somewhat to her surprise the boys opened the door after a few minutes, and she was allowed to enter the classroom.

The students ignored her, and the contact she tried to make with them, moving wildly about the room and occasionally interspersing their own rather manic conversations with some aggressive and offensive remarks about and to Mrs J. All her efforts to start the class working met with little response. Some students left the room, and others made a token gesture of acknowledging her authority before turning away from her.

By the end of the day, Mrs J left the school, feeling quite overwhelmed by powerful feelings of helplessness and despair. Among her overnight despairing thoughts were that she did not wish to return to the school, that she was a complete failure in her role, and that she had miserably failed these difficult young people she had been teaching for two terms.

There has been a holiday, and the students have been shut out from the school, the class and Mrs J's mind. It is also the start of the last term at school for these boys who are due to leave, and they are about to be permanently 'shut out' of the class and school. Two separations are in the air; the Easter holiday has just ended, and the time for leaving school is approaching. The exclusion of the teacher, through locking the door, is an indication of how strong are these feelings about separation; how definitive and non-negotiable the experiences seem to be. The effect is to push forcibly into Mrs J a sense of the power of these reactions to separation and loss. The manic state of mind of the students suggests an attempt to overcome an underlying sense of depression and lack of control. Since these are adolescents who have been excluded from mainstream schooling, they are thus positioned as 'excluded', and inscribed with this status. The action they take has the quality of a resistance to what they have experienced a taking up of a powerful role to reverse what they have experienced.

Mrs J is subject to intense feelings of a desolate, despairing nature. She feels like leaving, and she is full of a sense of failure, and of being no good at her job. She allows herself to be open to these feelings, and then feels overwhelmed by them and isolated from colleagues. On the other hand, she does not simply react to the students, but tries to give herself time to think and find a way of responding which neither inflames the situation nor avoids it.

The next day she found a different scene. Some students were absent, and the others moved more listlessly and quietly about the school. When she entered the classroom, students were sitting quietly, mindlessly and without energy. They passively acquiesced with Mrs J's instructions, but none of them seemed capable of attempting even the easiest of tasks. Mrs J actively engaged with them about their difficulties in learning, and one of the students said he felt he did not know anything, and never would. Some of the boys drifted, again listlessly towards the windows, and stood looking out of the class, into the school and beyond.

The students now seem to resemble, in their states of mind, the despair and desolation that Mrs J had felt the day before. The sense of failure that Mrs J felt is now located in the students, who now are listless, despairing and unable to work. The way the boys drift to the windows and look out recalls locking Mrs J out of the classroom the previous day, but here they are once more recipients of an experience which, probably realistically, is quite foreboding. Exclusion from the mainstream appears embedded in this image, and the pain of facing the world beyond school, while feeling ill equipped is evident. The boy who says, quite hopelessly, that he will never know anything plaintively expresses this.

Despair and failure appear to have been projected forcefully into Mrs J on the first day; on the second day, the students are more able to face these feelings in themselves, although this generates depression and listlessness rather than hope. The power and poignancy of this situation reflects the increasing emphasis on educational qualifications as a means of negotiating late adolescence. Therefore, a combination of powerlessness and anxiety about future vulnerabilities is especially acute in a context in which the power/knowledge connection is very much focused on, and institutionalised, through education. To leave school feeling that nothing is known, and no qualifications have been obtained, means also feeling that there is little or no agency available to oneself; no future.

Through not retaliating and allowing herself to experience these feelings and through thinking about them – at some personal cost – Mrs J experienced powerfully the students' states of mind. It is notable that on being excluded from the class, Mrs J was able to wait, to try to think, and on being admitted to the class, she aimed to make contact with the students, through continuing to try to work. These all constitute attempts to think and provide a reflective containing space in these circumstances.

In working with adolescents in organisations and institutions, the impact of emotionality is likely to be extremely powerful, partly through the processes that develop in groups and partly because of the level of disturbance, difficulty and damage in the adolescent population in these settings. This can be illustrated by work in an adolescent unit, where work is undertaken in the context of a high degree of suicidality and severe disturbance.

Case example

Bowley (1996) discusses a suicidal adolescent, Sarah, 14, who repeatedly over-dosed at times of separation or transition. One Christmas she refused to leave the in-patient unit and when her foster mother arrived at the unit to collect her, Sarah had disappeared. She later phoned to say she had taken an overdose. Since the unit was about to close for the Christmas period, it was not possible for her to stay there, and staff were furious with Sarah, feeling their work and care for Sarah was being attacked. In fact only the nursing discipline was still on the ward at that point, the others having left for the Christmas break. The nurses were filled with murderousness towards Sarah. Sarah was in fact admitted to a paediatric ward for the break, and staff on this ward was furious with staff on the in-patient unit for abandoning Sarah at this time.

Rage, as a response to the impact of separation, spreads like contagion through staff in the unit and then in the paediatric ward. Hinshelwood (1999) discusses distortions in individual identity in institutions and organisations in terms of contagion. 'Emotional states are coordinated across a group or crowd' who have something in common – 'a common internal object' – with which they all identify, to the extent that 'it is as if the individuals have suddenly contracted an infectious illness' (p. 155). In this case, the staff are 'infected' with violent rage and murderousness. It is easy to see the potential for interdisciplinary and inter-agency fights breaking out as the meaning of these intense emotions splits these groups and distorts the meaning of the incident.

The powerful communication that ensued from Sarah's reluctance to move from the unit to the foster carer, and then her disappearance and her overdose, stir up terrific animosity and hatred, so that the accusation of abandoning Sarah runs through both institutions. The nurses feel abandoned by the other professionals in the unit and are then accused of abandonment by the paediatric unit. They are attacked with both sides of the same coin, so to speak. Thus the split and violent aspects of Sarah's inner world are projected into the staff, and mirrored there by the split between a child who is furious at feeling abandoned and a hospital which is furious about an 'abandoning' unit.

Sarah's background was very important both in understanding her suicidality and the particular impact it had on those involved in her life. She was physically abused as a baby and through her early childhood. The staff in the unit found themselves very disturbed by the way they got to feel violently towards Sarah:

> In the in-patient unit, 'when we found we could feel the same level of violence towards her [as she had suffered herself] it was very disturbing. This would cause staff to overcompensate with Sarah for fear of acting on feelings of retaliation. It was difficult to show her anger or to stand up to her. Contact with Sarah was fraught with difficulty and she seemed to get under one's skin very quickly. For example I asked how she was, and she put on a phoney smile and said "fine"; when I wondered aloud about how she really was she said, "I'll throw you a fish if you like". She made me feel like a seal, uselessly flapping my hands together'
> (Bowley, 1996, p. 13).

The experience of being the recipient of cruelty as a baby and child pervaded Sarah's interactions, and at this point in her adolescence, she was actively cruel in her interactions with others, though this involved using herself, and her body, as the target, provoking violent reactions in others. Her attacks on others included an episode where 'Sarah put some strong cleaning agent in the other adolescents' drinks unbeknown to them. One girl was very sick' (p. 13). This particular piece of cruelty projected into others the sickening quality of what Sarah felt she had had to take in herself in her abuse at the hands of others.

The staff in receipt of these emotional communications from Sarah feel themselves to be in projective identification with an abusing parent, or, through trying to compensate for this state of mind, they become passive. Ordinary attempts to make contact with Sarah lead to her rejecting the help and in the process making the staff feel useless and helpless, like seals. The attempts to keep hold of these feelings and thoughts through reflection enables the workers to persist in the attempts to make emotional contact with Sarah, and understand her.

Being swept along with adolescence

The impact of these emotions on the staff makes for extremely difficult and demanding working experiences. Professionals contend with being filled up with intense emotions. In working with adolescents, there is a pull towards responding to the anxiety generated by becoming either passive or controlling. Organisations specialising in work with adolescents may develop specific institutional defences[1] against the impact of adolescence. In organisations where working with adolescence is part of the whole range of work, the organisational defences against the impact of adolescence may create a counter-culture, or alternatively affect the whole organisation.

Brenman Pick (1988), in discussing the emotional impact of work with adolescents in an analytic setting focused on the intensity of the forces which are mobilised in the adolescent and their impact on the worker. In adolescence, 'the power of the force by which the post-pubertal adolescent feels carried along by the impulses and defences he constructs against them', and in turn the adolescent has the potential to have this effect on the therapist. This leads to the adolescent trying to 'sweep the parents along with him, or angrily turn away and be swept along by the adolescent group' (p. 188). The therapist may be 'swept away' into 'colluding with his ideology or trying to sweep him [sic] away with a rival ideology' (p. 188). Brenman Pick compares two adolescents in analysis. The cases complement each other, for while 'John was carried away by the adolescent culture, Jane had the power to carry adults away with her', through a seductive superiority which aroused adults' envy (p. 189). John got 'drunk not only with alcohol and drugs but with his power to act out and have a good time'; Jane got the therapist 'drunk' on her seductiveness, and through projecting her sense of her superiority.

Thus both the therapist, or individual worker, and the organisation may develop a 'culture' which coheres around an adolescent ideology (drunk on adolescence). These defensive cultures can include impulsiveness, rather than strategic thinking, individualisation of methods of work, relying on charismatic leaders, having grandiose or manic overestimation of the work. These defences may indicate that the organisation is vulnerable to the power of the forces of adolescence and might be swept away with this power. Alternatively, the culture may cohere around an ideology which is an alternative to the adolescents'. Defences then have the aim of protecting the therapist from the fear of adolescent pain, especially the painfulness of change and separation. These defences aim to control the upsurge of adolescence. The 'forgotten' abjection of adolescence (Jacobs, 1990) is felt to be threatening and to stir up fears of losing control of a more rational and balanced approach. Boundaries separating adolescents and adults in these circumstances may be strictly maintained, so that the pain of adolescence is not felt consciously by the adults.

Defences against the fear of adolescent emotionality

Complementary defences against the fear of adolescent emotionality are those of promoting a 'rational' adolescent who has no unconscious, and the converse, seeing adolescents as packages of risks, without developmental potential or the ability to be affected by the environment. This mirrors the distinction made between 'warehousing' (packaging risks) and 'horticultural' (seeing growth but not limitations) approaches (Dartington et al., 1981).

Adolescents do have the capacity for reflection and negotiability, and the increase in cognitive capacity through adolescence is an important developmental factor. They too may be subject to particular pressures and projections in their family and school environments, and their difficulties are responses to these. As well, though, the intellectual capacities of adolescents, and their rationalism, can be used defensively to offset more abject aspects of themselves and their vulnerabilities. A particular kind of problem develops when notions of adolescent rationality seduce the adults in organisations into seeing rationality as the whole rather than a part of adolescent development. The importance of the adolescent's needs for adults to be available to receive projected anxieties and to contain these is then underestimated, or split off.

Case example

Watson and West (2001) discuss the impact of changes to the structure of residential care in a Social Services Department. This account highlights the following features. The reorganisation created smaller units, more closely located to the city centre from where the young people in care originate. 'Another reorganisation' is common in turbulent organisational contexts, and the anxieties about change were located between the workers and their managers. Because of the anxieties, a process of consultation was begun for the staff in which the consultants introduced the idea of obtaining the views of adolescents themselves. Staff felt powerless and that they did not have any control of the process of change. They were anxious about the future, and especially for their careers. They were anxious about running the units and about having the skills that were necessary. The staff wanted reassurance from management that they were well thought of and needed. When feedback from the adolescents was discussed, it showed that they were accepting that the changes had been carefully considered, that on balance they were probably beneficial, and that it was worth 'giving it a go'. The adolescents agreed to pull together to make sure that things went as well as they could as long as the promised benefits – greater contact with family and friends – accrued.

The adolescents were full of the spirit of interdependence and co-operation, resilience and flexibility, apparently unaffected by yet another change in their lives, while the staff were full of terror and trepidation. It seemed that some of the adolescents' anxieties had been projected into the workers, increasing their anxieties and leaving the adolescents free to be more rational. This picture of adolescent rationality and maturity does not fit with the realities of residential work with adolescents, who have usually experienced multiple disruptions in their lives, which have damaging consequences for their development. They are likely to act out in impulsive and destructive or self-destructive and explosive ways. Alternatively they may be very defended against the pain of these experiences.

The obverse of denying adolescent disturbance is noticing only the pathology and omitting to take into account the developmental dimension. This occurs particularly in psychiatric paradigms, where the diagnosis is central, and where the usefulness, or otherwise, in applying diagnostic categories to adolescents is a continuing debate. Diagnoses may be misleading in adolescence where there is potential to change, develop or turn away from destructiveness (Flynn and Skogstad, 2006) in a way that is not always possible in adulthood. The diagnostic approach connects with the current pre-occupation with risks from adolescent behaviour, including risks of violence to others, self-harm and suicidal behaviour. Rather than using risk assessment to inform therapeutic work, it can be used to replace the aim of making relational contact. Assessing risks can have the function of protecting the worker from the emotionality of the psychosocial difficulties (Souter and Kraemer, 2004).

It is now common in adolescent mental health services to feel overwhelmed by the amount of work and the levels of difficulties. The field of risks appears to increase, and with this so do workers' anxieties. Cases are getting more difficult is a common assertion, which overlooks both structural factors – for example, the realignment of services to bring these more problematic situations to the attention of health workers – and subjective factors: levels of difficulty may be seen in relation to how understandable, or not, these appear to be. Suicidality is a particular example of this, since its presence often stirs tremendous anxiety. Being flooded by risks is an inevitable consequence of the organisation of services within the 'logic of inspection', when there are widespread societal anxieties about particular aspects of adolescents and their problems.

Mawson (1994) emphasises the importance of maintaining a position which is neither unrealistically over-optimistic nor overtaken by despair. This means being radically and deeply affected by the emotionality of the work. It is crucial, he concludes, that 'in painful and stressful work staff need to be given space to think about the anxieties stirred up by the work and the effects of these anxieties on them' (p. 73). Discussion of the anxieties makes it possible to retain a stance which steers a path between over-optimism and despair. To this account must be added the need to find a path between undue pessimism and despair, which results from the risk-identification approach to adolescence. Over-pessimism, backed by a belief in the efficacy of the science of diagnosis and evidence-based practice can lead to a kind of professional authority which is removed from the emotional experience of the work and is impervious, avoiding feelings of impotence that arise when facing troubled behaviour and experiences in young people beyond the professional's control. The worker thus becomes split off from the context of adolescent development and the psychosocial meanings of particular difficulties. By shutting out this opportunity, adolescents feel misunderstood and unable to make emotional use of professionals. Over-optimism can take the form of 'empowering' adolescents, promoted by a belief in rationality and a philosophy of taking a positive approach, and splitting this off from the adolescent's intense needs of others. Beneath the application of this philosophy may lie a fear of setting boundaries, and thus being exposed to confrontation from the adolescents. As a result, the adolescents' defences are encouraged, and without a reflective stance, workers are open to the projection of adolescent anxiety and disturbance. This leads to confusion of adolescent needs for containment, contact with others and intimacy, and the wish to be more independent in supporting themselves in gaining a greater sense of autonomy. The confusion of need, vulnerability and defences against the pain of being hurt in relationships, with strivings for autonomy can be extremely disabling for the staff and the adolescent, especially where the adolescent has experienced significant loss and deprivation.

Case example

Julia, a 15-year-old in a residential home, was very private, to the point of excluding others from her thoughts and wishes. She had experienced a disrupted fostering and refused to contemplate a further placement. Thus she communicated that the pain of exclusion and rejection was so unbearable that she would not become involved again in an intimate relationship, in which there was the possibility of further experiences of this kind. Her workers experienced her as a rather unrewarding girl to relate to, as she invariably pushed away attempts to get close to her. This could be understood as an expression of retaliation, making active what she had passively suffered from those in parental roles. Her perspective, however, was that she wished to have more independence and autonomy. Her residential workers became anxious about approaching her on many issues which were worrying, including her conflictual relationships with family members and difficulties in her relationships with peers and teachers at school. Occasionally Julia would reveal that she was worried, especially when a meeting with a family member was arranged, but it was very difficult to address these anxieties with her.

Julia found it difficult to acknowledge her needs of others, and her wish for independence aimed to protect her from painful emotional contact. That Julia stirred up anxieties in others showed that she did have vulnerabilities and that she was not switched off from these feelings. Though she was felt to be immensely controlling, Julia also seemed fragile. The workers feared confrontation with her controlling defence and were anxious about the potential explosiveness if Julia felt herself to be touched emotionally. This fear of breakdown in the adolescent was frightening to them. The workers tended to reassure themselves that supporting her wish for independence was a helpful way to proceed.

The risk of breakdown confronts the institutional defences of workers in these situations, who develop an optimistic view in order to contend with the extent of the pain and deprivation that they face in the adolescents they work with. The optimistic or positive approach thus becomes a way in which workers keep themselves going, in the face of the kind of emotionality to which they are constantly exposed.

In Julia's case some consultative meetings with the workers focused on reflective discussions about the difficulties of making emotional contact with her. This allowed the underlying fears about Julia to be explored and discussed. Putting anxieties about her fragility into words provided the workers with a more reflective and flexible position from which to think about her, so that it was possible to separate out times when her needs for adults to take care of her and times when she was making more authentic bids for autonomy, rather than withdrawing defensively. This did not remove the difficulties, but it did provide the possibilities of greater emotional contact, and a sense of being able to think about ways of working with Julia.

Reflection provides the opportunity to put together splits which occur when working with disturbed adolescents. Focusing on disturbance without noticing possibilities for development and focusing on development without noticing disturbance constitute splits which can be constructed at the level of rival professional ideologies, and thus pull professionals apart.

One requirement, therefore, is to create a container for this kind of reflective practice. Warman and Jackson (2006) describe the model of 'work discussion'; developed initially for clinical settings, the model has now been widely applied with beneficial effects. In their evaluation of the application of 'work discussion' in educational settings (secondary schools), they found that staff using the work-discussion groups had lower rates of absence through sickness. The process, in the work-discussion-group method, of exploring the emotional impact of the work, and attending to meaning, not only supports the worker but reduces the risk of 'infection'.

Yes, despite the recognition that work discussion is a model of good practice (DoH, 2006), it has not been widely adopted, as yet. This reflects some of the major dilemmas and paradoxes in current service provision of adolescents. Though it is recognised that adolescent mental health is a major issue, and presents a 'global challenge' (Patel et al., 2007), services for adolescents have not, on the whole, been able to overcome recognised shortcomings (Kleinert, 2007). These include the shortage of adolescent specialist mental health workers and multidisciplinary dedicated adolescent teams, and the low motivation on non-specialist mental health workers to provide high-quality care for adolescents (Patel et al., 2007).[2] One of the notable paradoxes is that in UK, the Children's National Service Framework (DoH, 2004) placed mental health at the centre of one of its main aims (Lindsey, 2005) but re-established the cut-off point at 18 between child and adult services, a decision that flies in the face of the evidence of how adolescence is constituted today as not ending at 18. This leads to unnecessary transfers of young people to adult services, which are often inappropriate and which have not grasped the changes for young adults and to threats to existing adolescent specialist teams (Bowley and Bratley, 2005). Perhaps, as Kleinert suggests, this reflects the 'deep suspicion' (p. 1057) with which society – including policymakers – regards adolescence.

Working with adolescents in turbulent organisations

Societal and organisational turbulence impact on organisations working with adolescence. Changes in organisations and the increasing speed of change add to uncertainty. Repeated reorganisations can be obsessional attempts to control anxiety, uncertainty and ambiguity, a way of taking control to avoid the fear of losing control. Professionals working with adolescents have to contend with a kind of mirroring, in that organisational change can have similar structures and effects to the emotional impact of adolescence on the adult.

In the turbulence of recent and current changes, organisations are significantly concerned with negotiating loss, and with issues of control and the fear of loss of control. In organisations there are conflicting ideologies, characterised by Cooper and Lousada (2005) in the context of changes in welfare as a whole, as the replacement of a 'logic of compassion and development' by a 'logic of control and inspection'. This is certainly the everyday experience of health, educational and social care professionals in the UK, where audit and inspection, clinical governance and, increasingly, clinical guidelines based on a particular view of outcome research constitute an increasingly regulated framework. It can seem that the primary task of the organisation has shifted from providing services for young people to meeting government targets, while attached to failure is the fear of being publicly shamed. The relationship between worker and client which is based on a link to emotional experience is abandoned under these pressures (Cooper, 2000, p. 124), and this threatens the possibilities of providing reflective, containing spaces.

Bell (2000) gives an example where a cruel, omnipotent organisation is perceived to blame staff for all mistakes, creating a culture of blame and punishment. Thus, in the event of a mistake the omnipotent organisation 'would hold staff completely responsible and ensure they were punished' (Bell, 2000, p. 35). Bell discusses the impact of a suicide of an adolescent in a residential unit.

> At the first meeting after a suicide had taken place, the staff were understandably stunned, especially as the patient was not thought to be in much immediate danger. However organisational stresses had preoccupied the staff who then began to feel guilty that they had neglected to discuss the patients. Soon there emerged the idea that if we had talked about the patient we would have saved her life (ibid., p. 35). This became a pervasive sense that suicide was everywhere. I suddenly found myself wanting to use the meeting to talk about any patient under my care who was suicidal. I then remembered that it is often the patient whom one is not particularly worried about who actually commits suicide. So the category 'suicidal' widened its reference until it included all the patients under my care.
>
> (Ibid., p. 35)

Of course the suicide of a young person is an extremely difficult experience, which can test judgement and which is extremely painful. Balanced judgements are more difficult to attain in turbulent organisations, where the external social changes mirror the impact of adolescence on the professional, and where anxiety is high because of the pervasive anxiety. Morale may also be affected, leading to a stance which is easily overtaken by despair. The capacity to hold professional judgement and to manage risk means, however, that assessments need to be made on the basis that risks exist. Uncertainty and anxiety is part of professional judgement making, and in turbulent organisations, decision-making takes place on a ground which is in motion, not from a centred, solid, unmoving certainty.

In 'omnipotent' organisations 'the fear is that the entire professional team, including social worker, paediatricians, psychiatrists, and hospital managers, up to and including the chief executive, will then be blamed and publicly shamed in the media' (Souter and Kraemer, 2004, p. 260). This is contrasted with organisations in which a boundary exists between the responsibilities of staff and those of the clients. For this boundary to have a reality and represent a meeting point where work can be done, there has to exist the possibility of failure, and the presence of risks that cannot be eliminated but have to be lived with. In these conditions, organisations reflect and are representatives of the societal position that young people cannot be entrusted with responsibilities (Graham, 2004). It also confirms a polarisation in which adolescents are feared, blamed, treated with suspicion and mistrust. Adult remembering of the abjection of adolescence is the first duty for professionals and policy makers (Briggs, 2005).

Reflection on adolescent emotionality in a psychosocial space

Making sense of the impact of adolescent emotionality on professionals requires space to think, to discuss the impact of these emotions, and to use this kind of discussion to understand meaning, using, for example, the model of work discussion. Through this process it is possible to get to know something of the quality of the adolescent's projections. The examples in this chapter illustrate the way that adolescent emotionality impacts on the professional and the potential for understanding the adolescent, which is obtained from reflecting on these experiences. This applies the ideas about counter-transference that were developed by Heimann, in which the analyst has the means of

> comparing the feelings roused in himself [sic] with the content of the patient's associations and the qualities of his mood and behaviour, the analyst has the means for checking whether he has understood or failed to understand his patient.
>
> (1950, p. 10)

The aim is to 'sustain ... feelings as opposed to discharging them'. Brenman Pick's idea that adults get swept along with adolescent emotionality and ideology is a specific application of this theory to adolescence. In reflective containing space discussion aims to understand the feelings raised in the therapist or professional worker through the impact of contact with adolescence. A process of differentiation – which emotion is coming from whom or where? – takes place alongside an acknowledgement of the multiple or plural layers of meaning, involving simultaneously, the adolescent and the organisation in its context. The reflective space for thinking about adolescence takes on the qualities of a psychosocial space if the context of adolescence and the context of the worker are taken into account. Thus discussion about anxieties raised in the course of work can be self-reflective of the organisation's work through including reflection on the meaning of adolescence that is attributed in specific contexts.

Making contact with adolescents in turbulent organisations and contexts

Contemporary therapeutic services for adolescents are concerned about the difficulties of engaging and maintaining contact with groups of vulnerable young people. Adolescent attendance at therapeutic services is notoriously irregular. Young adolescents do not often self-refer and many adolescents drop out of therapy prematurely. Since severe difficulties in adolescence tend not to be resolved with the passage of time, and are likely to persist into adulthood, in at least as severe if not more severe form, the problem of attrition rates is a serious one. 'One suspects that those who drop out are often those in greatest need' (Mak-Pearce, 2001, p. 15). Making contact with adolescents in a way which sustains possibilities for therapeutic help, is a major issue for organisations offering therapeutic services to adolescents. The new diverse contexts of adolescence and the changing nature of organisations present both risks and threats and possibilities for these services.

Developing outreach services in order to locate and engage young people that do not willingly make contact with therapeutic services and developing these in contexts at which adolescents are usually present are key current policy objectives. These services require particular skills and attitudes in the worker, since the problem of being 'captive' is one that many adolescents do not willingly accept. Problems of confidentiality and boundaries in general can be intensified in these contexts for therapeutic service delivery. The new contexts put as great a premium on trust as seeing adolescents in traditional clinical service settings. Outreach enables some young people who probably would not make contact in more traditional settings to have access to therapy. However, changing the point of delivery of services does not in itself guarantee engagement. The main factor in whether someone is engaged meaningfully is the quality of therapeutic relationship that can be established, a mutual task requiring emotional effort on both sides, both in the relationship itself and in the ways that initial offers are made.[3]

The approach developed through outreach services, driven by adult anxieties about difficulties in engaging adolescents, seems conservative compared with initiatives that have used the Internet. This does mean reaching out to young people and one of their preferred means of communication. Ladame and Perret-Catipovic (2005) describe the development of a Web-based approach to suicidal adolescents, in which a young person can post a question on the website CIAO[4] which is responded to by a member of the therapeutic team. This approach brings new risks and opportunities. The aim is to encourage engagement through trying to become a 'third party' by responding to adolescents' questions. It does reach out into a space – the Internet – in which adolescents can feel they are on their own territory.

For terrestrial services for adolescents, maintaining emotional, therapeutic contact with vulnerable adolescents involves trying to look at the process through the adolescent's eyes, and through this, reflecting on and being able to recognise how the adolescent might in fact see the adult's positioning. Empathy requires some pre-orientation to the ways that adolescents think and view the world, a willingness to be open to the quality of communications and also the specific skills required to work with adolescents.

Mak-Pearce (2001) argues for a rapid response for adolescent requests for therapeutic help, and a methodology of focusing on the future transference. 'The future transference is a term I use for the current feelings about how the relationship with the therapist will be at some point in the future. To my mind it is the key to engagement. … What kind of figure will the therapist be? How potent, how useless, how intimate, how loved, how hated will the therapist be?' (p. 19). Alongside this is the importance of making space for thinking about the hopes, fears and expectations that the adolescent brings, the pre-transference (Wittenberg, 1970). It is always useful for the therapist to recognise that the adolescent may have some ideas about what the therapy and therapist will be like, and what it is like, therefore to be in this situation. Beyond initial recognition, it is very useful to develop this to share a picture of what attending therapy means, and for the therapist to tune into the emotional nuances of this. It is always important to take account of what communication an adolescent makes through their legs, which may bring them to the therapy, or away from it, despite what they may actually use.

This approach creates a focus for the reflective stance of the therapist. Other suggestions about ways of making contact include:

- Offering a number of modalities of engagement, including face-to-face therapeutic consultation and completing questionnaires in the therapy setting. The use of questionnaires can augment the process of making contact with adolescents (Radonic, 2001) and of understanding their relationships with others. Radonic reports on successful contact made thus with an adolescent who appears to be not psychologically minded.
- Actively providing information about the aims and objectives of therapeutic consultation, so that these can be discussed.
- Structuring the interview to take responsibility for the direction of the session, and not to leave the adolescent in silence. Questioning which shows an interest in the adolescent and the adolescent's preoccupations may facilitate a sense of feeling listened to (Baruch, 2001).
- Supporting a vulnerable adolescent's attempts to attend therapy by arranging for an adult to bring them to sessions until they can manage this on their own.
- Structuring sessions on a regular, weekly basis, and providing possibilities of a number of meetings, in order that the adolescent can get used to the therapeutic process.
- Involving the adolescent in the process of referral, even when the referral is made by others who are worried about the adolescent (Anderson and Dartington, 1998, p. 4).
- Thinking with the adolescent in terms of threshold states (see Chapter 1) or experiences of a particular transition, and engaging with the way that they picture or characterise these.

Positioning adolescents as negotiable, and negotiating with them, and so providing choice wherever possible, are important ways of bridging the power relations between adolescents and adults. Sometimes the adolescent needs a space made for her/him in the midst of everything that is going on around her/him through a direct invitation to a consultation. Other adolescents need to have the adults in their network get together to contain their anxiety about them before a therapeutic consultation is offered to the adolescent.

This is particularly important with vulnerable adolescents, particularly those who are in care and who have a wide network of adults involved with them. Consultations with networks contain the anxieties about adolescents and either provide the professionals, carers and parents with a more reflective basis for thinking about the adolescent, or allow the adolescent to feel able to emerge from within the anxieties and concerns of the networks and claim space for herself/himself. Some adolescents need encouraging into contact and others need to be left with space to choose to make contact. Some need informal contacts in the community, through professionals skilled in outreach, while others need to be given the space and privacy of an appointment in a clinic setting, perhaps at some geographical and emotional distance from the home and community. Some need the reassurance of meeting someone who is felt to be the same, and others prefer to move into a context of difference.

All of this suggests plurality and the need for multidisciplinarity in meeting the challenge of making contact with vulnerable adolescents. Noam's case, Rosa, was quoted in Chapter 3, to illustrate the need for flexibly allowing adolescents to experience belonging in 'contexts of affirmation'. Some vulnerable adolescents make a link with a therapeutic organisation and despite not attending or missing appointments clearly have the therapist and therapy in mind. Sometimes effective work takes place through the existence of this kind of link! While acknowledging difference and plurality and trying to provide flexibility is important in engaging adolescence, thinking about the best approach to each adolescent needs to be undertaken within a framework or ideology which offers a rigorous approach to reflective thinking about the emotional contact with the adolescent and its meaning. A usual structure of weekly meetings, which are time limited, provides the framework for the therapist to maintain a reflective space, which is crucial for the understanding of the multiple levels of meaning that emerge in work with adolescents.

There are many ways in which adolescents make contact and these demand internal flexibility in therapists, and organisations. Attrition forms a prominent anxiety in contemporary work, connected with the need to reach adolescents who find it difficult to use therapeutic organisations. However, the principle of making emotional contact is an important focus of work with all adolescents, and the principles are the same; by detailed reflective work and discussion the therapist attempts to understand the meaning for the adolescent and struggles to find ways of communicating about the adolescent's emotional states and their impact on the worker. This involves considering deep anxieties. A case example may illustrate some of the vicissitudes of this kind of work, addressing a particular anxiety, the silent adolescent.

Case example

Daniel was 14 when he first came to therapy. After his first session I came away with a strong feeling of not liking him, which, after a struggle, I let myself think might mean that he had a sense of not liking himself. In the second session this was exactly what he told me – he didn't like himself. He was brought up, as I have said, by a young single mother and had very little contact with his father. Recently his father had written to say that he would like to make contact and Daniel was trying to work out how to respond. He did not know how to get hold of the – probable – mixture of excitement, resentment, anxiety, pain and wish for revenge which was milling around inside him. Moreover, as he was clearly getting a sense of himself as probably gay, the invitation to meet father held poignancy in terms of his developing sexual awareness of himself.

Daniel had no difficulty coming for his therapy, but he was almost completely silent in the sessions. It was not a silence that led me to think he was about to walk out and never return, but rather one which was extremely awkward and which gave me a feeling of being really quite unable to speak to him. I felt extremely perturbed by this very restrictive context, and I began to feel a sense of dread when it was time for his session. Daniel arrived very early for his sessions, sometimes over an hour early. He sat in the corner of the waiting room under the care of the receptionist, who perhaps could have been seen by him as a 'mother in an apron'. He came reluctantly from the waiting room, as if the therapy session had interrupted his quiet sojourn there. So despite being so early in the building, he was often late for his session. I sometimes felt I might 'forget' to call him, to leave him uninterrupted, and I experienced both a sense of relief at the thought of not having to face him and a sense of guilt about wishing to avoid him.

At some point, I realised that the situation mirrored Daniel's dilemma in the external world. Should he leave the comfort of mother to meet father? Should he leave the waiting room to see his male therapist? I knew that I could not interpret along these lines, it would be not only indigestible but I think felt to be a cruel penetration of him. His father's letter was felt to be an intrusion and he resented it, but for father not to write would have been worse. I now began to feel the silences as a wish for and a fear of penetration. If I spoke I was penetrative; if I was silent I didn't care. But still what eluded me was a way of trying to communicate some of these thoughts in a way which would be containing, rather than inflammatory. I felt I was in a position with no room to move, no choice. In the silences of the session I began to feel something competitive, seductive, and ruthless, focused on a decision about who leads, who penetrates whom.

In some consternation, I discussed with colleagues what to do. Daniel had said that he struggled to put things into words and one suggestion that was made to me was that I should offer him some drawing materials. My first reaction to this was that it would have an effect not dissimilar to a lead balloon, and I feared Daniel would see this as me patronising him by treating him as a smaller child. On further thought I wondered if there might be some merit in the idea. I decided to try it. I obtained the materials – some pens and a note pad, and I discussed it with him. I said that I had wondered if instead of feeling that he had to always speak to communicate to me, he might like to write or draw. He was non-committal, neutral, but not objecting. I said I would think about it some more and I would then decide what to do. The next week I said to Daniel that, as he could see, I had decided to put some pens and paper on the table for him to use, if he wished.

Daniel did not use the pens and paper, but he did begin to talk to me. At first he would wait for a prompt from me, but eventually he began to take the initiative. The feeling in me, in which there seemed to be nothing between intrusive penetration and passivity, was also transformed, and many of the issues that had been unspeakable were opened for discussion. He did not use the pens and paper – but then he did not write to father. It only occurred to me later that I had presented him with a mirror of his dilemma – does he want to write or not. Somehow, he felt that he had been given choice, but there was a deep sense of loss too, a decision that he would not write.

The struggle to make contact with Daniel illustrates the process of working within a reflective space, in an organisation and in contexts of difference and turbulence, and the way that Daniel made use of the organisation and the therapist within it. The process of reflection on feelings and meanings within a structure or framework underpins thinking about adolescence, and can be applied, flexibly, to different adolescents in different contexts.

Summary

- Relationships between adolescents and adults, in role as professionals in organisations, are subject to anxiety, the projection of intense emotions, and these can be disturbing.
- Containment of intense adolescent projections is provided by thinking about the meaning of the emotional experiences that

workers are 'subject to', rather than being 'swept along' by adolescent emotionality. The intense experiences that workers are subject to may or may not be held in the structures of the organisation. The emotional impact of adolescent emotionality, especially in the very disturbed adolescents who are in residential care, can affect staff across institutions and between groups in organisations, creating professional conflicts.

- Defences against the impact of adolescence range between control and passivity. Splits between adolescent rationality and potential for development, on the one side, and focusing on disturbance and not noticing developmental possibilities, on the other side, are also typical defences used in working with adolescence.
- Organisations, in the current social context, are turbulent through involvement in processes of rapid change. Professionals working with adolescents have to relate to a subject – adolescence – on the move – from within organisations which are also in flux.
- In the context of change and turbulence, making therapeutic contact with adolescence is a priority. These processes are complex and require, in general terms, the capacity to respond flexibly, while maintaining a rigorous framework for thinking. The need for reflective space to think about the work is paramount.

6

ADOLESCENTS AS TEMPORARY OUTSIDERS: ANTISOCIAL BEHAVIOUR

Dartington (1994) proposed that taking up a position of 'temporary outsidership' is a necessary part of adolescent development, and that it provides a way of assimilating the transition from being a child in the family to an adult in the social world. This chapter discusses difficulties in adolescence from the perspective of outsidership. The concept of temporary outsidership is explained and applied to issues in adolescent development, leading to a focus on the anxieties and difficulties in maintaining a position on the boundary, between the inside of the family and the outside of the social world. Failure to reach and sustain the position of temporary outsidership leads to distinctive adolescent difficulties. Some of the difficulties which may be thought of as characteristic of adolescents as outsiders – especially antisocial behaviour, offending behaviour and drug use – are discussed.

Temporary outsidership

The idea of the 'outsider' originates in a modernist discourse, derived from notions of the 'outsider' as rebel, philosopher or seer. It is an idea which has a number of applications and meanings. The idea of the outsider is developed from thinking about groups:

> The outsider is one who is part of a social group but who, for a variety of reasons, takes a position on the fringe or the edge of the group. … The outsider is one who is part of a social group but who, for a variety of reasons, takes a position on the fringe or the edge of that group. The role of the outsider must be clearly

distinguished from the outcast. The outsider is of the group and definitely performs some function *for* the group. Of course he or she may become an outcast, but only if he or she becomes too much of a threat to the cohesion, structure and belief system of that group.

(Dartington, 1994, pp. 91–2)

The outsider is also necessary for the group in providing a capacity to observe the group, though this may be welcomed or felt to be persecutory. The outsider is likely to have to endure rejection. Dartington quotes from Camus' *The Outsider* who 'drifts in the margin, in the suburb of private, solitary, sensual life'. Thus:

The outsider is well placed to observe the world. The marginal position is a potentially creative one because the intellectual and emotional distance from familiar experience makes it a space for a new viewpoint or an original thought to take place.

(p. 92)

Dartington argues that the adolescent needs to take up a position of 'temporary outsidership' in order to develop a scepticism towards the rules, attitudes and beliefs of the group – family group in this case. Thus the outsider is both concerned with a quest for truth and authenticity and for thinking thoughts based on experience. The position of temporary outsider aims to learn from experience rather than to take as read the inheritance of other's thoughts.

The 'outsider' has a difficult position to maintain, since particular emotional and cognitive capacities are required in order to sustain the quest for truth and originality. In particular there is a precondition that the adolescent has a sense of finding some solitude and aloneness rewarding, rather than being persecuting and therefore lonely. This depends on the internalisation of good experiences, and the presence within of a coherent and cohesive sense of self (Stern, 1985). Becoming an outsider may be driven by a number of experiences or internal configurations. It is easy to confuse this constructive or creative withdrawal, to be alone with one's own thoughts, with a retreat from the difficulties in relationships, and it may constitute a retreat from relating.

The position of outsider can be developed quite concretely in adolescent group life. Socially, it is a feature of adolescence, usually most evident in those who have been called traditionally 'mid'-adolescents, that an outsider position is adopted through congregating around telephone boxes, garage forecourts, outside a shop or in some other specific vantage point. Adults witnessing this divide into those who fetch in the police to move the teenagers on before there is trouble and those who lament the lack of facilities for adolescents. Philanthropic efforts then lead to the construction of a café, or, in a more commercially exploitative mode, a 'teen disco'. But the café remains empty or the teenagers attending the 'teen disco' stay outside for most of the evening!

In truth this is a partial analysis. Accounts of the 'teen disco' provide a compelling reading of the varieties of adolescent 'outsider' relating. The 'teen disco' trades on the wish to be 'grown up' and to imitate the over-18s. Over-18s are barred. Staying outside is associated with wishing to take alcohol, which is not allowed inside the disco. An account in the *Evening Standard*, under the heading 'Homework, Hip Hop and Hot Pants' highlights that inside the disco there is a sense of merger in the same sex group:

> 'The cloakroom is a rail of identical denim jackets. "Don't lose your ticket", the frantic-looking cloakroom lady is saying'. Maybe she can be thought of as being the recipient of projected anxieties about the loss of individual identity, for which the cloakroom ticket is in fact a return ticket to individuality. The same story explains the reversed use of the word 'boo' to mean good, not bad, as in the phrase 'wicked, I got a lot of boos'. One participant, a teen DJ, on the other hand, retains his sense of his position as an adult in waiting, and thus his individuality, and his sense of his position 'on the boundary'. He retains a connection between being a 'kid', a child to his parents, and having 'adult' aspirations, being separate and being a DJ. He says, 'I want to be an adult. I'm going to be an adult for the rest of my life, but I can never be a kid again.' At this juncture his mobile phone rings and he hears his father is waiting round the corner to collect him. His phone rings again and he answers, 'hello mum – see I am a kid'.

(Buttolph, 2001)

The distinctive representations of the temporary outsider change and repeat over time. Contemporary adolescents recreate sameness through allegiance to tribes; according to a survey conducted by the Social Issues Research Centre[1] (Marsh and Taylor, 2004), almost half of UK teenagers (49%) reported the need to fit in with their 'tribe' dictates their behaviour, music tastes, dress sense, hairstyle and attitudes to drugs. This defines tribe allegiance. In the UK the ten leading tribes were identified as Academics/Geeks, Gangstas, Goths, Indies, Moshers, Scallies, Skaters, Sporties, Townies and Trendies.[2]

The multiplicity of tribes illustrates another aspect of pluralities in contemporary society, and the distinctiveness of each generates inside the tribe a sense of secrecy, and privacy while also attracting adult gaze. The tribe is often misunderstood; for example, Goths run websites that address some of the common misunderstandings such as whether Goths are vampires, evil, etc. Hoodies became 'folk devils' (Cohen, 2002) at Bluewater Shopping Centre and succeeded in engaging the government of the time in a significant exchange! The hoodie illustrates a global style and the generation of anonymity, mystery and anxiety (*The Guardian*, 2005).

In teaching groups of professionals working with adolescents the idea of the 'outsider' resonates with personal recollections of adolescence or current contact with adolescents. One teenage memory which was told in this context is of sitting on a wall, with friends, across the road from her home. From here the friends could monitor every movement in their own and each other's homes and discuss their and each others' families. Looking into parental homes was presumably accompanied by a wide range of thoughts and phantasies.

In early adolescence, exploring the inside of one's own family and in particular the minds and attributes of parents can be a difficult and inhibiting experience. By late adolescence, a narrative about one's parents is an essential aspect of identity. This process may be accelerated by exposure to change and loss in the family, forcing the adolescent to think about aspects of her/his parents she/he would sooner not yet know. The capacity to know another's mind depends on the ability to develop and maintain a sense of separateness from the other, and the experience of separateness may prove to be difficult to manage, raising anxiety.

Adolescents may take up these rather concrete positions of temporary outsidership with some difficulty, relying on the group and projecting ambivalent feelings into adults. There is a sense of strength through solidarity in the group which covers anxiety and fragility in the individual. A parent described her daughter and her friends, in their early teens, gathering in the entrance hall of her house. She had to walk round them for some time, as they stood there in a kind of indeterminate state in which the passage of time seemed to play no part. She found herself oscillating between passivity, on the one hand – leaving the adolescents to whatever they were doing, while being aware of them, in their gathered state – and being filled up with a sense of wanting to say 'for heaven's sake, make your mind up; either come in or go out!', on the other. The adolescent is much more able to maintain a position at some distance from the inside of the family, and to contemplate the social world outside when in a group, than when alone. In this positioning a projection can nudge adults to take up passive or controlling positions in return. Uncertainty, ambiguity, ambivalence and guilt may all be involved in these projections.

In this sense the outsider position, is formed from a spatial image, in which there is movement to occupy a position on the boundary. It is a position which is inevitably anxious. On the boundary, the anxieties may be of a kind consistent with sitting on the fence – or more tortuous – sitting astride barbed wire. Because the outsider position in adolescence stirs up anxiety, there exists the likelihood that anxiety will be projected into others, but also, there are opportunities for the adolescent to 'test' the ways in which she/he can draw on internal experiences of containment in order to tolerate anxiety. The experience of outsidership thus holds the possibility for the adolescent of getting to know about anxiety, risk and limits. Strengths and limitations may become known and thus the adolescent uses the position of temporary outsidership to augment identity, and a sense of herself/himself in her/his own body and mind.

Potentially, there are multiple experiences of outsidership, as the adolescent makes the transition from child in the family to adulthood. In particular, there are three ways in which the experience of temporary outsidership opens up a potential or transitional space.[3] These can be summarised as

- **Space to feel one's own emotions and to differentiate them from others**. If outsidership is a tolerable experience, anxieties may be engaged with. If it is not tolerable, anxieties may need to be repudiated, denied or avoided. The adolescent may oscillate, perhaps intensely, between moments in which the outsider position is taken up, and those when it is repudiated. At the extreme, subjectivity may become fixed or frozen on either side of the 'boundary' of the temporary outsider position.
- **Space within relationships which permits some freedom of movement.** If the adolescent experiences the potential contact with others in the outsider position as introducing a gap between self and others, a process of becoming separate is begun, of which increasingly complex possibilities in relating to self and others are the consequences. If the gap and complexities pose threats which cannot be tolerated, there are defences against difference

by attempts to restore sameness, merger or destructively breaking links with others. There may be omnipotent attempts to 'fix'
relationships and the sense of self relating to others through the
use of drugs, sex, or adhesively maintaining contact rather than
permitting separateness.

- **Space within the self for flexibly developing different aspects
of the self, in love, friendship, intellectual, artistic and cultural
connectedness.** If the 'outsider' experiences the self as having
new opportunities, and anxiety can be tolerated, possibilities are
opened for increased awareness of different aspects of the self,
which may be fragile or perhaps uncoordinated. If there is too
much anxiety, or terror, from the plurality of these experiences,
and the notion of internal division that is driven into awareness,
terror of catastrophic fears of inner fragmentation are stirred
up, so that defences against this fear are generated, in varying
degrees of control, violence and mindlessness.

The concept of temporary outsidership is best represented as providing space for thought, awareness, creativity and increasing complexity.
These are possible if there is fluidity of movement across the boundary, rather than getting 'stuck' or frozen on the inside or outside, or
at the threshold. Britton's thinking about the container–contained
relationship, as discussed in Chapter 1, showed that the two elements
of sanctuary and meaning required a capacity to be 'inside' as well as
'outside'. His patient Miss A was paralysed at the 'threshold' because
of the claustrophobia of the inside and the dangers of the outside. In
attachment theory, the capacity for exploration is dependent on a secure
base. The adolescent who is fluidly able to move between both subject
positions – outside and inside – retains the possibility of reaching into
the family, or outside into the wider social world for exploration.

Failure to reach the position of temporary outsider

In contrast to the positioning of those adolescents who can tolerate
experiences of temporary outsidership, there are those adolescents and
their families who cannot tolerate the in between states which require
both attachment to a secure base and a capacity for exploration.[4] In her
account of the temporary outsider, Dartington provides examples of
families who fail to attain a boundary position. In these families there is
a sense of being either locked into a closed world or being pulled apart
in a kind of centrifugal process. In Chapter 4, the closed dyad of Simon
and his mother is an example of being 'stuck' on the inside.

The consequences of the intolerance of temporary outsider-ship can be severe. For Dartington, the meaning of this 'right in or right out' mentality is that the wish to separate is synonymous with hatred, which may not be survived, and which may lead to a catastrophe. This has some congruence with Blos's views that if the process of separation is not sustained, adolescents may try to replace the emotional work of separating through concrete actions, imposing geographical distance between themselves and parents. Alternatively, through succumbing to regression the adolescent will be taken over by a longing for a return to childhood unity, or an idealisation of the state of being on the inside.

Adolescent difficulties may be related to the problem of maintaining a position of 'temporary outsidership'. It is one of the functions of therapeutic work with adolescence to provide, literally, a space outside the family and other social networks, which is, however, through the content of the therapeutic discussions, not cut off from either of these. Thus the psychosocial space of therapeutic consultation occupies a boundary position.

Establishing the boundary position means the adolescent has the capacity to move backwards and forwards – to progress and regress, to seek nurture and develop relationships within the family, and yet be free enough to move outwards and experiment, try things out in the wider social world, and get back again. Once a 'temporary outsider' position is maintained, the adolescent can begin to exert some active control over information flow and have opportunities for maintaining some selectivity about what parents and family get told. Similarly, not everything in the family need reach the world of social relationships outside the family. One emblem of adolescence – the diary – indicates the capacity of the adolescent to reach a position on the boundary, where all need not be said, and much of what is said can be contained by oneself, with the help of the diary. On the other hand, breaches in the 'secrecy' of the diary, or its adjunct, the address book, can be thought of as indicating a leak in the adolescent's 'adolescent' persona.

Adolescent problems and the temporary outsider position

Getting stuck on one side of the temporary outsider boundary is indicative of the kind of problem an adolescent is having. Some adolescent difficulties relate to being stuck on the inside – for example school phobia, being the victim of bullying, eating disorders.

WORKING WITH ADOLESCENTS AND YOUNG ADULTS

Other problems, especially acting out sexually, antisocial behaviour, such as delinquency and criminality, becoming immersed in drug cultures and gang behaviour, are more indicative of being stuck on the outside. This is, though, a crude distinction. It is more helpful to think of outside 'stuckness' as indicating a position with regard to difficulties experienced in intimacy and the need for others, disowning a sense of one's own vulnerability. The inside stuckness has the meaning of being unable to separate, or move away from the position of childhood dependency, or finding within oneself the means to undertake the work of separation. This chapter will discuss adolescents stuck on the outside and in Chapter 7 there is a discussion of those who are stuck on the inside.

Stuck on the outside

Adolescents who appear to break links with adults and families, in various ways are left stuck on the outside, without recourse to a return to emotional connectedness with parents. Blos (1967) describes the stuck 'outsider' as 'in his actual separateness and independence he experiences an intoxicating sense of triumph over his past and slowly becomes addicted to his state of apparent liberation' (p. 82). This forms a starting point for a discussion of delinquency, and drug taking.

As Ann Horne (2004) has noted, psychiatry has colonised the notion of delinquency under the term 'conduct disorders'. Time trends in adolescence show that conduct disorders are increasing (Collishaw et al., 2004). This fits with media views of adolescence that highlight violence, especially knife and gun crime, and the increased awareness of bullying. Conduct disorders also includes 'non-violent' but quintessential adolescent delinquent activities – stealing, lying and disobedience. Horne (2004) shows that, though the term 'conduct disorder' arose as a reaction to the medicalisation of behaviour that had its roots in social conditions, particularly poverty and exclusion, it 'paradoxically deprived mainstream thinking of the subtlety that a psychoanalytic perspective adds both to our understanding of delinquency and our capacity to intervene on behalf of the young delinquent' (p. 331). Treating delinquency as adolescent and therefore developmental behaviour, in context, provides the capacity to link experiences and behaviour as a psychosocial or mental health intervention. The persistence of gang behaviour, which can involve gun and knife violence, can be understood as linked with hegemonic masculinity, exercising power and pride while rejecting vulnerability and dependence on parents (internal and external). Popular conceptions of gangs and gang behaviour often oversimplify the meaning of gang membership for individuals, who may be much more ambiguously in or out of a gang, and whose membership of the gang may reflect temporary absences of containment from parents rather than a permanent positioning. The importance of tracing individual nuances of gang (or tribe) membership is highly relevant to gaining understanding of the meaning of the gang for the individual.

Relatedness to parents, containment of adolescent emotionality and development and delinquency forms a central configuration in understanding antisocial behaviour. For example, adolescents may be pushed into delinquent acts through being in painful predicaments with parents.

Case example

George, 17, hesitantly telephoned to ask for a therapeutic consultation. Between this phone call and his appointment, he and a friend broke into a shop. George said that he had second thoughts after his phone call and he had not intended to keep the appointment, but that now he was very worried about what he had done, and he feared being caught. George told me his father had left the family when he was 13, and, though there was a mystery about why he left, George thought he was in trouble with the police. I was struck by the timing of the break-in, between referral and appointment, and also that there seemed to be a connection, through offending, between George and his father. George said he had no premeditated plan to do the burglary, and he still did not know why he did it. He thus seemed to be 'subject to' intense internal forces of which he knew very little.

Freud (1916) wrote about criminals from a sense of guilt, whose actions indicate they acted upon expression of an intolerable sense of guilt internally, to which the subject had no direct access. Breaking and entering may be considered as an expression of being forcibly kept out from, together with a wish to gain access to, and thus control from within, an unavailable object. The burglary seemed to represent George's fury at being abandoned and a rather self-destructive identification with father. Another example is of a teenager who was 'looked after'.

Case example

Terry's had been looked after since he was seven. His mother was not at all available to him, and he spent four years in a foster home. This was

disrupted when he was 11, and then he spent some time living with rela-
tives, in foster care and in residential homes. Each placement ended when
the relative or carer felt that Terry had become too demanding or too dif-
ficult. At critical times in these placements, Terry would either leave, go
missing, or get involved in a violent episode, either within the home in
which he was staying at the time, or in school. These events tipped the bal-
ance against him, and he was excluded. Terry was contributing actively
to worsen his situation, which reached the point that he was not taken
in either physically or emotionally by anyone. When he was 15, a new
social worker made a determined attempt to find him a more enduring and
meaningful environment, and she worked hard with him, the network and
within her own agency to achieve this. When she found a placement for him
that would take care of him and provide education, Terry went missing,
and was later found sitting outside a house, which he had broken into.

Terry's break-in, and the fact he waited to be caught, seemed to
vividly convey his feelings about his relationship between himself
and others. Not only was he an outsider, and requiring others
to find him somewhere to belong, but the relationships involved
breaking and entry. This seemed to vividly express his sense of
permanent exclusion, outsidership turned outcast. The only kind of
relationship in which there could be a transition between outside
and inside, for Terry and George, was one which necessitated a
violent mode of entry. The experience of absent, dead, unavailable,
neglecting or abusing parents provides an almost impossible task
for adolescents in mourning these losses and maintaining a sense
of integrity, identity and development. George's situation provides
further illustration:

George's father's departure left him with a mother whose mental health was
fragile. She suffered recurring periods of intense depression, and sometimes
took an overdose. George was painfully involved with his mother's illness
and propensity to self-harm. He was worried about his mother and wor-
ried by her, feeling very exposed to her behaviour and responsible for her.
He hated being in the home, and occasionally found ways of escaping – to
play on a friend's computer or to watch his football team. He felt unable
to concentrate on his own life. He did not take GCSE's, and this left him
extremely frustrated and ashamed, feeling that he had let himself down. He
felt bitterly that he had more potential than this. He half-heartedly tried to
find work, but could not feel free enough to engage in the process of find-
ing a job. Several times he started to get work and then did not follow this
through. His fragility was such that when he was in his therapy, he was

quite genuinely shocked if I showed I had remembered things he had said to me. He told me he thought this remarkable, that he did not think people did this. This had the effect of stirring up within him complex, intense and ambivalent feelings about what he had lost and his current predicament.

Being stuck outside, not having parents who were able to attend to his developmental needs and to keep him in mind left George feeling preoccupied with his parents, worried about his mother and pained and angry with both parents. These preoccupations filled his mind to the exclusion of a capacity within himself to maintain a focus on his own life. His tentative move to ask for therapy was an attempt to find some space for himself, and it caused a backlash within him, which led to his offending before his first appointment. Being in therapy meant contending with considerable turbulence within himself.

Delinquency, antisocial behaviour and outsidership

The adolescent's delinquency and deviance is part of an inheritance of traditional ideas about adolescent conflict, turbulence and rebelliousness. It is the aspect of adolescence which gets adolescence hated and from which folk devils (Cohen, 2002) arise. Blos (1967) saw the upsurge of violence as internal and inevitable due to the increase in instinctual tension and the loosening of infantile ties to the parents. Some 'acting out' is therefore to be expected, and it constitutes a 'holding position until progressive development is rekindled again' (p. 82). But if acting out becomes excessive or prolonged it indicates a 'an attempt to escape from an overwhelming, regressive pull to infantile dependencies, grandiosities and gratifications', and thus 'the adolescent who runs away, drives off in a stolen car, leaves school, "bums" his [sic] way to nowhere, takes to promiscuity and to drugs' is 'resorting to emergency measures' and attempting to accomplish internal separation by external means.

Bowlby, Winnicott and Erikson took a slightly different approach to delinquency, emphasising the impact of the environment in a more concrete form. Deprivation is the cause of delinquency. The delinquent 'was not to be regarded as feckless, bad or evil, but as an individual seeking to rectify that which did not feel right inside' (Wilson, 1996, p. 395). Thus, in the face of depriving experiences, there was a note of protest in the delinquent act, 'as something positive, self-affirming and, above all, hopeful for the individual' (ibid., p. 395). In certain circumstances, delinquency has meaning and affirms authenticity, through its paradoxical 'doing wrong, it carries with it an unswerving sense of rightness' (ibid., p. 394). Though Winnicott's writing on adolescence is often accepting of the unacceptable (Perret-Catipovic and Ladame, 1998) the connection between meaning of the delinquent act and the background of deprivation and disruption fits the examples of George and Terry. Thus it is the extreme rupture or trauma that breaks up the identity of these adolescents, so that the impact of the environment is to render the adolescent a more or less permanent outsider, whose delinquency, or 'antisocial tendency' as Winnicott called it, 'is a reminder of a hurt or disturbance brought about by environmental failure' (Wilson, 1996, p. 395). The adolescent's delinquency is a form of resistance, within power relations.

On the other hand, the remorselessness, and imperiousness of delinquency cannot be separated from hating and/or envying others, who possess something that the adolescent desires and wishes to possess. This puts lying, stealing and violence in the same field, in which the adolescent aims to take, inauthentically, from a competitor or to wipe out the competition, internally or externally. Lying, another conduct disorder that is increasing, also tells of the link between acts and experience. Horne (2004) gives an example of a delinquent, Angus, who 'lied as a matter of course. ... His capacity to lie almost automatically seemed to indicate a return to mistrust of his objects and a need to keep them at bay, while also implying an attempt to hold on to difference and separateness' (p. 334). Lemma (2005) makes a distinction between self-preservative and sadistic lying; the former protects the vulnerable individual from intrusive or invasive others; sadistic lying enacts revenge on others.

Violence arises also in subtle relationship to internal experiences. Anderson (1997) takes a view about violence which has a point of contact with Blos. 'Putting the boot in', or apparent mindless violence is a response to the overwhelming feelings that are stirred up in some young people on encountering depressive anxieties. Feelings of vulnerability and dependency, concern for the other and being separate are repudiated, located in a recipient through projective identification and then attacked. The recipient can be another person or an internal, vulnerable part of the self, or both simultaneously. The problem is therefore the essential fragility of the individual, which cannot bear depressive anxieties.

Attention to the delinquent act suggests multiple, subtle meanings. For example, Waddell (1998, p. 139) shows that stealing – in the case of her patient, Christine, who stole from her family – can represent

- restoring a lost relationship, rather than mourning the loss and accepting separation;
- depriving someone else of their possessions (and it may thus be located in revived Oedipal conflicts, especially a jealous attack on the same sex parent);
- feelings of guilt which desire punishment (as in the examples of George and Terry), and an avoidance attack on the self by a jealous parent;
- depriving another through envy and rage; and
- a response to change and loss within the self.

Thus 'stealing is one of the most common manifestations of "acting out" [in adolescence]' (Waddell, 1998, p. 139).

The relationship between trauma and damage, 'acting out' and the capacity to make contact with, and to some extent, bear depressive anxieties are central to understanding these young people. Rustin (2000) in discussing two young adolescents placed for adoption shows that manic defences, 'excitement powered by hilarity and obscenity [hold] anxiety at bay quite effectively', and these two siblings clung together to relieve 'potential loneliness and the terror of facing so many worries about themselves and their future' (p. 80). The two, Lorraine, 14, and David, 10, seen together, played noisily and

> They squabbled, snatched and chattered abusively. David was full of dirty talk and kept up a torrent of verbal abuse of Lorraine and she retaliated by hitting his head.' Rustin comments that she felt she 'had two very wild toddlers in the room, in overgrown bodies.
>
> (p. 78)

The question that is then raised is how far either or both of these abused and disturbed adolescents have the potential to make emotional contact and *how* far each can tolerate their vulnerabilities. How far, it may be suggested, can they leave the manic 'protection' of the group-become-gang, or alternatively, how much will the hate, rage and envy lead to an obliteration of the desire for contact, so that a defence against contact prevents access to other people's minds in an empathic way, and delinquency or violence becomes a 'career' or a fixed subject position.

When vulnerabilities cannot be tolerated individually, a group may provide a way of sticking together to provide a sense of strength against powerful perpetrators of painful experiences, and functions through projecting vulnerability into a chosen target, within the group or outside. The gang 'turns their passive suffering into active cruelty' (Waddell, 1998) through identification of this 'target' who is then placed in receipt of aggression and murderousness. Bullying occurs when there is a reciprocal fit between the projection of murderousness into someone identified as vulnerable, with the victim of bullying projecting aggression into the aggressor. The gang need not be an actual group. In Rustin's example it is a sibling pair; and it is possible in these dynamic terms to see some use of drugs in this way.

Case example

Jill, 16, is in foster care and her relationship with her foster carers has become tenuous. She is developing a wild lifestyle of clubs, promiscuity and drug taking. She has a wide circle of friends, and she moves between them so that she is always able to be in contact with someone else. When friends or boyfriends are not available she has a mobile to which she is completely attached, and if this fails, she can get drugs from a dealer she knows. Although – given these aspects of herself – it may seem unlikely, Jill comes to her therapy, and she does have a capacity to make emotional contact, together with some awareness of the meaning of her manic defences. The end of her therapy sessions became a point of crisis for her, and she seemed to feel intensely a need to fill the gap or void between herself and therapy immediately. This drove her to action. One form of this was to make phone calls on her mobile before leaving the room. More extremely she went straight from her therapy to buy drugs. At these times Jill would not be aware of the causative impact of separation, but would rather talk about being unaccountably upset, or preoccupied with therapy being 'difficult', in order to try to make the overwhelming quality of her emotions more manageable.

Despite the fragility of Jill's subjectivity, she was able to bear emotional contact, and indeed longed for it, but this stirred up overwhelming feelings of loss and pain, which had to be kept under control. Feelings of vulnerability were unwanted and hated, and humiliating for her, but paradoxically she needed to feel some vulnerability in order to be able to be in contact with herself and others. Success for Jill was being 'cool', but when she achieved the desired 'cool' this also meant that she had split off her needs and vulnerabilities so that she was at risk of damaging herself, and her relationships. It was through getting into distressing and distressed states after something went amiss in one of these relationships that she felt a need for help, and this state of mind, her more vulnerable sense of herself, returned her to her therapy.

Drugs and subjectivity

The use of drugs is a complex subject. Social analysis asserts that pressure on adolescents to use drugs, alongside the development of a 'lifestyle' constitutes both a pressure on young people to take part in consumption, to develop a 'lifestyle', and also that it is an aspect of resistance. For example,

> In a moment where most young people can 'manage' little else, the body provides one important site for management and also becomes the primary vehicle for the achievement of pleasure. ... The use of drugs. ... And the cultivation of a particular fashion for oneself can, in this context, all be seen as attempts to stake out an independence from the parental and societal regulation of these bodies.
>
> (Pini, 1997, p. 163)

This analysis, which owes much to Foucault, sits alongside an older view in which adults are seen as hypocritical; they castigate the use of drugs but use their own, especially alcohol and nicotine. Graham (2004) points out that changing young people's patterns of drug (and alcohol) use requires a prior change in adult patterns of consumption. He adds there is not much chance of that, but there is evidence, mainly government led, which suggests some societal changes taking place; the focus on responsible drinking, and the ban on smoking are two examples.

Van Heeswyk (1997) proposes the idea of 'benign addiction' in which alteration of perception, through 'coffee, beer or heroin' changes how we feel. The hopeless problem before the use of drugs becomes easier in the 'benign addiction' paradigm. 'It may still be hopeless, but it is no longer serious' (p. 65). Clearly this approach to mental health problems has a parallel in pharmacological treatments, especially in the treatment of depression, anxiety and ADHD.

Bollas (1991) takes a different view, in which he asserts that 'hallucinating from ingestion of a drug is an act of violence against one's subjectivity' (p. 146). Writing specifically about 'tripping', Bollas points out that the alteration of mind through tripping is not the same as dreaming, since the drug usurps the function of the ego in processing 'lived experience'. The taking of a drug is a 'casual almost serene moment', in which the pill is 'dropped' like an atom bomb 'dropped' from a plane. The analogy of violence casually done places the taking of (some) drugs in a contemporary social context.

Between these positional aspects lies individual meaning. Jill took drugs because she was a member of a group of teenagers who were in that kind of scene. She also took them at particular points in time, primarily to express her fury at the fact that separation from others is a necessary and unavoidable experience in life, and she wished to avoid the overwhelming feelings that she experienced when she felt vulnerable. She also did it as a form of casual violence against herself and her objects, which was self-destructive (this was in fact her judgement of herself) and took drugs because she had to endure awful experiences inside herself, resulting from the abusiveness and deprivations of her past. The use of drugs then has multiple meanings in adolescence. It can indicate a group identity, a process of exploration, or a problematic and pathological situation. Rodriguez de la Sierra (2000) has proposed that alongside sociological explanations of drug use – peer group influence, experimentation, and rebellion against adult values – 'the use of drugs in adolescence is closely connected with failed attempts to deal with intense aggressive and sexual feelings, which the adolescent then tries to relieve by turning to pills or injections that bring deceptive tranquillity to his or her troubled mind' (p. 78). The relationship between the adolescent dug user and the social world can be masochistic, and also omnipotent, in seeking magical solutions to experiences of separation and loss. The same person may be involved with drugs for all these reasons.

The task of therapy, with Jill, was the rather awesome one of trying to find ways in which Jill could feel more able to bear her own emotions. This meant developing a sense of choice rather than compulsion; tolerating emotional contact with others, even though it meant at some points separating from them; managing to be alone, being 'inside', belonging, rather than fated to be an outsider, giving up, or relying less extensively and exclusively on manic, omnipotent and masochistic defences and relationships as a response to pain, frustration and separation. This, once more, constitutes a process of becoming 'subject of' rather than 'subject to' internal experiences in a given social context, or, in Williams' (1998) phrase, giving up dependency on an 'unreliable container'.

Summary

- The 'temporary outsider' is a term which describes the adolescent in developmental motion, an in between state, on the boundary between the family and the social world. It can be experienced in different ways as adolescents making the transition through from childhood towards adulthood.
- There is a hopeful, 'becoming' aspect of this if adolescents can tolerate the experience of a gap between themselves and others. Widening and deepening of relationships, awareness of self and a sense of power and capability are made possible by temporary outsidership, and the flexibility of moving between inside and outside in a fluid way.
- If the anxieties of the boundary position of temporary outsidership are too great, the adolescent may get 'stuck' on one side of the boundary – inside or outside, with consequent problems in development.
- The problems of being stuck on the outside include antisocial behaviour, delinquency, and drug taking and acting out. These are linked by an intolerance of experiences of separation and depressive feelings and the stirring up of violent and manic defences against pain. From different theoretical perspectives, there are multiple meanings for each kind of behaviour in different contexts.
- The case examples show that when emotional contact with others and a sense of belonging within intimate relationships are precarious, defences are mobilised against the turbulence aroused by intimate contact with others. Acting out is a means of expressing, resisting or obliterating the pain involved.

7

ADOLESCENT DIFFICULTIES IN ACHIEVING SEPARATENESS

Many adolescent difficulties relate to the problem of not being able to tolerate the 'gap' between self and other, upon which subjectivity is founded. We have seen in Chapter 6 that one particular aspect of expressing difficulty with and defending against the pains of separateness and intimacy is to engage in behaviours and take up positions that appear more adult or at least show intolerance of the pains of dependency. On the other hand, it is possible to identify adolescents that appear to locate the problematic arena in the outside world of peers and adulthood. These adolescents appear to be stuck on the inside, within the child in the family role. This has the meaning that the impact of internal, familial and social factors, often in inextricable combinations, slows down or brings to a halt the adolescent development towards separateness and relative independence of parental figures. Thus, either physically or emotionally or both the adolescent is unable to become a 'temporary outsider'. There is a range of adolescent difficulties that can be associated with being stuck on the inside. In order to explore the psychosocial aspects of these difficulties in adolescence, this chapter will discuss adolescents with phobias, body image disturbance and eating disorders and disabilities. This is followed by a discussion of depression and self-harm.

Not separating

The negotiation of separation from parents demands internal work akin to the processes involved in mourning. Becoming more separate is predicated on the capacity for closeness and intimacy with others, on having internalised a sense of self, and self-esteem, which is enduring and permits resilience when faced with difficulties. Both relational and individualised aspects are important in achieving subjectivation.

In early adolescence, if too much is demanded either in terms of close-ness in relationships or being independent, adolescents are likely to experience and demonstrate narcissistic fragility. Some adolescents who get stuck on the outside choose the route of an illusory self-sufficiency; for others it can seem that being self-sufficient is the last thing they can achieve, or would want to show to others. These ado-lescents stay close to their parents, sometimes literally, maintaining physical proximity, and sometimes through entangled interactions that cohere around the idea that parents have withheld, or failed to give something to them. Straightforwardly, this can be expressed as an imperative, in which independence is treated as though it is a gift, a consumable that parents could choose to give or withhold. For these adolescents a particular aspect of infancy – weaning – is activated in current relationships with parents, in which, though there is an aware-ness of the power of parents and their potential to give, there is also a resentment or grievance that this resides in the parents' control.

There are diverse manifestations of the failure to separate, and these form some complex configurations, for which the theory overlaps. To illustrate these different presentations and underlying meanings, I have selected three case examples, for each of which I will explore the meaning and relevant theory. The cases highlight particular problems, therefore, which can be located in patterns of not separating. The first, Colin, shows the adolescent's internal work of development delegated to parents; secondly, the example of Jeremy describes aggression projected into others, resulting in Jeremy being bullied and the third example, Sally, is an example of school phobia, expressing an uncon-scious conviction that to be separated leads to a catastrophe.

Case example: Colin

In this example, the task of working internally to achieve independ-ence is replaced by an imperative demand on others to provide separateness and independence as though it is a gift. This was stated very vividly by a 15-year-old adolescent, *Colin, who was in fact a very small boy – in appearance much more like a ten-year-old than a boy of his age, had a difficulty with eating, and with growing. He felt trapped in his smallness, weighing under six stones, not eating and worrying that he was losing friends. At the same time he said, 'There is a bit of me that is happy to be like this. It is like being in a cell with a heavy door that will take ten years to open'. And I can't find the box with the rusty nail in it. I need to spit it out. Colin felt trapped and faced with an immense labour to achieve more openness under his own efforts. His hopelessness led him to give up and ask for others to do it for him. He implored me to 'tell them [his parents] to give him his independence'.*

He could not contemplate or conceptualise undertaking himself, in conjunction with someone else, such as myself in role as his therapist, the emotional work that would bring about a negotiation of independence with others, over time. In his metaphor the rusty nail in the box seemed to have a deathly constellation, invoking a coffin. He felt that anything that took a long time meant things got worse. This also applied to therapy.

He said, 'There's no point coming here for a long time. Either you'll give me an idea that works or not. The longer you go somewhere things get less helpful'. At first he told me there were no problems in his family, but then he said that his mother was ill, and there had been deaths in the family. He was worried his mother would die. When we spoke about the difficulty of feeling someone was leaving him, or he was leaving someone, he said, 'it is difficult, it's like a death'.

When worries about separateness are linked with worries about loss and death the difficulty of separating becomes very frightening. Phobic defences get mobilised. The combination of parental illness and an intruding sense of death invaded Colin, so that he was stuck on the inside. Interestingly, he told me that he never drank milk, and he had been told that he had refused milk from the time he was weaned from the breast. The failure to mourn and accept substitutes went very deep in his relationship with his mother, with whom he could be thought to be overinvolved, so that there was a fusion between them, with Colin being ill because his mother was ill. However, we can also detect something more hostile in this, in Colin developing difficulties that also worried his mother, and which appeared to demand more from her, despite her own fragility. He seems to be challenging her to be a strong and not ill mother, rather than being more sparing of her.

Flynn (2000) discusses how different insider and outsider defences in young male adolescents – delinquent, phobic, obsessional and psychotic – all shared a 'continuously overly involved relationship with the mother ... based on incestuous patterns' (p. 62). In one of these cases:

He steered his way into his early adolescent experience very slowly and gradually by reluctantly relinquishing his latency pursuits and preoccupations. These included maddeningly abstruse games and procedures he would devise, and ways of talking and thinking that could be shared with practically no one but his mother, who seemed to be the sole initiate in Brian's one person cult.

(p. 62)

The wish for, or even requirement, of a special relationship with mother can leave young adolescent boys unable to tolerate separateness, and seemingly arrogantly or contemptuously tossing aside relationships with others.

Case example: Jeremy

Jeremy, 14, could not bear to be the same as other boys, and his eccentricities – seriousness and a 'nerd'-like refusal to join groups – were extremely provocative to his peers, particularly as he had great difficulties with his aggression, and projected it into others. He became extremely disliked by peers, which displaced an old grievance, his sense of feeling extremely disliked by his parents, who had not been satisfied with one child and had two more, his younger brothers. Being disliked by his peers brought a kind of satisfaction for him, and he was at times unmercifully bullied. Look, he seemed to be saying while taking himself hostage, what this eviction from the special relationship does to him. Desperately disillusioned, he felt that any closeness with others brought betrayal.

With Jeremy, there was no space on the boundary; he was right in or right out. His expectation of others was that they would have him, and only him or they were history. Being separate and sharing others' affections were unthinkable propositions. Dartington's view of the outsider was that when outsidership was felt to be impossible, it was linked with 'an unconscious conviction that the wish to separate is synonymous with hatred, that, in families, the reserves of love will not survive this hatred, and that family catastrophe will ensue' (p. 94). Phobic states are one defence against this fear of catastrophe.

Case example: Sally

Sally, 13, refused to go to school. She had been involved in an incident at school in which it seemed that another girl had criticised her, and since then she had absolutely refused to leave the home unless her mother was in constant attendance. Sally came to therapy with her mother and older brother, Sean, who was 17. Sally, dressed more like a smaller child than an adolescent, and she seemed completely overwhelmed by her mother, who was insistent that she must be seen by therapists who were parents. Sally's mother was adamant that if the therapist was not a parent, she could not possibly understand her. Eventually, Sally's older brother, Sean, taking the role of family historian, helpfully told us that there was another child, a girl, who had died in infancy. Both Sean and Sally were in fact terribly guilty that their own hostility and murderousness to this baby had some-how contributed to her death. Sean was ostracised for talking about this baby, as the family never spoke about it.

The indigestible, unmournable loss of this baby was a powerful unspoken presence in this family. The mother's insistence that Sally should be seen by therapists, who were parents, projected into the therapists the feeling that she had ceased to be a parent to her baby. Moreover, if Sally grew more separate then she would lose her too. Sally's role was to remain close to mother, and not separate.

Williams (2001) has written about the disorganising effects of silence surrounding a loss, and particularly a death of a baby, when these are projected into another child in the family. Sally was in more difficulty that Sean because her place in the family – the last surviving baby – attracted more projections from her mother. Sally was impelled not to leave her. The equation of separateness with death, or catastrophe, leaves the adolescent unable to reach temporary outsidership, because fear of the outside is produced through the projections of an aggressive nature on to the outside. The phobic and bullied states of mind converge. In Colin's case, the feeling of having something deathly, or deadly inside him prohibited the exploration of the inside space, and thus the outside world, and growth towards the boundary and separating, through projection, was invested as dangerous.

Disability in adolescence

Adolescents who are disabled get 'stuck on the inside', within a context in which physical separation and autonomy is perhaps restricted. Primarily, the experience is of facing difference – not being like others – within a context of negative attributions:

'Most of the people we have dealings with, including our most intimate relationships, are not like us. It is therefore very difficult for us to recognise and challenge the values and judgements that are applied to us and our lives. Our ideas about disability and about ourselves are generally formed by those who are not disabled' (Morris 1991 in French and Swain, 1997).

Organised by society as 'docile bodies' (Foucault, 1977), disabled adolescents constantly face experiences of difference or separation, especially through educational segregation. Special schooling can be excluding, or it may provide opportunities of experiencing similarity, in a kind of Diaspora:

> It [special school] was a liberating experience. It taught me how to like myself, to take pride in myself, and most of all to be sensitive to the needs of others.
>
> (French and Swain, 1997, p. 201)

Trevatt (2001) discusses how thinking about disability is a 'dangerous area to express views in' and how muddled thinking of adults can become between notions of normality and the limitations of disability. The idea that a disabled adolescent may have the same interests, desires and illusions as other adolescents is immediately countered by a differentiating process within the adult, as if to make decisions about what aspiration and desire a disabled adolescent may have, or may not have. Thus adults fall between ideas of nurture and growth, and of managing illness, disability and limitation.

Interestingly, Miller (1998), when working psychotherapeutically with learning disabled adolescents found that the experience of sameness and difference had a powerful impact in the therapy. She describes Beth, a 16-year-old with Down's syndrome, with a severe learning disability, who lived in a children's home. Beth caused many difficulties for the staff of this home, especially when she imitated other adolescents' aggressive behaviour in a contagious way. Beth's history was one of frequent disruption to continuous relationships, beginning when she was placed in foster care as a one-month baby, perhaps, or probably, because her parents were unable to face the fact of her disability. Miller describes the first therapeutic consultation with Beth, in which three professionals were present:

> When I suggested Beth might like to draw, she suddenly began to participate very actively in the session, drawing food and telling [us] to do the same, handing out paper and pens. She drew attention to ways in which we were the same; we all had black shoes for example.
>
> (p. 43)

Milller comments that the defence against painful difference could have been the focus of intervention, but if, imaginatively, the therapist tried to think about Beth's state of mind, there is a relief and freedom from thinking that 'we are all the same'. In a later session, Beth could not contribute to the session when she was faced with the idea of difference. She only found a way to continue when she could find another contact of sameness. Miller then discusses the implications for identity:

> When the [learning disabled adolescent] talks it is not clear to whom he or she is referring – to him or herself or the therapist – the direction is reversible. This mode of communication seems to lie somewhere between the concrete and the symbolic; there is meaning, but it is difficult to ascertain to what or to whom it can be attributed. It is as if there is a potential two-person relationship but the identities of subject and object are not clearly located.
>
> (p. 43)

The effects of the interaction between disability and experiences in the social world are extremely entangled. Beth had a deprived, abusive and disruptive background in terms of her relationships and the problems in identity cannot be separated from these or the limitations imposed by her disability itself. The problem arising from the phenomenology that Miller describes is that social experiences, which are internalised, complicate differentiation of self from the other. Beth is looking inside for contexts of sameness. When she has a notion of sameness with another, she can relate, play and creatively communicate.

Thoughts and feelings about the relationship between body and mind may become subject to multiple meanings. David, 18, who had been born without arms from below the elbow, and who had a foot amputated in childhood designated his disabilities as 'his bits missing'. Williams (1997), who discusses this case, describes how David had 'bits missing' in his childhood. His teenage mother and her family were not able or willing to continuously care for David, so that, in the absence also of a father he had never met, David spent time in children's homes. He had poignant memories of the frequent separations from his mother, which conveyed his wish to hang on to her as she left. Unable to do this with his arms, he focused on her with his eyes instead.

David's response to his predicament was to overcome it, and he did make himself very 'able' through physical activities and painting. Williams felt that 'I was asked, for a long time, to pretend that the disability and the many 'bits missing' in his body and in his life did not exist, or if they existed, that they did not matter' (p. 80).

Trevatt (2001) discusses the tensions for physically disabled adolescents who have fantasies for the future which are probably illusory and which can be painful for adults to bear, and difficult for them to challenge. He refers to young people who 'seem to live more in a fantasy world to the extent that they need me to believe that their fantasies are true' (p. 100). The strength of these fantasies is linked with anxieties about loss and death, reflecting a painful reality that some young people will have severe limitations in terms of their independence and autonomy, while others face an early death or a very uncertain future life expectancy. Williams' reports David moving between two states of mind, in one of which there was a sense of real achievement in which emotional contact was possible, and another in which he was swept away in phantasies of an omnipotent nature. In these moments, it was difficult to make emotional contact, and David seemed 'extremely elusive. He could probably only tell me about the pain of not being able to take a firm grip on his object by evoking this feeling in me' (p. 80). David used his eyes to compensate for not being able to make a grip on another in other ways. His eyes fixed on other people, and he only began to be able to let go of this rigid grip when he internalised containment of his anxieties. This included both an appreciation of his real achievements and awareness of the quality of his omnipotent phantasies. Williams formulates the transition from the necessity of the emotional need of another in the external world to relying on an internal world separate form others, in parenting roles, as requiring the 'internalisation, or at least the beginning of the internalisation, of a reliable internal object' (p. 88).

Eating disorders in adolescence

Eating disorders have been thought about as evidencing a difficulty in the adolescent to accept a developing sense of adulthood, and as a defensive reaction to emerging adulthood and sexuality (Plaut and Hutchinson, 1985). The low body weight of the anorexic girl and her loss of periods maintain a childlike bodily state and a rejection of the bodily world of adults. Williams (1997) points out that anorexic girls are 'often terrified of sexuality in general, but terrified of penetration in particular' (p. 118). To remain looking like a child means not facing the process of adolescent development and the world of adulthood, with its separateness and sexuality.

Eating disorders are however complex, and 'loom large as potent metaphors of our times' (Williams and Bendelow, 1998, p. 75) Giddens (1991) suggests that 'anorexia represents a striving for security in a world of plural, but ambiguous objects. The tightly controlled body is an emblem of a safe existence in an open social environment' (p. 107). The risks of engagement are not felt to be worth taking, since a loss of sense of self-worth is experienced through engagement. Giddens quotes the title of Sours' (1981) book *Starving to Death in a Sea of Objects* in this context. Bulimia and obesity present different images and ways of attending to the same dilemma – safety through control in a plural, ambiguous social world. 'Whilst bulimia represents the unstable double bind of consumer capitalism, anorexia (i.e. the work ethic in absolute control) and obesity (consumerism in control) embody an attempted resolution of cultural contradictions' (Williams and Bendelow, 1998, p. 75). These analyses of eating disorders include the idea that there is a tremendous asceticism in the trials, punishment and purgations that are done to the body, through which arises both a sense of achievement, which overcomes despair and which acts on the wish for self-denial and of being an active agent, through control. The validity of the methods and outcomes may be questioned from a psychoanalytic viewpoint, where the central problem – relating to others – is evaded by these compulsive, and often increasingly intensively cyclical defensive manoeuvres. Where Giddens talks of empowerment in this context, it has to be questioned whether the empowerment is real, illusory or simply defensive. On the other hand, the accounts provide a way of understanding the social and cultural pressures which affect adolescents; in particular, the problems of plurality and risk seem especially pertinent; subjectivity is avoided through eating disorders.

Social and cultural analysis of eating disorders emphasises the gender divide. It is a mainly female phenomenon, or, it can be said, girls and women 'pay the greatest material and symbolic toll' (Williams and Bendelow, p. 75). The gendered nature of eating disorders is connected in these accounts with the obsession with exercise, and body building in the 'asceticism' of eating disorders. Many more adolescent girls experience eating disorders than boys, but boys too have eating disorders – and are increasingly noticed as such clinically.

However, it is argued that there are particular gender specific pressures that bear on adolescent girls. On the one hand, the emphasis on thinness and the devaluation of women through negative societal images create a context in which adolescent girls may become ambivalent about their development as women. Much of this discourse centres on the body. On the other hand, girls are socialised differently from boys and their relationships with mothers are more tense, more divided and more including a specific tension with regard to identifying with their mothers (Sayers, 1991; Bordo, 1993). Under these pressures, one solution may be to remain as an insider and not to venture into the world of adulthood. Being amenorrheaic makes a powerful statement of not negotiating puberty, or retreating from it.

In that there is recent recognition of young male eating disorder, this may reflect some changes in the constitution of masculinity. Sayers (1991) characterises female adolescence as divided in relationships, and male as internally divided. For males to experience eating disorders there is a prerequisite, in this analysis, that they are torn internally, with ambivalence in relationships and fear of loss of control, rather than being split off from emotionality.

Psychoanalytic thinking has extended the understanding of the internal dynamics in eating disorders. Magagna (2000) argues that anorexia means not simply closing the mouth to food, but also closing the mind to emotional experiences, which means also withdrawing from the world of others and particularly the nurturing possibilities in relationships. Williams (1997) has described a 'no entry syndrome', in which the anorexic adolescent closes down the possibility of taking something in. This forms a defensive system, in which the fear of taking in is experienced by the adolescent as so acute that it becomes a dread. If the anorexic teenager feels something has to be taken in, then the impact of this is akin to a breaking and entering. Forced feeding thus breaks through the defensive system and simply reinforces the dread and sense of persecution; the emotional resistance to taking in is in this way reinforced. It is important in this sense to think about the parallel meaning of physical and emotional digestion (Briggs, 1995). The anorexic is not made better by putting on weight; in fact 'emotional anorexia' continues to dominate, in some cases, the mental life of the anorexic even after an increase in weight and an improvement in eating patterns. Instead of bursting through this defensive system, Williams advocates noticing and talking about the defence, being receptive to what the adolescent can take in (being prepared to use tea spoons rather than table spoons, so to speak), while at the same time maintaining vigilance with regard to the fluctuations in weight (weighing is usually undertaken by a professional other than the therapist, and this establishes a couple working with the adolescent).

The bulimic teenager presents a similar picture; emotional bulimia can exist alongside physical bulimia, in patterns of gorging or binge-ing followed by evacuation. For example, one teenager bought clothes which she wore once and stuffed into her wardrobe, and then periodically cleared out the wardrobe, putting the clothes into plastic bags and throwing them away.

These accounts suggest that there is something in particular taking place in the minds or internal relationships, of anorexic and bulimic adolescents. Williams argues that the eating disordered adolescent has experienced a particular quality of relationship with her par-ents, usually the mother, in which she has been the receptacle for undigested emotional experiences of the parent. That is, instead of the parent being a container for the adolescent, the roles have been reversed. She gives an example of a teenager, Sally, whose night-mare was being invaded through every orifice by tadpoles. This constitutes not only a fear of sexuality (tadpoles being recognisable as spermatozoa) but 'a more pervasive dread of allowing anything to come inside … every orifice is a possible access to persecutors' (p. 120). Thus though it is often the case that adolescents with eating disorders have had difficult and painful life experiences, some have been sexually abused, and suffered other traumas, eating disorders are underpinned by a problem in the arena of containment, which affects internalisation, or taking in from others.

A complementary approach which however emphasises much more the aims and motives of the eating-disordered adolescent's inner world, emphasises the attacks on life (Magagna, 2000) and the hidden – but active – murderousness (Lawrence, 2001). Lawrence in fact uses this analysis to demonstrate the internal dif-ference between the bulimic and the anorexic. Both the anorexic and the bulimic patient have a paramount need to control the other. In particular the problem which needs to be controlled is a sense of life and liveliness in others, which excludes the patient, and the prototype for this experience is the parental couple (Britton, 1989) whose fertility is evidenced by the existence of the patient. Since this experience of another's life and liveliness is totally unbearable and unimaginable, the eating-disordered patient tries to destroy liveli-ness, both through the impact of the eating disorder on her inter-personal relationship and in her inner world. The anorexic needs to render her 'object' helpless, and thus to be obliged to observe her destructiveness.

Case example: Anorexia

A distinctive case of anorexia in a teenager illustrates many of the above points. Samantha, a 16-year-old, came to therapy on the recommendation of her teachers, who were concerned about her. Sam's parents died in a traffic accident when she was nine. This had been an intolerable and indigestible emotional experience (Williams 1998), and Sam never talked about her parents. Avoiding contact with this, she 'got on with her life' and in particular concentrated on her schoolwork, where she had developed a reputation for extremely diligent work, and she had high expectations of herself. Her teachers said that she was increasingly difficult, she lacked concentration, and her work was very inconsistent.

It was very striking in her therapy that Sam had great difficulty in taking in from me. She would contest things I said, making a great deal of minor discrepancies and quibbles, so that the point of any interpretation was lost. Soon, she became very preoccupied with a wish to stop coming, and would raise the idea in each session that I should let her not continue. I had the feeling that it was important to resist this, but that it was also important to try to find a way of thinking about it with her, and that was a very delicate thing to do. My sense was that she presented me with a 'no entry', system of defences as discussed by Williams, and that beneath this was a powerful murderousness, which she was not really aware of. It also seemed clear to me that the discussion about stopping therapy was in some way connected with the loss of her parents, and that she was not consciously aware of her feelings about her parents, or, indeed her murderousness.

Eventually, though I had to wait a long time, she told me she had problems with eating. She told me she had begun to have difficulties with eating in her early adolescence – though no one knew, and she described herself at this point as bulimic, keeping her difficulties hidden by eating and then vomiting. In telling me this, she talked also about her parents' deaths, including many details of her feelings at the time and afterwards.

Instead of this bringing relief and improvement, Samantha's wish to face her difficulties and her past brought about a terrible struggle with her internal demons. She became seriously anorexic, in the grip of a terrible internal murder, which meant I had to face the feeling – and at times the prospect – of losing my patient in an awful way. I felt condemned to watch her, helplessly, just as she had helplessly suffered the loss of her parents.

That her parents' deaths was felt by her to be a very cruel experience seemed to be evident from the way she treated her therapy, making active what she had previously passively suffered, and putting both of us through a life and death struggle. In this example, there is a tremendous power of enactment, in which the eating disorder, in an extremely suicidal form, impacted upon me in a way which made me feel extremely helpless. It seemed to be the only way she could work through the indigestibility that had become frozen inside her. Eventually, however her murderous attacks on herself and her objects relented and she was able to relinquish her deadly grip on herself, and others, and begin to turn towards life and development. Eventually she left for university, leaving her therapy at the same time, and effecting a fundamental aspect of adolescent development – being able to leave parent figures, rather than being left by them.

The bulimic, more secretively, tries to conceal her destructiveness from the object. However it is control, which is paramount: the ultimate form of control is effected through an underlying phantasy of murder. The anorexic wipes out in her mind the existence of others, and then, through turning things on their head, in a perverse way, the wiped out and objectless world is idealised. Lawrence provides the example of a patient who dreamed that she was having intercourse with her boyfriend when suddenly everything went white, the boyfriend is no longer there, and the patient says how much she loves white. It is thus murderousness which makes active the impact of anorexia which is usually transmitted to others as passive. Murderousness towards the self actively places the anorexic in a life-threatening as well as self-damaging arena; there are also links between this kind of material and suicidal dynamics (see Chapter 8). The anorexic is caught between two opposing trends, one on the side of life and the other favouring death rather than growth. 'Both the life seeking and the death-seeking factors are writ large. This "fierce dispute betwixt damnation and impassioned clay"' (Williams, 1978) has the adolescent trapped at the threshold, and in long-term eating disorders, addicted to the state of near death.

The bulimic's vomiting represents a phantasy of killing internal objects, but the bulimic has less of a stranglehold on the object than the bulimic and the objects keep coming back to life, only to need killing off again. The bulimic needs to be a serial murderer. Lawrence illustrates through a bulimic patient who was unable to read before her analysis, but when she felt able to do so, read only books on serial murder. This is then linked with Klein's (1935) thinking about the manic defence which is employed to control dangerous internal objects, and in particular to keep at a distance feelings of concern and compassion for the object. In some case, even noticing the separateness of the object as another human being can trigger the defences of the eating disorder. Thus the eating-disordered patient gets involved in 'activity which to the external observer seems pointless. This often includes intense physical activity, but also the massive and unnecessary scholastic over-achievement found in many young anorexics' (p. 51). Though writing on the whole about adult patients, Lawrence also links her thinking about eating disorders with the adolescent issue which revolves around the place which is given in the adolescent's world for relationships with others, and what has been called the 'omnipotent quest' of adolescence (Greenberg, 1975).

Case example: Bulimia

Carol's descriptions of eating were characteristic of a bulimic teenage girl, bingeing on ice cream which she would take for herself from the fridge. She said, for example, she would eat three ice creams – but it could be anything that was there. Then something seemed to take over and it would become mechanical. She would keep eating and afterwards she would vomit.

Carol was worried about not being liked or popular at school and she thought popularity was in indirect proportion to her weight. When I saw her she was a small teenager of 15, whose shape was somewhat hidden by a bulky jumper. She told me she was just under eight stones at present, though her weight fluctuated and she had recently been ten stones. She thought that her bulimia had been an 'ideal solution' to her problems. By vomiting she was able to eat, and not gain weight, thus satisfying her craving without losing her popularity. She felt 'cheated' that, when her weight fell as she continually vomited, she lost her periods.

Carol's 'ideal solution' was seen in the way she continually bypassed emotional as well as physical processes. She avoided problematic feelings in her relationships with others, particularly her parents, and aimed also to 'bypass' the therapeutic process. Indeed any process involving taking in was to be treated in the same way, including learning at school. Bulimic interactions pervaded her world, including her view of her parents' behaviour. Carol wished to play down and evacuate her difficulties, to which she felt her parents overreacted.

She was worried that she upset her parents, and she just wanted to be rid of the problem. She added that she wanted 'a form of therapy that will soon be over'.

Carol spent time in my room greedily feasting on the objects in the room, especially, she would stare at the books.

I felt I was under considerable pressure to collude with her, especially to spare her from commitment and contact. Instead of thinking with her about her states of mind, she seemed to want me to let her raid my bookshelves, take away a book and return when she was ready. This I learned reversed her experiences with her parents from when she was very young. Both parents worked and Carol would let herself into the home after school, and prepare her own meals from food in the fridge. In Carol's life, people were turned into 'fridges' and this was how I felt in working with her. The fridge could be raided at will, whereas the communications with me were restricted to face-to-face meetings at specified time intervals. The fridge was an inanimate, cold storage object, but one which permitted access under her control. Live contact was thus controlled and devalued, at the tyranny of an infantile part of her who could not bear to depend on someone who was separate from her. The experience of separation was short-circuited and avoided, because it was intolerable and stirred up powerful feelings of being out of control. Carol was someone who could not bear the thought of therapy more often than once a week because it meant that the increased frequency provided not more help, but more experiences of separation. She needed to be right inside, or right outside, and the position on the boundary, tolerating separateness and accepting a limit to the control exerted over others, was too anxious for her.

Carol's pervasive bulimic state of mind, in which evacuation – churning out – was predominant exemplified issues of control and the need for a short cut through emotionality and relationships. This led to problems of subjectivity and objectivity. The lack of a perspective, of what is serious, is absent or changed into a kind of curiosity about how something works, while the 'I' is restricted. On the other side of this 'short cut' was a fear of overwhelming feelings, especially depression and distress, which became unbounded, in an enormous sense of loss and damage.

Carol binged and then became depressed. In her therapy she was able to become worried about the loss of her period and felt it may be lost forever. She communicated a sense of never being able to grow up and become a woman. She felt she had 'messed herself up' (an image of being covered in her own vomit). Fleetingly and elusively in these moments of this state of mind, there were possibilities of making emotional contact. In these moments, it was possible for thoughtfulness to be present. Painfulness could be digested, in other words, with thought, and the developmental possibility also emerged, and was witnessed in her therapy. Fleetingly a different kind of subjectivity was felt and experienced, and the self-destructive state was turned away from, with realisation of the damage that was being done to herself.

Obesity

Obesity, it has been well publicised, is a problem that is increasingly affecting us all; the number of seriously overweight young people is increasing through poor diet and not enough exercise. This is the common sense approach; sedentary lifestyles are to blame (Graham, 2004). One in five adolescents are currently overweight, and this rate is rising, and for many of these a simple societal explanation for being overweight is probably sufficient. Reflecting on this, however, it is possible to agree with Williams and Bendelow (1998) that being thin, well-toned and fit is the 'correct attitude' in contemporary society. This poses a dilemma about how to fulfil two contradictory demands to consume and to stay thin; in obesity, the demand to consume if in control.

For some young people who have problems of being overweight, internal factors are important. Becoming obese can involve using food to deny separateness. Maria Rhode (2004) gives a brief example in which overeating and thus obesity was a young woman's way of defending against a rather traumatic adolescence in which she felt guilty about reaching puberty. She identified herself with her father, who was overweight, and her mother, who had a history of alcohol abuse. She intended thus to deny separateness from both parents and to deal with terrifying, clear memories of being left in a residential nursery when she was a child. Through her identifications, this young woman provides a meaning to the view that obesity runs in families (NICE, 2006) and situates obesity as a response to traumatic memories. Food is used concretely to overcome fears of being separate and controlled, and this which is displaced on to the body being now out of control. The use of obesity as an addictive defence against traumatic experiences is illustrated by the following case example.

Case example: Alison

Alison, now 21, began to become overweight in her early teens. By the time she was 20, she had become so overweight that she needed physical support to move around, and after many kinds of treatment – physical and psychological – she was admitted to an in-patient unit. She had been sexually abused by her step-parent in her childhood. She eats continually, and says she cannot do without this. Though extremely traumatised in her childhood, and having constant medical attention throughout her teens, she does not give any indications of pain, unhappiness or depression, but speaks with a little girl's voice that was blissfully small and innocent. Thus Alison restored an idealised sense of childhood, including physical dependency on others and emotional dependency on food, and defeats all attempts to help her become more separate and able to relate to the deeply felt grievances of the past. There is an absence of any voice that can say 'stop' and thus introduce a limit or boundary.

Clearly with obesity there are narcissistic and aesthetic issues in contexts where thinness is overvalued and extensively promoted through the media. Adolescents encounter through these kinds of communications a super peer (Brown et al., 2006), creating pressures on norms and ideals. For young people to buck these aesthetic trends means accepting a more abject subjectivity or using this as a defence or shield against prevailing trends with regard to sexuality. Graham (2004) reports an ordinary kind of case of a 'plump' teenager who accepts not having a boyfriend, unlike most of her peers; managing the body in this way constitutes a way of protecting oneself from engagement in the mainstream sexual and bodily discourses.

As with all eating disorders, it is vitally necessary to link the adolescent experiences with patterns of feeding in infancy. Infant feeding difficulties stem from splits between physical and emotional care. In taking in milk, Klein thought, the infant also takes in love. When there is disturbance in the relationship between mother and infant, and a failure in the container–contained relationship, there are a number of possibilities. The container–contained relationship can be reversed and the infant then becomes a receptacle for indigestible experiences perceived as taking in foreign bodies. This is often accompanied by vomiting, in attempts to be rid of contamination. Secondly, there can be food refusal – 'no entry syndrome' – often accompanied by conflicts between parent and infant and an accompanying sense of rejection. Thirdly, there is 'comfort eating', food taken in to fill spaces, while the mind is elsewhere, literally a meaningless pursuit (Briggs, 1997; Williams et al., 2004). Thought, love and physical digestion are split off from each other. These patterns of disturbance with food map closely on to adolescent eating disorders. Feeding meaninglessly can increase weight to the point of obesity, and along with this is an inevitable sense of never being satisfied, no matter how much is consumed, because the essence – love and being loved – is absent. At this point infantile and contemporary social practices meet.

Body image disturbances

It is quite common for young people with eating disorders to develop a distorted sense of their bodies, particularly, being convinced they are fat when in reality they are not. Alongside this, there are other disturbances of body image, which can be experienced as a profound sense that something is wrong with the body, including the body's gender.

Body dysmorphic disorder (BDD) is an obsessive preoccupation with an aspect of the body which is felt to be wrong, or ugly, a view which, from the outside – 'objectively' – seems mistaken or distorting. The preoccupation can be so central to the person's identity, that massive energy is put into worry about the body part including, for example, hours spent in font of the mirror. Social interaction can be severely inhibited and drastic action contemplated to change appearance. The contemporary preoccupation with cosmetic surgery appears to promise a solution for people with BDD; here there is a conflict between the idea of the 'plasticity' of the body, that it can be surgically renewed and therefore under the control of the mind, and the more traditional view that the 'ego is first and foremost a body ego' (Freud, 1923). BDD expresses a particular split within both the mind and the body, which is located in one or more aspects of the body.

Case example: Martha

Martha, an extremely attractive but troubled 20-year-old was preoccupied with the idea that she had to change aspects of her body. In her therapy she frequently reported discussions she had with her cosmetic surgeon, who provided her with many procedures, including botox and surgery to her nose. In her therapy, Martha wished to engage me in protracted discussions about whether or not she should have further nose surgery, and this 'nose job' was the subject of considerable contention. The position I tried to hold, to her considerable annoyance, was that I was concerned with the meaning of her wish, not with her decision to have a further 'nose job' or not. Martha was convinced that her previous surgery had not corrected the original problem, that her nose was bent and ugly. Some sense was made of her preoccupation in that she thought her nose was like her father's, with whom she had a very ambivalent relationship. Alongside this she was able to accept, without any real conviction, that she wished to locate all her problems in this one part of her body, and then by undertaking surgery she had the hope that the problems would be removed magically, rather than involving emotional work.

The discussion with Martha generated some quite ugly feelings in the therapy, as she always introduced the subject with an atmosphere of hostility, loaded with an undercurrent of how I looked upon her. This is a point Lemma (2007) makes in discussing BDD patients, that they feel themselves subject to a hostile gaze. '"Looking" as in "understanding" may be so easily experienced by these patients as being watched from "on high". Thus the therapist is attributed as looking with 'a malignant omniscience – an ever present critical, CCTV camera type eye'. This appears to mirror how the patient looks upon herself when looking in the mirror or thinking about herself. In extreme cases, the paranoid sense of being looked upon malignantly can be all-pervasive. Another young woman, Carmel, 17, was so obsessed by the thought that she was being looked at with hostility that she was totally unable to go out unless accompanied. She stopped attending college, and had to be accompanied to her therapy. She gave strict instructions to her therapist that she should not look at her on her way into or out of the therapy room. It appears an unequal struggle is taking place between her rather fragile narcissistic organisation and a cruel, super-critical accuser, or superego,[1] which seems to wish to judge her ugly and loveable. In this kind of conflict, identity is compromised, and the focus on a seemingly localised embodied issue is the site for a battle to deal with a significant aspect of the self that cannot be integrated, a rejected and abject aspect of subjectivity. Underneath the localised symptom is an elemental conflict, about lovability, one which is potentially overwhelming, and which the BDD subject feels she/he has been the passive recipient. Being subject to this overwhelming experience stemming from primal rejection and humiliation, the aim is to reduce and localise the problem, in a way that is consistent with a dismissing attachment pattern. Activity in the form of surgery or other bodily modification defends against the fear of being out of control, subject to very powerful emotions and aspects of the self, and thus generates an illusory sense of control.

Parallel to and linked with BDD are problems of gender identity. This is both a special case of a lack of integration of embodied identity and also a distinctive area for discussion and enquiry. The first distinction to be made is between sexual identity, which denotes the preferences of sexual object and gender identity, which refers to the body (male or female) with which one identifies. Domenico Di Ceglie, who developed and leads the only unit specialising in gender identity in the UK, describes the seriousness with which the split between body and mind can be experienced by children and young people who have the conviction they are strangers in their own bodies (Di Ceglie and Freeman, 1998; Di Ceglie, 2002). He gives the example of his first case, in which a teenager

> was claiming that she was a boy but in a female body. The impact of this relationship was an unexpected one. … I got the impression that there was something very profound about her sense of identity of being a boy which could not be easily explained and that was fundamental to her (or his?) being. Colleagues were saying that she was confused about her gender. I discovered instead that *I* would become at times confused during the sessions about her identity, whereas *she* seemed to be very clear that she was a boy and that there was nothing more to find out about this. I was at times made to feel extremely curious in the sessions, only to find out that my curiosity would be frustrated and that it was pointless to pursue my enquiries.
>
> (2002, p. 487)

The question that arises is whether the definiteness of the young person is the end of the story, or whether it is a defensive concreteness, in which symbolic thinking cannot take place. The clue is in the sense of curiosity and confusion which are projected into the therapist. Di Ceglie's approach developed from this to emphasise development; the treatment plan would be to see what developed for each child or adolescent as they explored the split between mind and body. It is a non-dogmatic approach in an arena often dominated by strong ideologies and definitions, and one which aims to explore the meaning of developing gender identity for individual young people in and with their families (Wren, 2002).

Depression

Depression in adolescence is present throughout the discussion in this chapter and Chapter 6: it is ubiquitous, and presents in many different ways. Recently, clinical guidelines have tried to tie down this hydra and reduce it to a stepwise account (NICE, 2005). The problem is that depression is important and of itself explains nothing. Alternatively, relating to depression in young people means taking a holistic approach and seeking to understand the meaning of depression in a psychosocial field. We need to know not just whether an adolescent is depressed, but what this looks like, what kind of relatedness is there and how does depression relate to other factors. There is a major difference to be made between depressive affect and depression.[2] The former allows for the pain of loss and change to be felt and communicated; the latter is more accurately a sense of persecution within. Where there is depressive affect, in the therapy the quality of communication is in the field of concern, empathy and pain; depression in contrast generates criticisms, frustrations and also rage and fury.

In this chapter, the case examples all illustrate different facets of depression. Colin feels overwhelmed by the task of growing up; he feels small, weak and defeated by it. Jeremy in contrast has developed a masochistic defence against feeling depressed: he projects his aggression into others and suffers being beaten up as a result; Sally and her mother are locked together because of the chronic feeling of depression that comes from an unbearable loss that cannot be mourned; Carol's 'depression' is located in her difficulty of tolerating a gap – it evokes too much the absence of her parents when she was little. She tries to defend against depression by her short cut, but this does not work and she then has to know that she is depressed. Other adolescents are threatened by the pains of the depressive position, and feel these are too much to bear, too complicated; they retreat from these pains to a simpler paranoid schizoid way of relating to self and the world. This might include 'putting the boot' into aspects of vulnerability and dependence on others (Anderson, 1997). Working therapeutically with adolescents on the threshold of the depressive position can mean that a 'good' session is almost inevitably followed by a 'bad' one as hatred for the humiliation involved in demonstrating the need of others (the therapist) kicks in. Howard, in Chapter 1, is an example of someone who could express this hatred for 'making him think' rather than act and thus feel the pains rather than evacuate them.

Thus sometimes depression presents itself directly, and at other times we know of its presence only indirectly, through a sense of worry in the adolescent or someone close to them, or by the defensive positions that adolescents present, which infer that depression is somewhere a problem. As Hyatt Williams pointed out, 'During adolescence it is common to encounter depression. What happens during its course depends upon a bewildering variety of factors' (Williams, 1978, p. 309). Thus with some adolescents, it is manifest that depression is the issue that they are bringing to therapy and with others it is hidden from sight, defended against or low on the list of things the adolescent is concerned about. To illustrate the 'bewildering variety of factors' in adolescent depression, I will compare depression in two contrasting cases; in both of these the persecutory type of depression, rather than the encounter with depressive pains, predominates. In the social, external world, both have educational pressures to deal with. The cases contrast through, firstly, the nuances of the relatedness to self and others that produce depression and, secondly, through the quality of therapeutic contact and use of the therapeutic setting.

Case example: Lenny

Lenny, 15, feels overwhelmed and trapped by his own and others' expectations. In his first meeting his therapist noted immediately that he had a sulky, sad expression, staring at the floor as he walked and dragging his feet. After a brief moment of hesitation he talked about having pressure coming from all aspects of his life, and everything is falling apart. His voice was wobbly and he was tearful. He said that if he concentrates on one thing then everything else crumbles. He feels like he is failing at school, and talking through his tears, says he can't do anything; he tries his best but it doesn't work and he fails; he does not meet expectations. The therapist asked him whose expectations he was trying to meet, and he replied that they were his own, but also his parents' and his teachers'. Tearful and anxious, feeling overwhelmed, he goes on to describe – in his words – a complete breakdown recently when he was in his room crying. He felt suicidal then, and he has suicidal ideas, but he wouldn't act on them.

Freud thought that suicide 'is what makes depression so interesting and dangerous' (Freud, 1917, p. 252), and is always a possibility in depression. Here Lenny describes a classic conflict between severe expectations (superego) and a weak or overwhelmed ego. He is persecuted within by his sense of not being able to 'cut the mustard' and – though this is less immediately obvious – he resents his parents' placing him in this position, or not rescuing him from it. He evokes in the therapist both a sense of concern, being worried about his manifest distress and also a more persecutory feeling, in which one might want to get hold of him and tell him to 'pull himself together'. In fact he made a good contact with his therapist and in the course of a time-limited therapy was able to be less beleaguered by his internal persecutors and the external demands of exams.

Case example: Sharon

Sharon, an 18-year-old is about to take her A levels. She is depressed and cannot revise. Despite being in a relationship with a young woman of the same age who appears to care for her – or perhaps because of this – she has a haunting and almost vicious sense of being no good, and disliking herself. She dislikes her body intensely in the way some BDD and eating disordered patients do. She finds it hard to communicate to me in her therapy and I have to struggle very hard to not be defeated by her. She has recently requested therapy, but is very ambivalent about it, and I have offered her a series of consultation sessions to see how it becomes possible to think together alongside some meetings with a psychiatrist colleague. She comes on time, but from this point onwards throughout each session she seems to wish to backtrack from this level of commitment. For example, in one session she came up to the room on time, with a small smile but also a worried expression. After some silence I asked what thoughts she has and she complained about the warm weather saying that she doesn't like it because she is less able to cover up with lots of clothes. This led quickly to her saying that she really didn't like herself, the thoughts she has or her body. She said she was still thinking it was in her best interests to come here, but it is still difficult and she felt sick again on her way here but it's not so bad once she actually gets here.

It all feels very bleak, and I am unsure whether the process of being in therapy is too much for her, or whether, on the other hand, she is getting me to experience for myself what it is like being her, and how bleak and depressed she feels; there is a sense of something incipiently vicious about to break out, and at the same time, her presence feels very precarious. If it is in fact a communication from her, she succeeds, as I feel very disabled by the interactions with her. She seems to both be aware of needing help and being so frightened of it that she will defeat it.

Sharon brings not only a sense that she really does not like herself but also a sense of a very critical aspect of herself that seems to mock anyone's attention for her. She seems to have come to a decision that she must have therapy, but almost unworthy of it, and very frightened by it. How this state of affairs has come about will only be discovered through more exploration – though that promises to be a difficult journey for both of us to undertake. What is apparent is that this kind of depression does not generate a feeling of a sense of loss or sadness, but rather a terrible sense of persecution in a field which seems to have the quality of being dangerously 'landmined'.

Sharon may well be clinically depressed. She has many of the features; she is very despondent, dislikes herself almost intensely, cannot really bear contact, to see another or to be seen by them, and she is badly affected in her social functioning; for example, she cannot revise. Not being able to revise increases her self-loathing as she feels she is spoiling her own chances of being able to leave home to go to university. Leaving home is, she feels, the only way she will ever feel better, as she says she loathes home, is tormented by her better-achieving younger sister and has an old grievance against her parents for inflicting her with siblings. Thus underlying her depression is an ancient grudge that she should be the only child of her parents and a rigid refusal to negotiate within herself about this. However, she is actively inviting the prospect of failure, by not being able to study and seems subject to some other impulses to stay around and torment herself and everyone around her with her grievance. In other words, she is not ready to separate, yet, from her parents. This is a tortuous and tormenting situation, illustrating that severe depression is experienced as a very persecutory and persecuting state. She can be helped to an extent in this predicament, because she does come to her therapy and enables the therapist to experience some aspects of states of mind. This is a precarious situation, though, and one in which other kinds of intervention and containment may become necessary, particularly as she is invested in retaining her grievances. The task of trying to stay with this process is demanding, exhausting and can easily feel futile, at which point the persecutory aspect of the depression triumphs and defeats the therapy and therapist. In situations like these, consultation with a colleague is essential to maintain the capacity to focus on the task, and to review the level of risks posed.

Self-harm

There is a close relationship between depression and self-harm, which is defined as including a range of ways that young people harm themselves, either with conscious intent or without; it can also be an act of commission or omission (Turp, 2008). A recent enquiry showed that one in every fifteen young people self-harms, which, as the report puts it, means two in every classroom (Brophy, 2006). The report highlights the ways that young people who self-harm are treated with misunderstanding and hostility, and that trusting spaces for discussing feelings relating to self-harm are often not available. Professionals can get caught up with the projected despair and aggression, and enact this dyadic relatedness; it is as though the professional response becomes that of an abnormal superego (Briggs, 2008).

Making better contact with young people that self-harm has been one of the recommendations of recent studies, with particular emphasis placed on the opportunities provided by school-based work (Hawton, 2006). As we have seen earlier (Chapter 5), work discussion promises ways of creating the necessary thoughtful reflective space for this work.

There is often a distinction made between self-harm and suicide, as though these are separate phenomena. Some sources suggest that people that self-harm by cutting do not also make suicide attempts (Gardner, 2001), but it is also true that many do. In any case, self-harm should not be equated with cutting, and it is the most reliable risk factor for suicide (NICE, 2004). Self-harm is best understood as manifesting a dyadic relational conflict, in which one part of the self is attacking and hurting another part, and the body is used to take a conflict from the realm of the mind to the body, often with the aim of obtaining some relief from the pain of the emotional conflict. Self-harm can become patterned into a young person's life and identity (she 'does' self-harm) or can be a more impulsive response to particular tormenting circumstances. The more persistent self-harm can have addictive qualities, but can still be ameliorated through therapeutic work. When self-harm is less entrenched, there are often possibilities for understanding the conflicts that initiate self-harm and reducing self-harm more quickly. In these situations, the containment of the therapy promotes the adolescent's developmental capacities; development 'kicks in' leading to turning away from self-destructive relatedness. The following example is of a young woman who responded well to her therapy in a relatively short period of time.

Case example

Naomi, 19, refers herself for therapeutic help to, as she put it, 'deal with some current emotional issues that are affecting my day to day life to the extent that I have been self-harming and am scared to be left alone because I get so down'. She presented in therapy as indeed very depressed, tearful and panicky. She was preoccupied with suicidal thoughts and had taken some small overdoses, and one which was more serious. She had times when she would cut herself and these were usually at times when she had felt hurt or let down by someone. Particularly likely to trigger self-harm were occasions when someone else was not available and she felt left alone. This she experienced as completely unbearable, and triggering a furious part of herself, that attacked the passive, helpless part of herself that was unable to control others as she would wish. In discussing these issues, she was tearful, not sobbing but rather oozing tears, which seemed to almost leak out of her, as though through her skin (Bick, 1968; Turp, 2008), thus demonstrating a kind of helpless passivity. Through this and in other ways, the picture that emerged was that Naomi had difficulty in containing her emotional experiences. She was overwhelmed by her experiences of relationships, and passively felt 'subject to' emotions that she felt she could not control. However, she experienced her therapy as providing her with an alternative way of relating to her passivity and sense of being overwhelmed, one that was more tolerant and thoughtful about these feelings than she could allow herself to be. With this containment she began to manage better her panicky sense that she was abandoned when her demand for others was not immediately responded to. From this she gained a sense of being less lonely and subject to being abandoned by others. She gathered herself and showed a greater sense of muscularity, holding herself together in a more vigorous kind of way. Through her connection in her therapy, she began to feel better, without initially understanding why this was so, but the greater sense of mental and emotional space this provided came as a relief from feeling so tormented and alone. Thus she felt less depressed, and felt free from the torments of being depressed and this reduced the need to harm herself. More able to tolerate her feelings on her own she became more curious about how her emotions related both to her sense of herself in the world and the impact of others on her.

Summary

- The adolescent who is 'stuck on the inside' has disconnected from the adolescent process, and development towards adulthood has reached an impasse. These adolescents cannot bear to be separated from external parental figures (including therapists), and the task of relinquishing a hold on an external figure is felt to be terrifying.
- The clearest examples of adolescents who get stuck on the inside are those where there is a social refusal, such as school phobia. In these situations, the external world becomes invested with extreme dangerousness, where the fear of separation is closely connected with a fear of death. Actual, unmourned losses may play a significant role.

- There is an extremely entangled and complex interaction between social, physical and emotional aspects in the development of insider difficulties. In some situations, negative experiences emanating from the social world may be extremely important; in others experiences of deprivation, disruption and loss in childhood may powerfully affect development adversely.
- Transition from reliance on an external to an internal parental figure in stressful psychosocial contexts requires the internalisation of reliable containing parental figures.
- Fear of loss of control and the need to control the separateness and independence of others, are significant factors in the development of eating disorders. The eating disordered adolescent attempts, through the use of the body, to arrest development into adulthood.
- Eating disorders, which are emblematic of contemporary adolescent difficulties, are complex in that there is both a wish to retain a child-like relationship with parents and a wish to break links with dependency upon others. Thus in eating disorders there is not simply an insider wish to stay a child, but also a hatred of dependency and the emotionality of contact with others in relationships. The 'attacks on life' form an extremely important aspect of the self-destructive and at times suicidal eating-disordered adolescent.
- In disturbances of body image, including BDD and gender-identity difficulties, there are difficulties of subjectivity and problems of integration of mind and body.
- Depression is ubiquitous in adolescence and is encountered in many forms. What happens during the course of depression depends on many factors.
- There is a close relationship between depression and self-harm, which is defined as including a range of ways that young people harm themselves, either with conscious intent or without; it can also be an act of commission or omission.

8

PSYCHOTIC AND SUICIDAL STATES IN ADOLESCENCE

In this chapter, the extremities of adolescent difficulties are discussed, especially suicide and suicidality, and psychosis and psychotic anxieties. The psychosocial context is discussed in order to consider the intersubjective as well as the subjective contexts of becoming suicidal or psychotic subjects in adolescence.

Psychotic subjects

Novels such as Kafka's *The Trial* and Eco's *Foucault's Pendulum* describe a psychotic world, in which the internal becomes located in the external or social world, a feature of psychotic subjectivity. According to Kennedy (1998), 'In psychotic states, the elements of the subject are felt acutely to be "subject to" outside forces. Instead of being part of the subjective organisation, the social field is then experienced as outside the subject, and often then the place where projections are located.' (pp. 188–9).

However, the processes of projection from inner to outer are reversible in contemporary social contexts, so that a fragmented and dangerous external world is introjected and internalised. In the contemporary social world, the breakdown of expectancy and continuity has been described as destabilising and unstable. The social world impacts through the proliferation of images, and the breakdown of gaps between time and place, which is immediate, sudden, global and virtual. These images are also invasive – 'space invaders' – so that 'our reality is transformed and made flimsy by its penetration by invading images. ... Chaos, flimsiness and instability [is] our experience of reality itself' (Lash, 1990, pp. 14–15). The way the internal world is formed from the cultural context may be inferred from the way psychoanalytic descriptions of the internal world are taken from external phenomena. Rosenfeld's (1987) discussion of the 'mafia gang' and discussions of internal hostage takers and terrorists come to mind.

It is the boundary between two spheres – conscious and unconscious – which is subject to erosion. Bion (1962) described this as the 'contact-barrier', through which the unconscious and conscious domains are kept distinct.

'The contact-barrier is therefore responsible for the preservation of the distinction between conscious and unconscious for its inception. ...The contact-barrier permits a relationship and preservation of belief in it as an event in actuality, subject to the laws of nature, without having that view submerged by emotions and phantasies originating endo-psychically. Reciprocally it preserves emotions with endo-psychic origin from being overwhelmed by the realistic view' (pp. 26–7).

The contact barrier, in other words, creates balance while preserving the distinctiveness of difference. Adolescents, subject to internal change and social repositioning at the same time, are particularly vulnerable to the breakdown of the order of unconscious and conscious, or, primary and secondary process.

Case example

Judith, who is not psychotic, but who is subject to intense psychotic and depressive anxieties, illustrates the confusion of internal and external through the actions of powerful projective identification.

Judith was extremely sensitive to pain, and she reacted strongly to any sense of being 'touched', in which she would become verbally very defensive. She told me of a memory of early childhood when she felt furious with her cat for scratching her. She was not just hurt, but mortified, so that physical pain and outrage were both present. In murderous retaliation, she shut the cat in a cupboard. She felt better for a time and then realised she needed to release the cat from its confinement, as she began to feel responsible and guilty for its imprisonment. She opened the cupboard door and found the cat looking at her directly. She was terrorised by this, feeling that the cat was accusing her, and she felt unable to cope with the level of accusation, as though it went through her. Her acute pain and mortification returned and she shut the door, leaving the cat incarcerated.

In her adolescence, repeated experiences of sensitivity to pain led to the same configuration of attempting to shut out the identified source of the pain, and then feeling overwhelmed by facing the resulting hostility and rage now located in the other. In feeling hurt or wounded by any painful experience, however slight tremendous hatred, which threatened to take her apart from the inside, was stirred up. She withdrew into a solitary, lonely state, in which daydreams of overcoming human pain, such as achieving immortal recognition as a great person, occupied her mind, or, alternatively she took drugs and alcohol, primarily to remove herself from this intolerable predicament. Return to the world of others was then feared as others were invested with feeling intense hatred towards her.

In her therapy, the predicament was repeated in patterns where either she or I felt shut in and trapped. On occasions she missed her sessions without informing me and I found myself feeling intensely troubled, and, at times suffocating, rather like the cat shut in the cupboard, waiting for release either by her arrival or the end of the session. When Judith occupied the position of the cat, she experienced panic attacks, which had an intensely claustrophobic quality, so that, for example, she suddenly felt the need to get out of where ever she was, unable to control her mind, her thoughts and feelings. Judith was aware that she was being attacked from within, and that she had no one, in her mind to reach out to. Her 'objects' had become suffused with hatred. In recounting these experiences, Judith was desperate, feeling fearful that one day she would have a panic attack from which she would not re-emerge, as if, being shut in a cupboard forever. On other occasions, she felt that if she faced herself, she would descend into a bottomless, awful and intolerable depression, a pain which would be beyond endurance.

Judith was facing a sense of breakdown. Her sensitivity to pain, her narcissistic sensibilities, and the feeling of being overwhelmed by her emotional experiences were accompanied, in a rather hidden way, by severe judgements on the self and others. These led to a cycle of retaliatory manoeuvres; the cat should suffer for hurting her; she hurts because the cat suffers; the cat does not wish to repair, or forgive; she experiences new hatred, and retaliates again, etc. Sense is made of these interactions if they are thought of as projective identification, in which she and the cat have a similar identity, which is reversible. The violence of her splitting leads to a nightmare like internal and external world from which the only escape is some kind of annihilation, of the mind or the body. At the same time, the overwhelming fear is of annihilation, being trapped forever in a psychotic part of her mind, an eternal panic attack. She felt she was at risk of being trapped inside her object, and she continually tried to pull away, but then she found that this merely brought about a repetition of panic, or, alternatively depression. Depression, which she felt to be intolerable and unbearable, was prominent when she was more in contact with others, and vulnerable, or when she questioned herself, her own grandiose daydreams.

The image of the cat concretises and makes solid an emotional predicament. The absence of containment of emotions, and problems of self-other differentiation, leads to a confused and intolerable state. It is possible to see in the confusion of inner and outer and the cycles of projective identification. There is the absence of an outside perspective, of someone (a 'third' person) who will disentangle internal and external, reaffirm boundaries and the difference between inside and outside, and make an attempt to transform the emotionality – especially in Judith's panicky state, in which, almost, a pure culture of hatred exists. In this sense, the concreteness of the cat imagery stands for a failure in the container–contained relationship, in which, instead of reverie there is both the refusal of ingress and invasiveness. Emotions in a world without a container are homeless and potentially attacking, or invading.

Bion described 'beta elements' as 'things' which travel, like missiles, through space, looking for somewhere to land. These are not thoughts but parts of the personality, which have been disowned with the aim of not facing painful reality, or transforming or modifying frustration:

> Beta elements are not amenable to use in dream thoughts but are suited for use in projective identification. They are influential in producing acting out. They are objects that can be evacuated or used for a kind of thinking that depends in manipulation of what are felt to be things in themselves s if to substitute such manipulations for words or ideas.

> (Bion, 1962, p. 6)

Projective identification, used in this sense is not so much about communicating, more about stripping the personality of everything with which it feels encumbered, so that frustration, disappointment and disillusion do not have to be faced. These projective identifications *may* be used as communication, by therapists who are prepared to be permeated by these feelings, in order to try and think. The length of time that it takes to return the projections in modified form, so that the patient may begin to think for herself/himself means that the risk of enactment is high, and the acceptance of the return of the projections depends also on the development in the therapeutic relationship of a sense of the dependability and reliability of the therapist, which the patient can respond to, without this being too threatening. In other words, there needs to be a non-psychotic part of the personality which can be working with the therapist.

Working with psychotic adolescents

Dubinsky (1999) has discussed three adolescents who broke down and 'crossed the frontier into psychotic and borderline states' (p. 170). Each of these is discussed within a familial context, so that Dubinsky concludes that they shared features in common, 'the mother was emotionally unavailable, the father was distant, rejecting or cruel', and she carefully follows the chain of events which led to the breakdown. Thus Debbie, 18, became ill under the pressure of school examinations, when her fragility as a child who seemed not to have parental protection and her projection of her own rage and jealousy into others created a world in which 'painful and frightening similarities between her two worlds became increasingly blatant. In her phantasy world she was absorbed in violent, exciting phantasies in which she was the victim. In real life she became an easy target for playground bullies and later for her abusive boyfriends' (p. 153). All three adolescents had 'an incapacity to withstand psychic pain in the absence of a containing maternal object' (p. 170). Thomas, 17, suffered from panic attacks. His father had left the family when he was ten, and his grandmother also died at this time. 'Death, ugliness and a tremendous sense of unfairness and loss seemed to have suddenly invaded Thomas' world' so that he felt growth and life was impossible. He found sexuality frightening, so that when he started to have a girlfriend, he wanted this more from the point of view of finding another way of merging with mother than as an adult sexual relationship. He was terrified of sex, so that the prospect of having sex with his girlfriend triggered a revival of his panic, so that he felt he was falling apart.

Dubinsky emphasises that Thomas' problems revolved around his repudiation of masculinity and his wish not to be a man. He had 'identified with a pathetic and fragile male figure' so that all his aggression, rage and violence were projected into 'macho' males, whom he tried to see as 'other'. This account comes close to the view of adolescent breakdown held by the Laufer's (1984), in that Thomas's difficulty in identifying with his father led to him to renounce masculinity. However, Dubinsky's account also emphasises the intolerance of frustration, and disappointment and the process whereby the internal world of the adolescent is subject to violent fragmentation. The experience she records of her experience of working with these patients is important. In working with the third adolescent, Tania, 19, she:

> felt violently controlled by her and at times almost immobilised. The atmosphere could feel threatening. For a long time, I felt I could hardly speak of our relationship, of her need for help, of feelings of helplessness. I felt she would want to hate me, get up, leave and never return. All these feelings needed to be lodged in me. I felt impotent, inadequate, small, excluded. It was only when Tania was more trusting of me and felt that I wouldn't abandon her that I could start talking to her about these feelings and we could think together about the underlying fear that her envy, competitiveness and possessiveness would destroy us both.

Thus the 'missile' like projections from Tania at first need to find a home in the therapist, though these cannot be spoken about for some time, and the therapist experiences the intense pressure, of being used in a very concrete, bodily way as a recipient of projections. Premature returning of projections would be experienced as extremely invasive and attacking – like being looked at by an angry cat, to refer back to Judith.

Fragmentation of the self

Breakdown in adolescence begins with the failure of the 'contact barrier' to differentiate inside and outside, internal and external, past and present, conscious and unconscious. In relation to the social world, the individual both projects outwards, either in a more benign, communicative way, or through the launching of missiles, in the form of split off parts of the self. Two particular situations where intense primitive forms of projective identification produce madness are war and racism. This statement is true in reverse; racism and war produce primitive forms of projective identification. Racism constitutes a distinctive kind of 'madness' in which reality and true sameness – being human – are denied while instead the 'empty category' (Rustin, 1991) of race becomes a receptacle (rather than a container – there is no alpha function) for split off envy and hatred. Social groups 'contain' psychotic aspects and anxieties. In some times, which may be thought of as well functioning, these aspects are kept under control or institutionalised. However, some 'madness' is evident even in these times. According to Segal (1995), 'groups behave in a way which in an individual would be considered mad; for instance, almost invariably groups are self-idealising, grandiose and paranoid' (p. 194). Particularly, this is seen in 'national' groups. In times of turbulence, and the conditions of late modernity, the stability of groups is always in question, so that there is a high propensity for mutual 'invasion'. That is, that the group infiltrates the individual and vice versa. In contexts of racism and war, the group impacts on the individual through breaking through the contact barrier, and this is apparent through the presence, of a 'virtual' war in the home, through TV. During the Gulf War, I observed a family where the TV, playing constantly, showed missiles being launched and landing, causing destruction. In the family, feeding of the one-year-old baby resembled a war zone as mother, attempting to gain control of the baby's mouth, insisted that the food-refusing baby ate. Spoonfuls of food became missiles which were treated to the interception of the baby's anti-missile devices – a tensely closed mouth and spitting. The father, returning home after the meal, commented that it looked like a bomb had gone off. Bick (1968, 1986) wrote about the need for a 'psychic skin' to keep together the fragmenting parts of the infant's mind. At the boundary between the inside/family life and the outside/political/group there is no functioning contact barrier, and the inside is not held in a skin. Alternatively a fragile skin is burst through the invasion of the social world, or a thick skin is impervious and therefore unable to respond to the external situation of danger (or opportunity).

Suicidal subjects

In adolescence there is a close connection between psychotic anxieties and suicidality. That is not to say that suicidal adolescents are psychotic, but that the experience of breakdown may be experienced as leading to cessation of development, through the death of the mind (psychosis) or the body (suicide). The combination of the two are vividly illustrated in Anderson's (1999) example of a young man, who made many serious suicide attempts and said that he *imagined jumping out of a window and flying away leaving his battered and scarred body to fall to the ground. This was not an ordinary religious belief, but a delusion that he could solve his terrible internal state by creating a split between two parts of himself* (p. 165). The delusion of outliving the body, which Campbell and Hale (1991) call the 'surviving self', indicates the difference between psychosis and suicide as an outcome for adolescent breakdown, in which suicide aims to 'solve' the psychic problem through destruction of the body. Splitting the body and the mind – an idea incidentally 'embodied' in western thought as Cartesian dualism – is the key to suicide, and the relationship with the body is central to understanding suicide. Adolescents at risk of psychosis are often suicidal, but suicide is not the outcome in many cases. Suicidal adolescents are not always manifestly 'psychotic' but there is an element of suicidal thinking in which there is an avoidance of reality, and this can become delusional.

Working with suicide risk

Working with adolescents who are suicidal means being exposed to intense and extreme emotions. These include predominantly anxiety, guilt, a sense of responsibility and fear, both for the adolescent and for oneself. Suicide risk is an important and complex aspect of working with adolescents; it is a high-profile social issue following the international concern about rising rates of suicide, particularly amongst young men during the 1990s. Suicidality is highly problematic to work with for it is highly unpredictable – literally, prediction[1] of suicide is an inexact science, and because it appears to be essentially heterogeneous. In other words there are multiple or plural 'kinds' of suicidality rather than it being associated with one clinical feature. In psychiatric terms suicide transcends diagnostic categories, and in psychosocial terms, there are a number of different 'categories' of suicidal adolescents. As Freud noted, commenting on the complexity of suicide, referring to one of his cases, a young woman of 18 who had made a serious suicide bid, *'several quite different motives, all of great strength, must have co-operated to make such a deed possible'* (Freud, 1920, p. 163).

Case example

Sonia, 17, referred herself for therapy on the advice of her doctor, and wrote a letter in which she said that she took an overdose because 'she gave up on life'. Her passive hopelessness was immediately striking. She was a very distinctive young woman. She had never known her father, of Chinese origins, and during her adolescence, coinciding with her mother becoming very preoccupied with a relationship and more unavailable for Sonia, she had developed an increasing curiosity about him. This curiosity developed in a context of thinking that nothing she could find out would be good. She developed a number of thoughts about her father, that he was dead, a drug addict, a member of a Triad group. She felt increasingly that he had abandoned her, and that she felt worthless. She then herself abandoned her efforts to find him, and, at this point, she took an overdose and 'gave up on life'. Feeling hopeless about herself, she was attacked from within by a cruel, raging, damaged and sadistic father who seemed to tell her she was useless and worthless.

In this case, the problem of suicidality was out in the open. An attempt had been made and the task was to understand the complex processes involved in this young woman's predicament. This situation can be contrasted with those where a suicide bid occurs without previous history, near the beginning of therapeutic contact. The predictability of *knowing* that the adolescent is suicidal is replaced by suicidality exploding into the work with sudden and shocking rapidity.

Case example

Gemma was a bright, vivacious and attractive girl of 18 when she was referred for psychotherapy by a school counsellor. The counsellor, an experienced person, did not indicate she had thought that there was a suicidal risk. Gemma's early adolescence was characterised by risk-taking behaviour and early sexual experiences. She idealised her parents and felt guilty about her behaviour, feeling that she constantly let them down. She seemed quite cut off from her own feelings and quite split between a sense of herself as being very successful, especially in her schoolwork, and of being a burden and a failure. She seemed to try to manage these feelings by playing down their importance to her. She was very sceptical about her therapy, minimised her problems and tried to maintain a superficial attachment to her therapist. She missed sessions, and she was barely engaged in her therapy.

After five sessions, spanning eight weeks (including the missed sessions) she said – not immediately, but some minutes into the session – that she had overdosed since the last session the previous week. She said she had been at a party, and her current boyfriend had ignored her. Feeling he was involved with someone else, she went home and took between 30 and 40 paracetamol. Her parents heard her vomiting and she was taken to hospital. She said that she had told the hospital that she was in therapy and she was discharged.

The sense of detachment was quite stunning. It is not much of an exaggeration to say she finished her story and went on to the next subject. I thought, rather irrationally, perhaps, that if I had not been able to be at her session today, I may never have heard about this. This thought mirrored the fragility with which her overdosing was found by her parents after a serious suicide bid.

Gemma refused to discuss the reasons for the overdose in more detail on the grounds that she had not, and did not, have any suicidal ideas at all. She did not know why she took the paracetamol, and she never formulated to herself the idea that she felt suicidal. She did have to admit that her actions showed she was, or had been, suicidal. She was however concerned that she had set a very bad example for her younger sisters, and she felt guilty about hurting her parents, who had been good to her. The feelings of revenge and murderousness towards others, which had surfaced in her suicide bid, became almost instantly inaccessible.

The impact of Gemma's reporting her suicide bid was intensely alarming, and set in train two almost parallel but equally urgent trains of thought. The first, stemming from a sense of responsibility and guilt, both realistic and omnipotent, of a failure to know, protect and control the suicidality, was to analyse whether some clue to the suicidality had been overlooked. The second was to attempt to think about the meaning and causes of this bid.

The sense of responsibility is partly a professional response to a serious situation. Should there have been some greater awareness of the potential for suicidality and should more action have been taken. Partly, it is driven by a wish to escape blame. This is heightened in organisations, which, operating under the impact of the 'audit explosion', as discussed in Chapter 5, become omnipotent when fear of outcomes becomes the sole driver in an organisation.

The stressfulness of working with suicidal adolescents, and being engaged in the assessment of suicidality cannot be overstated. It does demand a particular kind of containment for staff, in which purposeful discussion of cases, the capacity to make judgements of risk, and the capacity to maintain a perspective are paramount. The sense of perspective is gained, in part, by making a difficult and delicate separation of responsibilities. The therapist's responsibilities are not total, and the adolescent has some responsibilities too, but the delicacy lies in maintaining a sense of therapeutic boundaries in a field of knowledge – suicide risk – which is unpredictable, complex and uncertain.

Suicidal dynamics in adolescents: cruelty

We can compare the two cases – Gemma and Sonia – to consider some of the key suicidal dynamics in adolescence. Sonia's situation is striking for the immediate presentation of a passive hopelessness, a quiet resigned despair. Interacting with this is a vicious, cruel and attacking part of her which seems to be identified with her father, and which seems to tell her she is worthless. In *The Ego and the Id* (Freud, 1923), Freud discussed an internal conflict like this:

> [T]he ego gives itself up because it feels itself hated and persecuted by the super-ego, instead of loved. When the ego finds itself in an excessive real danger which it believes itself unable to overcome by its own strength, it is bound to draw the same conclusion. It sees itself deserted by all protecting forces and lets itself die.
>
> (Freud, 1923, p. 58)

In this pitiful state, the ego cannot raise a single cry against the accusations, and has to succumb. It is a powerful description of a precondition for suicide that, for a moment, or longer, there can be no voice to be heard from within on the side of life.[2] Hopelessness and despair are implicit in this state of helplessness. The sadistic attacks of the superego and the helplessness of the ego are complementary aspects, suggesting that, while either sadistic attacks on the self or hopelessness may form the presentation of the suicidal state, each presumes the existence of the other. A helpless, giving up ego indicates the presence of a savage, merciless superego and vice versa.

The merciless cruelty of the superego may be related in Sonia's case to the experience she had in her mind about being abandoned by her father, as a very cruel act on his part. In this way she had identified internally with the abandoning father. This follows Freud's original and enduring ideas about the problem of mourning (Freud, 1917). When a loss involves an ambivalently loved and hated other, instead of grief and separation taking place, the other is taken in and identified with, so that the other is felt to be a part of the self. When the identification is with a cruel and attacking other – or alternatively someone who has been cruelly attacked – the impact is that the self is attacked and hated from within and this gives rise to the self-reproaches of depressive (melancholic) individuals. When the identification is with a remorselessly cruel 'object' the result can be that there appears to be no escape from the relentlessness of these attacks, except through death.

Suicidal dynamics: getting rid of the pain

Gemma's suicidality appears differently from Sonia's. Whereas Sonia is aware of despair, and suicidal wishes, Gemma is not, and her detachment from her suicidal intention creates a strong sense of denial. Gemma shows how sudden, impulsive and explosive, uncontained feelings of rejection, abandonment and revenge can be triggered, and how much this suicidal behaviour was linked with Gemma not being able to know about these feelings and her *inner* relationships. She was aware of sudden, intensive feelings of rejection and abandonment, which she seemed to feel she needed to get rid of immediately. This represents a violent defence against perceptions of vulnerability and need in herself, and which is turned against herself through her body. The brief, fleeting contact with a sense of vulnerability and need threatened to humiliate and over-throw a sense of a competent, independent and omnipotent self.

This explosive kind of suicidality, in which depression is not eas-ily visible is often the kind encountered in young suicidal males. The absence of visible or acknowledged depression in suicidal adolescents is puzzling, until the difference between depressive ill-ness and depressive pain is held in mind. Depressive illness occurs, according to Klein, through an inability to manage the pains of the depressive position. Thus there is a difference between the pain of awareness of damage done, psychically, to the object, and the anxi-ety and pain that arises from feeling persecuted. Bell (2000) points out a different kind of depression, 'a particular kind of tormenting psychic pain which arises from the feeling of being internally perse-cuted by the recriminations of damaged objects – as if so to speak, they are saying "we are all suffering, look what you have done to us"' (p. 25, footnote 1).

Case example

Gary, 16, felt furious about feeling excluded by his parents from their separate lives – in which each of them had younger children – and robbed, menacingly, a group of smaller boys. He said he was not at all remorseful about this. However, during the following few days he got into violent arguments with his mother and a teacher culminating, on his father's birthday, in his mother telling him to leave. He then made a suicide bid.

Gary makes active the experience of which he was first a passive recipient, that is of feeling 'robbed' of the love of his parents, and replaced by new siblings. He then intensified his sense of being excluded by arguing with his mother and getting himself rejected, again. He then turned this round again, to 'rob' his parents of their child, himself. The torturing kind of depression is somewhere in this configuration, and powerfully acted on, and reacted against.

The lack of space, or time, between the experience of rejection and the suicide attempt in Gemma's case indicates an impulsive inability to wait, while her evacuation of these intolerable feelings was directed into her body. Thus, as in psychotic anxieties, a 'missile' of projective identification was being launched, but rather than being directed into the outside world, searching for an external object or just being launched into outer space, it was aimed into herself, first, through her body and through thus taking herself hostage, she indirectly targeted someone else, who would be left to suffer or repent of the lack of love and consideration she was given. The impulsivity thus reveals a particular relationship between the container and the contained, in which the container is put under terrific pressure to respond to an impossible request, immediately, and fully. This is a configuration of internal terrorism, which can be particularly powerful and chilling when it is ruthlessly put into practice.

Many adolescents have suicidal ideas, from time to time, but far fewer are seriously worried about them and less act on them. In contrast, those who are seriously troubled by suicidality, and likely to act, are in serious inner and interpersonal difficulties. Adolescent suicidality constitutes a crisis of inner relationships, and adolescents who are at risk of suicide are not passing through a transient phase of difficulty which is cured by time (Perret-Catipovic and Ladame, 1998).

Suicidal internal dynamics have been thought of as a series of distinct but overlapping internal relationships. The 'motive force' in suicide is found in these relationships (Campbell and Hale, 1991; Hale, 2008):

Merger: The aim of the suicide bid is to solve a problem of separation, in which being separate is intolerable and being in intimate contact is engulfing. The 'solution' is to idealise a state of merger, or fusion. *For example, Penny, 16, described a difficult relationship with her mother who was critical and attacking, calling her 'bad' and 'dirty' and at time humiliated her in public. In her misery, Penny fantasised about being united with a star, which she called 'her star'. She thought how she might be transported to be with the star, and contemplated a suicide bid by jumping from a bridge.*

Revenge: As discussed in the case of Gary, above, revenge, on the principle of the talion law, is the 'solution' for the pains of being left or abandoned. There is an aim of triumphing over others' remorse, and parents, in particular, will regret not having loved the son/daughter better.

Self-punishment: The aim is to resolve conflict in relationships through punishing the self. Freud (1924) wrote of self punishment that, 'in order to provoke punishment from [the superego], the masochist must do what is inexpedient, must act against his own interests, must ruin the prospects which open out to him in the real world and must, perhaps, destroy his own existence' (p. 169). Often, sexual guilt is involved (Penny, above, was self-punishing as well as merging) and Flaubert's *Madame Bovary* is an example from literature. Either the self-punishing suicidal individual reaches the point of despair and 'gives up' or there is a self-sacrificing or atoning quality present.

Elimination: The case of Gemma has been discussed as an example of 'elimination' in which the aim is to 'get rid' of the painful state of turbulence. The delusion is that this preserves the individual through expulsion of the unwanted states of mind.[3]

Dicing with Death: Adolescents are particularly likely to be found 'dicing with death'. On one level, it means experimenting with risks and taking an omnipotent view of things. In suicidal situations, the adolescent aims to overcome despair, misery or failure through undertaking a risky enterprise which might end catastrophically, but which may also produce a high. At the extreme the stakes are highest, and then the 'game' is like Russian roulette, when death is not feared. Parental care is rejected and replaced by an omnipotent gamble. The suicidal 'dicing with death' adolescent oscillates between misery and abjection and manic invulnerability. The drug user's 'unreliable container' is close to this configuration, and drugs are often used as the means of the 'gamble'. *For example Nick, 17, told me that he had crashed his friend's motorbike. He was not hurt but he seemed to be communicating to me that he had felt the need to do something, which was quite dangerous. I raised with him that he had previously told me that he sometimes had suicidal thoughts. He said that he does not have an active wish to kill himself, but when he felt particularly bad he would take on a gamble in which he might get damaged, or killed, but which might also lead to a sense of triumph.*

Suicidal relationship to the body

These internal configurations are thought to power suicidality, though what distinguishes suicidal and self-harming adolescents from others is the relationship they have with the body. Earlier, in Chapters 2 and 7, I have discussed the adolescent body as a 'site' for the interplay of internal and sociocultural experiences of subjectivity, and as a means of resistance. Suicidal adolescent bodies are disowned, hated and felt to be impediments to arriving at more peaceful and less turbulent states of mind (Egle Laufer, 1985; Laufer and Laufer, 1984; Anderson, 1999; Fonagy and Target, 1999). Laufer and Laufer (1984) emphasise that suicidal adolescents dislike or hate the body. They discuss the development of the body in adolescence bringing about unwanted separation from childhood, and thus the development of sexuality is hated as confirming the loss of childhood and the emergence into the adult world.

Adolescents relate to their body as though to an attachment figure. In a study of suicidal adolescents, using an attachment theory framework, we found that adolescents' patterns of relating to their bodies was consistent with their overall attachment patterns (Wright et al., 2005). Insecure dismissing adolescents deny, negate or understate relatedness to the body, insisting that they did not think about their bodies, for example,

> When I was a child I probably didn't care about it. I didn't think about it at all. It was just like 'it's my body'.
>
> (p. 487)

This introduces an ambiguous idea about 'not caring' for the body. Insecure preoccupied/entangled adolescents talked anxiously and at great length about their bodies, often building a picture of feeling trapped, out of control and fearing negative peer judgements. Suicidal adolescents' hatred of their bodies is expressed defensively, through these attachment patterns, not necessarily therefore directly as hating.

A suicide attempt causes a rupture to bodily and emotional containment, which attacks meaning and freezes subjectivity (Ladame, 2008). Painful phantasies, and emotional experiences are denied and annihilated by the bid. Thus there is a loss of alpha function, and the skin – containment is also attacked, ruptured or obliterated. The suicidal adolescent is more likely to be defended in relation to the body, not knowing about its qualities, not thinking or feeling the rhythms and perceptions that are located in the body. Suicidal adolescents are more likely to objectify the body, and to split it from the mind, creating a Cartesian fallacy. Foucault thought that resistance meant that there was action on bodies to 'transform themselves in order to attain a certain state of happiness, purity, wisdom, perfection or immortality' (Foucault, 1988, p. 18). However, what Foucault had in mind was the maximising of pleasure, beauty and power rather than the destruction of self – and, through the dyadic nature of suicide, the inflicting of terrible pain on others.

Protection from psychosis and suicide

Kennedy (1998) has written that 'the psychotic subject has a precarious subjective organisation, made up of "loose" elements that can fall apart and can be experienced then as physical objects. Perhaps one could pay more attention to the details of what holds the elements together, the psychic "glue" so to speak' (p. 188).

In this discussion, both psychotic and suicidal subjects are 'subject to' fragmentation, and yet, the plurality, multiplicity and diversity of modern life create potentially fragmentary experiences which require reflection so that some kind of order can be made from turbulence. In the inner world, especially in the Bion-Bick model, the experience of the mother's reverie pulls together the potentially fragmenting infant, who thus gets to know both the sense – providing and integrating function of the mother, and also the fragmentary state which she protects her/him from.

Amiel (2001) describes a young man, John, 19, who after a psychotic breakdown, arrived for his therapy one day carrying a *'tatty carrier bag which split, pouring disconnected bits of his life on to the floor; old letters, combs, rotting food, medication. Together we taped up the bag and slowly put all the bits back into it. Much later in his therapy he was able to see this moment as a metaphor for the process which he had undertaken and the reintegration he had been able to begin to achieve'* (p. 31).

Kennedy suggest that attention should be paid to the psychic 'glue'; Amiel's example is a vivid example of the concreteness of the psychotic breakdown, and the jumble of objects which are unlinked, meaninglessly, in the carrier bag, container, which itself is split and likely to leak its contents. The suicidal 'subject' aims to break the container and to fragment the contents. Amiel also shows, as did Dubinsky, whose work was discussed earlier, the demand on the therapist to hold these events in mind over time, before a more symbolic form of communication can be achieved, or regained.

Containment is a binding, linking force and process, which problematises fragmentation and aims to provide connections between parts through meaning and symbolisation. The 'skin' is a boundary which has to bear the pressure and stresses of holding on to fragments. Linking with another offers a potential for hope, and self-containment. *An 18-year-old, subject to self-destructive attacks on herself, became explosively furious and impulsively decided to throw herself in front of a passing car. At the pavement's edge she stopped and thought to herself that she did not wish to jeopardise her therapy.* On the brink of potential self-destruction, she found a different voice in her mind, which pulled her back, into a connectedness with her therapist, with the idea that it mattered. Being felt to be kept in mind, she could protect herself (precariously) through keeping in mind herself an integrating and meaningful relationship.

Summary

- Psychotic breakdown in adolescence is discussed in terms of the processes in which the domains of inside and outside, conscious and unconscious are confused and broken down, through the operation of violent projective identification.
- Psychotic experiences are heightened in postmodernity, so that a fragmented and dangerous external world may be internalised, as well as a fragmented inner world projected into the external world. 'Psychotic anxieties' are widely experienced, but these do not lead to psychosis unless there is a failure of containment.
- The absence of containment of dangerous aspects of the self leads to a confused and intolerable, concretely experienced inner world. Bion's concept of 'beta elements' is discussed to make sense of the concreteness of these states of mind.
- The therapist working with potentially psychotic adolescents will need to be able to take in the unbearable states of mind which are projected, and to hold on to them for some time. Case examples were given to illustrate these processes.
- Suicidal adolescents split the body and the mind, and can develop delusional ideas that killing the body solves the emotional problems that underlie suicidality.
- Suicidal adolescents present heterogeneously. Some are depressed and know consciously that they are desperate. Others may be more cut off from their emotionality and seem to deny their own suicidality. Case examples were used to illustrate these differences, and discussed in terms of the dynamics of cruelty and getting rid of the pain.
- Psychotic and suicidal adolescents are 'subject to' fragmentation internally, and containment helps to bring these fragmented parts together, providing connections between parts of the self, or 'psychic glue', which acts as a protection from suicide and psychosis.

9

EMERGING INTO ADULTHOOD

The process of entering adulthood is, as we have seen, increasingly complex, and diverse. Overall, adolescence is extended into the third decade, though some adolescents who are among the more disadvantaged take a 'fast track' route into adulthood. For others, the 'slow track' route, taking longer to fully enter adulthood, implies that the process into adulthood needs reconceptualising to include thinking that the transition to adulthood can last at least the period up to the mid twenties. Chapters 1 and 2 explored this new thinking about the transition to adulthood. Amongst the many ways of characterising the route from adolescence into adulthood, we have focused on the tensions between individualised and relational aspects of subjectivity. This chapter explores the different ways that adolescents enter adulthood – or emerge into it. How taking up different adult roles impacts on subjectivity is discussed.

Working with adolescents and young adults has to be informed by the contemporary context rather than traditional theories. The fast track route, which equates more closely chronologically with the transition to adulthood, is likely to lead to marginalisation and exclusion. Usually, these adolescents need to be approached now from the perspective of responding to the potential vulnerability of their situation. In contrast, slow track adolescents are not usually avoiding the tasks of growing up, and it is crucial to orientate to the particular conflicts and tensions they feel about partial independence, continuing dependence on parents and the short-term nature of their immediate goals, in whatever sphere of becoming more adult. Often these young people can respond best to more focused, time-limited interventions that attend to part of the difficulty rather than a thorough revision of their life to date (Ruggiero, 2006). This can be experienced as tuning into the situation they are actually in, and it does not need to be the only therapeutic experience they have. Crisis theory can be applied through breaking down the problem into manageable parts.

Do adolescents still 'leave home'?

As we have seen in the discussion in Chapter 1, for many adolescents the process of leaving home happens in stages. Rather than forming a simple transition from family of origin to family of destination, the transitions from school to employment, and away from the family home are subject to a more fragmentary process. More often than not, there are repeated leavings and returns with intermediary stopping off places and arrangements. There are, therefore, comparable piecemeal internal processes of entering adulthood. The crucial process concerns the ways that adolescents tolerate becoming more separate and interdependent, developing greater capacities to be alone, while also having an ability to depend upon others and be depended on by them. Diversity externally and internally is the hallmark of ways in which adolescents become 'more adult', and this is probably a more meaningful way to describe the late adolescent transitional process than the traditional formulation of leaving home.

Adolescents are dependent upon, and subject to, economic possibilities and restrictions, for education, housing and employment. As has been discussed in Chapter 1, rapid changes in all these spheres have destabilised the context of the process to adulthood, producing 'difference, exclusion and marginalisation' (Giddens, 1991, p. 6). Adolescents 'embark on journeys into adulthood which involve a wide variety of routes, many of which appear to have uncertain outcomes' (Furlong and Cartmel, 1997, p. 7). Thus the experience of leaving home is experienced as a 'calculative attitude to the open possibilities of action, positive and negative, with which, as individuals and globally, we are confronted in a continuous way with contemporary social existence' (Giddens, 1991, p. 28). Leaving home becomes individualised, as traditional structures and institutions are obscure; everything is presented as a possibility, and yet constraints loom from all sides. Loss, as well as risks and hazards, looms large.

Facing loss and separation

Loss in the process of transition from adolescence to adulthood is experienced in relation to the social world. Becoming engaged in the opportunities, constraints and risks of adulthood usher in an intensification of the awareness of the loss of the past, of the ending of childhood. Waddell (1998) emphasises the enormity of the task during the transition to adulthood:

> It is a time of hope and expectation, but for many, also of extreme sadness and distress, and even of breakdown for the few who find themselves unequal to the task. ... At the heart of the matter lies the degree of the person's capacity to experience loss, a loss especially stark as childhood is definitively left behind and engagement with the adult world becomes a necessity.
>
> (pp. 158–9)

It is the urgency impelled by the non-negotiable fact of transition to adulthood, to take up adult roles and positions, that propels so many late adolescents to therapy. Whereas in early adolescence, engagement in therapy, like life and responsibilities, are avoidable unless parents or school are very definite about their necessity, at various points in the transition to adulthood, adolescents often refer themselves for therapy. Many of the examples of young people in therapy discussed in this book fall into this category. Though the transition is usually later than previously, in various ways an urgency is generated. Whether this is around feelings stirred up by exams, choices and decisions about relationships or employment, or moving out of the family home, and whether this sense of urgency is experienced at 16, 18, 21 or 24, the action of external pressure, or reality, on internal states triggers tension and the need for help. Whereas traditional formulations of the move into the adult world are characterised by the urgency of making decisions for 'commitments for life'[1] (Erikson, 1968), contemporary young people have to make the commitment to be engaging in the calculation of risks and opportunities in a range of individualised decisions. The transition into adulthood takes many forms, and there are many different kinds of late adolescent transition – depending on the contexts. There are risks and hazards in deferring work and responsibilities, even through the institutionalised moratorium of the 'gap year'.

Case example

Peter was contemplating a period of travel during his gap year. He felt propelled to get away from home. Tentatively he tried to discuss his plans with me, but inevitably he stumbled on the same problem, that he both wished to get away from his therapy, and thus to evade his difficulties, and he was frightened of leaving. However, his plans progressed and he announced boldly that he had made the decision to travel. Then he crumpled before his fears about leaving. He said he was ready, and not ready. He said his friends had been winding him up by saying that he would be back within a week. He asked what I would decide about his therapy. I said that we both had something to contribute to that decision. I added that, if I said I'd see him when he got back I would not be taking into account his anxieties, expressed through his friends, that he might need me before then. If I said I'd see him next week as usual I would be undermining his attempts to make his plans succeed. He said he would phone if he came back early.

Peter's plans are for a temporary absence, rather than a permanent departure, but it is nevertheless full of anxiety, and combines constructive and destructive aspects. He is anxious about himself and also about how he will be thought about in his absence. Will I keep a space for him, or will I fill it with someone else? This appears rather delicate. Too fulsome an offer from me could lead him to feel trapped and 'subject to' my wishes; not enough of an offer will leave him feeling unsure whether he has a place in therapy, and in my mind. Peter is involved in a calculative process, engaging with subjective risks and weighing up the options.

The anxieties involved in the late adolescent transition demonstrate the falsity of the traditional view of adolescence. This is satirised as being *'kick started by puberty and cruises slowly to a halt at adult identity, the point at which the petrol is getting low and we need to think about saving it for the long, straight road ahead'* (Van Heeswyk, 1997, p. 3).

Positioning as adults

The positioning of adolescents as adults occurs within the power/knowledge discourse. In the context of wide sweeping changes in the social structures affecting transitions into adulthood, adolescents 'are increasingly held accountable for their own fates' (Furlong and Cartmel, 1997, p. 8) and yet there are strong external and internal forces which the adolescent is 'subject to'. Transitions are subject to the limitations of specific fields, socially and internally. There is often an illusion of choice and control, and a gap between possibility and expectation. Knowledge, as educational knowledge and credentials, is a powerful factor in the transition into adulthood, and this has increasingly become a continuous or frequently recurring process that is continuous throughout the long transition to adulthood; it happens at 16, 18, 21 and into the mid-20s.

We have seen how Mrs J's students (Chapter 5) were abject at the imminent prospect of leaving school with no qualifications, and therefore feeling quite vulnerable in taking up adult roles. This is extremely realistic, since one effect of radical changes in the social context of late adolescence is to place educational attainment at the centre of the complex routes into adulthood.

Exams also constitute a rite of passage into adulthood, increasing the tension and anxiety about performance, and highlighting the difference between those who are equipped to succeed and those who are more vulnerable. George (Chapter 6) did not take GCSE's, because of his state of mind at the time, when he was preoccupied with the difficulties in his family. Providing a powerful discourse or route into adulthood, exams test the authenticity of the adolescent's credentials for making it in the adult world. Success in doing and passing exams provides reassurance that the appearance fits the reality, and that the adolescent has 'qualified' for continuing along this route into adulthood. Success positions adolescents as more adult, which is a more powerful state, and yet brings with it new vulnerability and fragility, of facing future uncertainties, and raises questions about how emotional needs for dependency and financial needs will be met. Paradoxically, success can bring about separation from parental figures and simultaneously increase dependency upon them. Anxiety about exams can rock the sense of identity, testing internalisations and containment, as has been discussed in the case of Lenny, Chapter 7. This can become acute if it seems to point out to the adolescent that something is wrong, that the test, symbolically, is only the first of many in adult life. Samantha (Chapter 7), for example, lost a sense of herself as a competent, successful student during the year of her A levels. Her fear of loss of control began to become manifest when she got behind with her work and then she felt panic that she could never catch up. This is not to say that the exams were a cause of her breaking down for that would be superficial. The tension and pressure around exams, together with the underlying meaning that they lead to separation through leaving home and going to University, and that in that process there will need to be self-reliance, revealed problems and weaknesses in her identity. It was then that problems had to be faced rather than shelved.

Taking a driving test comes a close second to exams, in terms of ritualistic passage to adulthood, though the greening of society may soon make this redundant. Adolescents are often extremely crushed by failure and thrilled by success. Failure seems to stand for a judgement for a refusal to enter adulthood, and enjoy the fruits of adult power – driving, and the driving examiner can be represented as a demonic figure, guarding the gates to paradise. Driving may be more important to some young people than having a home (Joseph Rowntree Foundation, 2001). In this case, leaving home becomes a less significant goal than owning a car. Both however lead to the possession of keys, which symbolically confer power. The power/knowledge concept points to the relationship between self-knowledge and power. To have an awareness of oneself, one's subjectivity is the means to power/knowledge, but trying to respond to one's sense of vulnerability by seeking more powerful positions can lead to repetitive behaviour. Driving tests can be repeatedly failed by adolescents who 'know' that they can drive, but their performative skills let them down. Omnipotence breaks down under the experience of pressure from external realities. Anxieties about taking up a more adult position, fragmentation in the face of these anxieties and underlying Oedipal competitiveness provide deeper explanations.

In the context of the long transition towards adulthood, there is a movement towards becoming, which is harnessed to adolescent ideas of knowing that certain positions are desirable. Taking up more powerful subject positions means losing or giving up on other positions which are less powerful, but allow access to being dependent. Relinquishment of these relationships means experiencing loss. Thus vulnerability may be heightened. (cf. Urwin, 1998, Chapter 2). Relationships between adolescents and adults, including therapists, are important in developing what Noam calls 'contexts of affirmation', sorting out realities from omnipotent illusions and providing a space to think about the meaning and implications of proposed routes. In the transition towards adulthood, the process of becoming a subject is one of completing, testing and monitoring how the impact of adult positioning in one domain or another will affect identity. At this point the adolescent is acutely aware of a gap between her/himself, and others. This leads to anxiety, and an increase in the need for containment. The openness of this moment, the imperative for action and the opportunity to reflect back in time and to the future brings to bear a sense of the enormity of the new conditions in the transition from adolescence to becoming more adult.

Becoming positioned as adults replaces leaving home. In the movement from leaving adolescence to entering adulthood, four aspects of 'becoming' are important:

- becoming a parent
- becoming a student
- becoming a worker
- becoming a sexual partner

These four aspects are subject to wide diversities in terms of the meaning of the experience – working, partnership, parenting and student role. Diverse routes into each of them ensure that the meaning of these experiences needs to be located firmly in the individual and social context.

Becoming a student

Becoming a student, that is entering post-secondary education, used to be a traditional way for middle-class adolescents to partly leave home and enter into a last stage of childhood. Contemporary adolescence is different, and the role of a student is taken up by a majority of young people, in diverse ways. Not taking up post-secondary education is now an indicator of potential social exclusion. The explosion of the student population – driven now by government agendas for the need for increasing the skills base – is one of the significant changes in the landscape for young people, alongside the centrality of education as the primary source of power/knowledge. Becoming a student is a diverse experience, which raises other aspects of the late transition, especially with regard to relationships with family, with boy/girlfriends, and with choices and decisions about future directions. Thus becoming a student is always part of a field of transition. Many of the case examples in this book discuss the processes of separating that are linked with student roles. Howard, in Chapter 1 experiences a sense of fragmentation at the end of his university experience, and the uncertainties of identity began to impact upon him then, rather than earlier in adolescence. Some young people experience the end of a university course as returning them, painfully, to an uncertain and difficult set of experiences, in which they are often vulnerable, facing turbulent and rebuffing contact with the adult world of work and facing limitations to independence from parents. They are, in their 20s, thrust back into the whirlpool of discovering what they will be and do.

Others may experience the student role as a period of temporary outsidership, which enhances the capacity to reflect and bear emotions and thoughts. The overall effect of the new way that the student role impacts is that it lengthens the period of adolescence and leave young adults facing adolescent issues anew.

Often, relationships with peers as well as experiences of study are vital experiences of being a student. Some find shared living with other students a supportive and enhancing experience. Others experience this as presenting many conflicts within complex group dynamics. The way young people engage with the role of student can be defining for them, for it is hardly possible to move from adolescence to adulthood without having negotiated a student role of some kind; the alternative is likely to be the role of being NEET (not in education, employment or training). How the role of student connects with other more adult positions can be seen in the following example, in which becoming a student has implications for relationships and thus on the role of becoming a sexual partner.

Becoming a sexual partner

Case example

Sasha's dilemmas about starting university formed an important aspect of her therapy. It meant also working out a relationship with a boyfriend, already long standing, but which caused her considerable ambivalence. Initially, when she began therapy she felt that she would have to separate from him, recognising at some level within herself that she had become involved in order to avoid the pains of adolescence, rather than making a positive decision to become involved in a sexual partnership.

As her fear of separations began to be held in her therapy, she felt more able to think about a future which might include her boyfriend, and the renegotiations of their relationship, which would need to take place. Between them, they did negotiate a way in which they could continue their relationship and both go to different universities, to keep in touch, have time together and also have some elements of separate lives. The precariousness of the separateness was expressed through awareness at everyday levels. For example, Sasha discovered, to her furious disbelief, that her boyfriend's new mobile was on a different network from hers.[2] Reluctantly, another aspect of separateness had to be faced.

The painfulness of leaving home was expressed in the ending of her therapy. It had been agreed at the outset that her therapy would continue up to the point she left for university and would then end. Sasha raised the question of whether this was to be a temporary parting, or a permanent ending? There emerged a qualitative difference between negotiable and non-negotiable facts. On the one hand, she could leave home, go to University, return home, go to see her boyfriend, he could visit her – so why could she not return to her therapy? She raised this in a way that left me feeling extremely mean and cruel in trying to stick to the agreed boundary that the therapy would end. I wondered why I felt this was necessary; sometimes it is possible to arrange for continuing contact, during vacations etc. (though this can also be a mistake). I seemed to have pushed myself into a corner, in which to back down would mean feeling humiliated by Sasha's assertions that she knew best, and that I was making a mistake. However, when Sasha spoke about to me about her resentments about her brother, a different aspect emerged, so that the meaning of separating from home and her therapy also carried the meaning, in the transference, of being left, as an infant, by a mother who had another child. Through this Sasha lost the sense of a space with mother, which was just hers. Thus the aspect of the meaning of separating to go to university which was complicated by the influence of the non-negotiable infantile situation alongside the purely 'adolescent' issue, that her sole space with mother was lost forever when her younger brother was born. The definite ending of the therapy brought the non-negotiable infantile issue to the foreground and through this a differentiation of different kinds of separation and separateness became available for discussion.

The relationship Sasha developed with her boyfriend may have begun as 'a pairing-off, which ... despite appearances [has] little to do with a genuine transition from adolescent to adult states of mind. ... Indeed such couplings can constitute precisely the opposite; that is, a defensive bonding in the face of anxiety about what stepping into adulthood might really entail' (Waddell, 1998, p. 158). In her therapy, Sasha was able to find, with difficulty, and at times agonisingly, a path between two polarities. One polarity was to be stuck in a retreat from adulthood in a relationship which denied separateness. The other was to jettison her boyfriend, who at this point also represented her brother, in a frantic attempt to undo the relationship, because a key motive for the involvement was to retreat from the pains of separateness. The latter would have also caused both of them pain, and could be construed as masochistic. Developing the capacity to become attached and separate was undertaken within the relationship, which became transformed by this process, though

still in some ways precariously so. Nevertheless, after these considerations had been thought about, Sasha's ambivalence about her
boyfriend lessened and was replaced by a more tender disposition
towards him. The complexities of becoming 'repositioned' as being
in an adult sexual partnership were complicated through growing
into them, so to speak, from within the partnership, while both of
them grew up. But, again, that could be defined as an adult quality,
that is, the capacity to keep developing within a relationship. For
Sasha, taking up an adult subject position in her relationship ena-
bled her to begin to differentiate between infantile and adult aspects
of relating.

The juxtaposition in contemporary contexts of later and more
piecemeal transitions to adulthood, which cut across traditional
timings for becoming involved in relationships, are differently
experienced in different cultural settings. The following example
illustrates the tensions that arise when the traditional age for marriage occurs at the time that the young person is embarking on new
studies.

Case example

*Prasad had a very different route towards adulthood. When she began
university she put thoughts of leaving home and having a relationship out
of her mind. She would have liked to live in student accommodation but it
would have created too many problems in her Bangladeshi family. Also, she
believed that the right course for her was to adhere to traditional cultural
values. She was accepting of the limitations this put on her social life, and
especially when she felt herself to be in a marginal position with her friends
at university. When Prasad started to go out more to see student friends,
her parents became anxious and followed her, and she was quite upset that
they seemed to mistrust her when she was so 'good'. She was also furious
that they did not seem to know about her ideology and beliefs. She began
to feel that she had to be more rigorously self-reflective, to really be sure
that her ideas were her own, and belonged to her, and she realised that as
she continued her studies she may change her views. She began to think it
would be possible for her to be in a relationship, and this stirred up a fear of
difficult conflicts ahead within herself and with her parents.*

Prasad had complicated reasons for taking up her traditional and
conformist position, and she was anxious about experiencing
change within herself, precipitating conflict within herself and in
her family. Ghuman (1999, p. 119) gives an example of an Indian girl

facing a similar context. She said, 'my father would not let me go away from home to a university in London. Then I suggested that I could stay with my uncle and travel daily to the university. He agreed. ... Then my parents were concerned that I was getting too old (22 years) and they should arrange a match for me. I said "definitely not from India". To which they agreed. Then I said: "Let me finish my diploma course". After that I turned down several boys and chose the one I really liked; it was a sort of compromise. ... There was never any question of dating, or going out with boys.'

For this girl, the move towards adulthood was accompanied by developing a sense of agency through the capacity to negotiate with parents about traditional values and expectations.

Becoming a parent

The preparation for taking up parental roles is a complex one, based on separation and differentiation from one's own parents, and the development of a sense of being different from as well as the same as one's parents. Subjectivation, the process of appropriating ownership of one's body, thoughts and passions, depends on achieving 'a mind which is rooted in and yet also distinct from the sources and models of identification that are visible in one's family, or in the wider school and community setting' (Waddell, 1998, p. 158). Becoming different from, but having a sense of being the same as, creates the foundations for belonging and individuality, attachment and separation. From this bedrock, taking up the role of parent follows this ordering, and of course, traditionally, requires the prior establishment of a sexual couple. However, vulnerable adolescents take other routes to parenthood. If becoming prematurely involved in a sexual relationship can constitute a retreat from the anxieties of impending adulthood, and also an attempt to become repositioned as an adult, becoming pregnant may have the same meanings. The following case example is of a group of young people who are extremely vulnerable in contemporary society; this vulnerability consists of being in conflict with and unsupported by parents, leaving education early and becoming a teenage mother.

Case example

Tanya left home at 16, after an argument with her mother. She moved into a house shared by other young people, an 'intermediary household',[3] became pregnant and decided to keep the baby. Soon anxiety about her capacity to care for the baby became very high, and the potential risk to the baby led to social work involvement. Tanya was unsupported by her family, her conflicts with her mother increased and conflict pervaded her relationships with professionals. Tanya accepted an offer of individual therapy, and the therapist was able to establish a rapport with her, despite her very strong sense of persecution. The therapeutic relationship provided an important link for Tanya, through the period when child protection procedures were focused on her. When the baby was born she was devoted to her, and her intolerance of frustration reduced, so that she was less volatile and able to put up with a difficult environment and limited support, externally, from her family. The capacity to make a link with her baby, and with her therapist, provided her with a sense of having some internal resources. Resilience emerged in a way that was quite unexpected.

Teenage pregnancy is both a contemporary 'moral panic' and an objective indicator of vulnerability. Often it is seen in the same way as premature 'coupling' as a way of avoiding the anxieties of adulthood. Ambrose (2001, p. 84) suggests:

Separation usually involves physically leaving home as well as emotionally leaving. This is very difficult for many young people, particularly if they are enmeshed with their mother. They may be scared of coping alone. A gradual loosening of bonds may be too difficult and pregnancy may be a way to leave. It may be seen as a way to leave home, separate, be seen as a grown up, independent, different. Alternatively since pregnant teenagers often stay with their mothers it may be a way not to leave home, solving the dilemma for the young person. The boyfriend is unimportant in this case. Pregnancy avoids painful choices about the future.

Ambrose provides a wealth of examples which illustrate the role of pregnancy in conflicts between the adolescent and, especially, parents. These teenagers range from knowingly seeking to get pregnant, to denial, hoping it would not happen to them.

Case example

Mary, a 17-year-old, asked for therapy through her social worker. She was about to leave care, and she had become perturbed by an increasing sense of loss, of not knowing who her father was, and the rejection she had experienced from her mother. The social worker had thoughtfully, over some time, discussed with her the idea of having therapy. When she made the referral, the social worker felt confident that Mary did wish to have therapy, though she also felt that she was quite fragile and anxious about what would happen in her therapy. Mary did attend her first therapy appointment, but between making the referral and the appointment the social worker learned that Mary had become pregnant. Mary was clear she would keep the baby. She did make emotional contact with the therapist in her consultation, but indicated she would not now wish to continue with having therapy.

Mary seemed to have thought about therapy for herself, but to have made a choice to have a baby instead. There did seem to be a sense in which she felt that the anxiety about the past, for the baby part of her who felt so rejected and needed attention, but facing therapy was too difficult for her. Mary seemed to feel that being in the role of parent to her baby would be more manageable, emotionally, than being actively involved in experiences of her own infancy, in therapy. Tanya, on the other hand, taking a similar route into adulthood, found therapy supported her taking up a more adult position. The anxiety about Tanya when she was pregnant mobilised both responses to potential risks, and support and attentiveness. These had been absent in her earlier adolescence, which she felt to have been particularly abject. Teenagers who become pregnant are likely to be extremely vulnerable, having probably experienced deprivation, abuse and loss of family, through being in care (Garnett, 1992). But Tanya's relationship with her baby opened up a negotiable aspect of her and provided her with some opportunities for becoming more grown up, needed and loved (Musick, 1993). In the face of limited familial, internal, educational, and economic opportunities, parenthood appeared to become a chosen option (Phoenix, 1991), which had opportunities and possibilities as well as risks and hazards, as a precarious more-adult position.

The great divide: leaving home, leaving care

The timing of when young people leave home on a more or less permanent basis reveals a great deal about their social, emotional and financial capital. Noam (1999, p. 52) points out that 'even in the past, the adolescent moratorium required some money in the bank as well as some educational capital in the home'. The process of leaving adolescence is now more closely tied to educational capital and the capacity of families to support young people emotionally and financially through the vicissitudes of the long transition to adulthood, as has been discussed in Chapter 1. Thus young people may remain dependent on families for an extended period of time, and this 'rests on the dubious proposition that families are able and willing to submit to the authority of their parents during this period' (Furlong and Cartmel, 1997, p. 52).

Young people whose families cannot offer this support, or who have difficulties within the family, face a different prospect. It remains anomalous that, despite the continuing focus in policy and practice on looked after children as a most vulnerable group of young people, these most vulnerable adolescents are required to be more independent earlier than those who have educational and financial capital through, mainly, family support, available to them.

Julia (Chapter 5) was prepared for independence when she was 16. This meant developing practical skills for living alone, and moving into a semi-independent flat. The anxiety about the risks faced by young people leaving care can nudge staff towards colluding with pseudo-independence, hurrying development. Julia found it very difficult to make contact with others emotionally, and to allow contact, which might become painful so that the veneer of maturity masked a desperate internal need for others. Leaving care means that an emotionally deprived adolescent, who has probably been subject to many changes and disruptions faces the difficult and challenging task of developing the resources to contend with 'independence'. This splits the adolescent into a part that is still a child, and one that has to be adult. The adult, independent position is often the more appealing, since the disappointments and pains of relating to parental figures have left mistrust of others, and a painful residue of damage. Anxieties about holding together a self which has not been contained within continuous relationships, can leak through the attempt to maintain a sense of self-control.

Case example

John had been in foster care until the placement broke down when he was 16. He returned to her mother's care and revived many of the difficulties which had led to him being accommodated when he was nine. John and his mother therefore resumed a conflictual relationship, which was painful for both of them. John asked for a place of his own and was provided with a bed-sit. At this point both were in an agonised state of not being able to bear leaving and being left. A therapeutic consultation was arranged for them both to be seen, but separately. In his consultation, John was very tearful, crying a great deal about the pain he felt about his mother rejecting him and the pain of leaving her. Towards the end of the interview he started to talk about how much better he felt it would be to be in his own place, and that his move was about to take place. He wrapped himself in his coat, and seemed to tighten it around him, as if to hold himself together. After he left, the therapist was extremely anxious about a delicate and fragile boy, who had gone, unprotected, into the outside world. This was a powerful and evocative worry, raising the question as to whether he would survive. An infant part of John had been left, along with the tears, with the therapist. When John next returned to see the therapist, he had moved into his flat, and his talk was about college and friends, and he conveyed a sense of an active life connected to his friends.

John put into his therapist a very powerful feeling of being an abandoned baby. Thus the abandoned infant part of the young person was projected into the therapist. Being able to take in this lost relationship of a child with his mother, left the therapist worrying about him, as a parent would worry about a child. The therapist's emotional availability for taking in this aspect of John's situation appeared to free him to take up a more adult position. John was fortunate in the strength of his peer network, and, as he positioned himself as living independently, he gained the benefits of these relationships, and he was able to feel, and be, more resilient. Resilience requires both the capacity to face, at least, some of the truth, as well as the flexibility to make use of what resources are available. This is often too much for young people who have moved repeatedly during their childhood, where disruptions of placement result in disruptions to schooling, relationships with peers and extended family. Thus a split can develop between a hurt infant or child part of the adolescent, and a competent, or pseudo-competent, adult part. The latter may involve a defensive reaction to the feelings of despair and helplessness; hope for the future requires both the vulnerable infant and genuinely striving to be adult parts of the adolescent to be recognised and thus thought about. This is a difficult combination to hold together, and often the two aspects – competence and vulnerability – are split off form each other.

Case example

In a leaving care team, workers became embroiled in a conflict over the methods of work. The problem came to light when only half the team was available to take on new cases. The members of the other half of the team always had full caseloads. In exploring this division, it emerged that two opposing and different approaches were being taken to the work. The group that were available to take on new cases were being reactive to their clients, so that if they requested help, this was provided, but the workers did not seek out those young people who did not themselves ask for help. They also made short-term contracts with the young people, defining work in a task oriented way. They assumed that young people would find follow up intrusive. The other team members, in contrast, were proactive in visiting the young people, and were more actively involved in building relationships with the care leaving adolescents. They felt that their cases were not ready to be closed, and that doors needed to be left open, in case of need. Cases would be followed up for years, rather than weeks.

This split represents different views of vulnerability and need. The short-term model was based on a sense of 'getting on with the present' and making do with resources and limitations as they are. The long term model included the concept of caring for the infant in the adolescent/young adult, and acting on the fear that the adolescents would not survive without parenting. Within this split are dilemmas, which are not easily reconciled. The practical needs of young people leaving care (and home) become vital, so that the function of parenting (external and internal) can become represented by commodities. Thus two youth workers came for consultation about responding to the emotional and mental health needs of homeless young people in a van, loaded with a fridge, cooker and a washing machine. Mothering can be thus reified. Emotional contact can get lost in the emphasis on practicalities, or they can provide opportunities for thinking about meaning and understanding.

Increased homelessness of young people, in Britain, in the last years of the 20th century was probably caused by the restructuring of the economy of late adolescence, especially the increased centrality of education, the fragmented routes through late adolescence towards independence, and the extension through these of the period of semi-dependence. The burden of this fell on the most vulnerable, those with extreme family difficulties and those who had already experienced multiple transitions in care. It is a powerful argument that the absence of an internal home, emotionally, stems from the problems in internalising parenting, through its lack, absence and deficiencies, and that this manifests itself as the inability to make a home in the adult world. To move into the adult world after experiences of such damaging quality requires the capacity to take a calculative approach to options, in a context of risks. The experience of contact with someone in a therapeutic role that can bear the anxiety and pain of loss and risks is helpful in keeping together the infant and more adult parts of the adolescent. The question arises for young people in these contexts of how, and in what circumstances, sufficient internal resources can be obtained. Recent innovations in thinking about looked after children include the strategic use of 'transitional therapy' for young people whose placements have been disrupted (Wakelyn, 2008) and the possibilities of work and recreation in contributing to resilience (Gilligan, 2008) through generating competence in specific areas.

Becoming a worker

It is in the arena of becoming an adult worker that great changes have taken place in the context of the late adolescent transition. Young people seeking employment undergo a number of moves involving complex patterns of full time study, part-time work, part-time study, vocational training, full-time work and unemployment. This has been thought of as consisting a change in British society in which 'The pattern in Britain is therefore becoming more like that in continental Europe, with young people living with their parents until their late twenties or early thirties, when they are established in work and have some savings' (Joseph Rowntree Foundation, 2001). Alternatively, the relative higher rates of employment of young people, and lower rates of post secondary education place Britain as more similar to Southern than Northern Europe (Bynner, 2005).

Some young people are excluded from the opportunities that are available within the complicated routes from school to work. Those who did not reach their potential at school get stuck in low-paid and unrewarding jobs or become NEET; those who have social difficulties may become long-term unemployed. For many, it is not so much the lack of opportunities, but rather the uncertainties that cause the problems. The risks and hazards of the route to work include, probably, a period of unemployment for school leavers and graduates, requiring the capacity to move between different positions, putting together bits from part-time work and training. The point is not that things are 'worse'. Twenty years ago, two thirds went straight from school into a full-time job (J. Rowntree, 2001), but most of these jobs were in manufacturing industries. The predictability of this route provides few opportunities for change and development. Currently, the shift towards unpredictability, and change, and the need for young people to flexibly adjust to different roles – of student, part-time worker, part-time trainee – and to be able to maintain an active pursuit of their future that typifies transitions towards adulthood. It is an anxious process.

Erikson (1968) wrote that 'In every technology, and in every historical period there are types of individuals who can combine the dominant techniques with their identity and *become* what they *do*'. This would be a dangerous technique for most young people, who need to be able to move between finite, time-limited and changing conceptions of what they do, in work, and to be able to lose, mourn, relinquish and realign (or, as Giddens put it 'reinvent'). The problem, in terms of work identity, is to steer between commitment and flexibility without losing either authenticity or adaptedness. Perhaps this is true of relating as well as working. These requirements demand a great deal of the internal world and the capacity to make sense of experience. Experiences of a flexible and receptive containment in infancy and during adolescence are the prime requirements for young people 'leaving home', as these provide opportunities to move between different and overlapping subject positions without losing a sense of self, through fragmenting or becoming rigidly stuck in one way of relating to the social world.

Becoming adult

The question that has been avoided is what it means to be adult. The gathering of experience through adolescence leads to participation in an adult world, which is complex, changing, and mirrors, in some ways, adolescence. Becoming adult thus, might imply being able to be a 'good' adolescent. The turbulence of society means that, in Emery and Trist's phrase, quoted in Chapter 1, 'the ground itself is in motion'. The capacity to maintain authenticity and integrity while changing, and experiencing loss, requires a particular kind of flexibility; the capacity to mourn, and to relinquish, to be introspective and to be aware of destructiveness, the need to repair, where possible, and to face what cannot be repaired; the capacity to bear anxiety and to have a calculative approach to risks. The adult process is not unlike the adolescent process. To Freud's idea that maturity is the capacity to love and work, needs to be added the capacity to weigh risks and bear the consequent anxieties. Thus, it is possibly a useful preparation for adulthood to have an adolescence which has, to a tolerable extent, exposed the individual to the experiences of change and loss. The adolescent may have felt the possibility of fragmentation, and, provided with this awareness has, through connectedness with others, created a sense of the value of others in performing containing functions for these emotions. Thus self-reflectiveness, an awareness of subjective experiences and inner states of mind provides possibilities of digesting diverse experiences and making sense of them. An adolescence, in which the complexities of relationships are discovered, along with the capacity to love, provides the possibilities of moving between different positions, in which power and vulnerability are reflected upon and experienced. Waddell (1998, p. 175) refers to Bion's view that he worked as a psychoanalyst in order to learn how to become one. This combines the positions of learner and worker, child and adult, apprentice and master, in a reflexive flexibility, which summarises the aliveness and fluidity of the potential and possibilities in the turbulence of late or post modernity. Adolescence provides the opportunities and hazards that follow from the exposure to external and internal turbulence, and the possibilities of making and maintaining a link between immaturity (childhood) and maturity (adulthood). Vulnerabilities and potencies, dependency and learning, independence and agency are linked through the experiences of adolescence and the contact that is made through these different aspects of the self. Through linking childhood experiences and maturity, the importance of the prolonged phase of adolescence is, indeed, immense and vital in so many ways, for the achievement of a capacity to contend with the demands of adulthood.

Summary

- Leaving home is a complex and often piecemeal process in contemporary society, and the sequences in which adolescents move into adulthood are diverse, depending very much on context. Fast-track routes to adulthood are now linked with vulnerability; slow-track routes increase tensions around independence – dependence and hence also the sense of agency.
- There are special tensions internally in the transition to adulthood, which create a sense of urgency for adolescents. These can be thought of as intensification of the processes of loss and mourning, and of emotional struggles involved in taking up adult positions, in terms of power and vulnerability.
- Some adolescents are particularly vulnerable to the late transition and risk becoming socially excluded and/or facing unbearable pain. However, case examples have been chosen which illustrate capacities for resilience, sometimes of a surprising nature. These include those who experience teenage pregnancy and leaving care.

- Adolescents take up adult positions in terms of work, education, sexual partnership and parenting, rather than simply 'leaving home'.
- Since adult society mirrors adolescence to some extent it is a helpful preparation for adulthood to have experiences of change, uncertainty and potential fragmentation, as long as these are tolerable and that containment makes sense of these experiences. This equips adolescents to be flexible *and* authentic at work, and in love.

NOTES

Introduction to Second Edition

1 Graham (2004), who advocates this approach suggests, for example, reducing voting eligibility to 16, or even 14 years.

1 Contemporary Adolescence: Still the 'Age Between'?

1. The Department was formed in 1959, and is thus approaching its fiftieth anniversary. Dugmore Hunter was also a central figure in the Department's foundation.

2. Patton and Viner (2007) summarise the evidence for earlier pubertal development. Except for some research in the USA, the age for pubertal development is not starting at an earlier age three.

3. Bynner (2005) shows European national comparisons for age at marriage, participation in education at 18 years and economic activity for ages 14–24. The higher rates of marriage and in for being in higher education in some countries (Germany, Denmark, Holland, France) contrasts with higher economic activity in some countries (Britain, Greece, Portugal). He also shows how over three cohorts, born in 1946, 1958, 1970, in the UK, the age at first child rose; in the 1970 cohort more than 75 per cent men and women are 30 or over, against 50 per cent in the 1946 cohort.

4. Part of the muddle about adolescence is the numerous and different timescales that are applied. One common banding is 14–24; another is 16–25. Alongside this, in the UK there is an incremental approach to the appropriation of adult status: 16 to marry, 17 to drive, 18 to vote and buy alcohol etc. Jones (2006) summarises many commentaries when she points out that these do not connect with developmental processes.

5. This refers to Freud's taking the Greek myth of Oedipus to be a cornerstone in individual infantile/childhood development, in which the infant's desire for the opposite sex parent and competition with the same sex parent creates a passionate – and bloody – set of 'phantasies'. The 'Oedipus complex' has a number of significant aspects and variations, which placed in a 'modern' context, as we shall see, has a continuing relevance for understanding development.

6. The idea that brain changes accounts for adolescent behaviour was popularised by *Time* magazine's (2004) article 'What makes teens tick?' and

makes use of Giedd's (1999) studies using MRI scanning. Giedd identified and explored the twin processes of brain cell growth and 'pruning' whereby the brain 'selects' the cells and connections (synapses) that are most used.

7. He used masculine examples throughout 'Identity: Youth and Crisis'.

8. Narcissism is a complex and controversial concept within psychoanalysis. Freud (1914) developed the idea based on the myth of Narcissus, who was in love with his own reflection and preferred it to the company of others. Thus, narcissism is linked with self-love, grandiosity and turning away from loving and being loved by others. The fate of Narcissus, in the myth, was to drown in the water in which he saw his reflection. Hence there is a destructive potential in narcissistic states. Controversy surrounds the development from Freud's work of the idea of primary narcissism, present from birth in which the earliest stage of development is the generation of self-love, and is thus 'libidinal'. Kohut (1971) saw early grandiose and omnipotent narcissism as gradually reshaped into a mature and realistic self through empathic interaction with the mother and, later, with others. Kleinians, on the other hand, conceptualise narcissism as a state rather than a stage, and one in which there is (destructive) withdrawal from object-relating. The role of destructive and 'libidinal' aspects of narcissism in adolescence will be further developed in subsequent chapters.

9. Esther Bick described the terror of fragmenting internally in the infant as 'being shot out into outer space without a space suit. The predominant terror of the baby is of falling to pieces or liquefying' (1986, p. 296). Maternal containment has the effect of pulling together the infant within the boundary of the skin, but if the function of providing a 'psychic skin' through containment is disturbed, the infant may make her/his own attempts to hold her/himself together psychically to contend with the terrors of fragmentation. This is described as an omnipotent attempt to replace dependency on others with a pseudo-independent 'second skin'. Becoming wrapped up in clothes may be a way of attempting to provide a 'second skin'. Muscularity and precocious verbal development are others. Adolescents may turn to second skin formation in the absence of understanding, containing figures, which can make sense of the feelings of potential fragmentation.

10. The term mother is meant to be inclusive of any involved caregiver. Technically, the projecting process that originates with the infant is 'projective identification'. Unwanted or overwhelming feelings are split off and projected into the mother, and these parts of the self are then identified with. Perhaps the clearest exposition of this is Klein's (1955) discussion of the novel, 'If I were you' by Julian Green, in which the subject, Fabian envies others more powerful and wealthier than he and through making a pact with the devil, takes over their personalities. The emptiness of the project is revealed when Fabian discovers that under the sway of his envy he had omitted to take into account the negative aspects of the envied person's life, which he has just inhabited, and a frantic attempt to return follows. Klein (1946) described projective identification as a defensive attempt to omnipotently control the mother/object. Klein thought about degrees of projective identification, in which either parts of the personality or almost all of it is projected. Bion used the idea of degrees of projective identification to distinguish between a defensive attempt to control the object and a

primitive form of communication. The latter is 'normally used, preverbally, to let another know something of what is felt and experienced, and thus it is a crucial aspect of the container–contained relationship where the mother gets to know her baby by letting her/his feelings enter her. See Hinshelwood 1989 for a further discussion.

2 Becoming a Subject in Adolescence

1. Blos's account has some weaknesses in thinking about contemporary adolescence. Firstly, the conceptualising of 'hatching' from fusion to separateness, based on Mahler's (1963) theory of infancy, oversimplifies the relationship processes of both infancy and adolescence. Secondly, rather like Erikson, Blos places the emphasis on progression towards autonomy, and this introduces the idea of a rather solid, unified adult self as an outcome for adolescence.

2. In the paranoid schizoid position the infant splits the mother, or object, into good, or loved, and bad, or hated, aspects. This is accomplished through projective identification, denial of reality, splitting and idealisation, in order to deal with persecutory anxiety in which the infant is threatened from within by bad, hateful and destructive feelings. The primary aim in the paranoid schizoid position is to protect the self from difficult, unpleasant and disturbing feelings. In the depressive position the infant becomes more aware of reality and thus that the attacks on the hated object are also attacks on the loved object. In an attempt to make good the damage that it is felt have been perpetrated on the loved object, there are attempts to make reparation. In the depressive position, tolerating ambivalence, pain and concern for the other person is strived for, and if the feelings become unbearable, there results either a return to the paranoid schizoid position, a retreat into a manic defence or an overemphasis on guilt, in a masochistic way. In the paranoid schizoid position, there is no separateness or toleration of separation, and through the projective processes that predominate, the boundaries between self and others are broken through and blurred. In the depressive position, the problem or difficulty is the management of the pain of guilt and separateness and of the sense of vulnerability that ensues.

The manic defence is important in adolescence. The idea is that to defend against pain and loss, the individual resorts to a denigration of the importance of relationships and of dependency, and also that, omnipotently, everything that has gone wrong can be put right again (see Hinshelwood, 1989).

3. See note 5, Chapter 1.

4. Kennedy (2000) makes a similar defining claim: 'subjectivity incorporates both intrapsychic and intersubjective positions, both phenomena within the subject and between subjects in the social field. Psychoanalysis has mainly clarified intrapsychic phenomena, and is only now paying more attention to the intersubjective arena. I am not implying that we should abandon the intrapsychic, for that would be to deny an essential component of the subject' (p. 878).

5. There is a connection with Meltzer's (1988) discussion of the aesthetic conflict. Rustin (1995) has suggested that this is a most radical position.

'This approach views imaginative understanding – conceived as an aesthetic experience of the beautiful and the sublime, in effect – as the true aim of psychic life. It is the encounter with the disturbance of new emotional experience – of which the infant's experience of the breast is for Meltzer the prototype – which creates the possibility of this state of aesthetic apprehension' (p. 240).

6. Bion's term 'the selected fact' had a similar meaning with regard to the internal organisation of the mind.

7. The myth of the 'repressive' hypothesis is for example firmly endorsed by the historian very sympathetic to Freud, Peter Gay (1984).

8. Frederick Buytendiyk (1974) proposed that 'There is no mode of being in which the polar unity of bodily and personal subjectivity manifests itself so clearly as in those situations in which he [sic] refers with words: being affected, upset, touched, moved, struck, shocked, alarmed, overwhelmed etc.' (p. 174).

9. Bion (1970) when discussing catastrophic change gives the example of someone trying to control (contain within the self) the intense experience through words, and the failure to do this – through developing a stammer for example. The 'container' is put under excessive pressure, in turbulence and the conditions of catastrophic change. This is close to the idea being discussed here.

10. Irigaray (1991) celebrates the flow and fluidity of femininity. Touch is prioritised over seeing while, taking the labia as a model, she proposes that female sexuality is always plural, always touching herself, without the need for mediation (pp. 204–5). But women's sexuality is 'far more diversified, more multiple in its differences, more complex, more subtle than is commonly imagined' (p. 207).

11. Kristeva is also responsible for developing a concept of 'women's time', which is cyclical, rather than linear.

12. Most writers comment on the performative shift which over the past two decades has seen girls achieve better than boys at school (e.g. Johannsson, 2007, p. 23) and this brings about concern about the problematic performance of boys (see also Frosh et al., 2002).

13. Girls worried about homosexual orientation were four times more likely than other girls to be suicidal. For boys the ratio is 2:1. The numbers reported in this study are low in terms of the overall population: only 3 per cent reported 'worries' about sexual orientation. This may be due to under reporting, but it is important that the category being considered here is those with 'worries'. Feeling gay and proud would not be an issue.

4   Parenting Adolescents

1. The longitudinal study was restricted to parent report, but it was found that the higher rates of difficulties reported by parents correlated with rates of later adult difficulties, including employment difficulties, less stable partnerships and poor health indicators. There are a number of other recent reports of adolescent difficulties published recently in the UK. These include a study of 15-year-olds in Scotland (West and Sweeting, 2003), showing that girls rather than boys were subject to considerable stresses including those

generated by educational demands, and the Camelot study (Brophy, 2006) on self-harm in young people.

2. 'Your sons and your daughters are beyond your command': The line is Dylan's from 'The times they are a-changing'; thus, not a new phenomenon.

3. Dartington (1998) points out that 'it is not unusual for young people to be quite ruthless in their experimentation at this period' (p. 14).

4. Hinshelwood (1999) develops Freud's conceptualisation that the child internalises not the parent, but the parent's superego (Freud, 1924). In this sense the superego conceptualises the way familial and cultural contexts are organised in the mind, through internalisation of parental values, attitudes, norms and prohibitions. The superego may have different characteristics, in that it can be a guiding force, even when strict, or it can destructively attack linking and thinking. In this model, the cultural values which are transmitted as unconscious processes are those relating to a sociocultural state which has past.

5   Containing Adolescence in Organisations

1. The term 'institutional defence' was developed by Menzies Lyth (1988).

2. Kleinert (2007) also refers to the failure in the UK to act on the report by the Royal College of Paediatrics and Child Health, 'Bridging the Gaps: Health Care for Adolescents', which identified a range of shortcomings in adolescent health services. Only USA, Canada and Australia have dedicated multidisciplinary adolescent health care centres.

3. Lowe (2006) gives an example of an initial letter sent to an anxious mother, a black woman, inviting her to an initial appointment of one and a half hours, which was to be videotaped. She did not attend. The art of the initial appointment letter, a considerable art in fact, has been subsumed by the needs of bureaucracy. In place of the carefully crafted individualised response to an adolescent's request for help, there is now, most likely, a bureaucratically driven thick wadge of forms necessary to fulfil all clinical governance requirements.

4. http://www.ciao.ch.

6   Adolescents as Temporary Outsiders: Antisocial Behaviour

1. SIRC runs the influential website, Frank, which offers drugs advice to young people. Marsh commented on the function of tribes thus: 'Like their tribal ancestors, teenagers today learn to understand who they are by defining themselves through social bonds and affiliations with a peer group. As they make the hormone-laden journey from child to adult, they forge a personal identity by first creating a social identity. Music tastes and appearance are the obvious ways to define oneself, but the ways in which young people talk about themselves to their peers also helps them to create a sense of self. To be an individual, we first need to be one of the lads or lasses' (SIRC, 2004).

2. Tribes occur across the world. French tribes for example include '"Lascars" (young people from the impoverished suburbs) collect trainers and prefer rap to literature. In Paris, "jet-setteurs" and "bourgeois-bohèmes" (leftish AND compulsive consumers) love to window-shop and hang out in trendy night spots. The "raveur" goes in for a lot of body piercing, the "skateur" worships oversized trousers, the "campagnard" is bound to be at a loose end and the "internaute" glued to his computer screen, incapable of going to cafés, museums' (France Diplomatie, 2007).

3. The ideas of transitional space and a potential space for creativity are Winnicott's (1971).

4. The concept of the secure base is Bowlby's (1988). In attachment theory security of attachment is a prerequisite for the capacity to move away from the parent, and to begin exploratory behaviour. Allen and Land (1999) discuss recent understanding of adolescent attachment behaviour. The absence of a secure base, or security of attachment leads to different patterns of relating, based on the distinction between ambivalent/anxious and avoidant responses to separation. Avoidant adolescents tend to try to pull out of emotional engagement, playing down the significance of emotional experiences. Anxious/ambivalent adolescents in contrast make a great deal of all emotional experience, indiscriminately, without prioritising. Thus they make mountains out of molehills, so to speak, while avoidant adolescents, in contrast, make molehills out of mountains.

7 Adolescent Difficulties in Achieving Separateness

1. The kind of superego that is represented here is, as Lemma (2007) points out, an abnormally harsh or critical one, which strips meaning and points accusingly at the self. This contrasts with a more benign superego, which, while possibly critical, is also a guide for the ego. O'Shaughnessy (1999) and Britton (2003) have recently developed this concept of the abnormal superego, which as well as applying to BDD has been thought of as a significant factor in eating disorders (Wiliams et al., 2004) and suicide (Briggs et al., 2008)

2. This discussion is developed further in Chapter 8.

8 Psychotic and Suicidal States in Adolescence

1. Rates of suicide among young men began to fall before 2000 and have continued to decline from the high levels of the 1990s. The causes for the rise and then fall of these rates are complex and contested. The rates represent small changes and the presence of suicidality in young people merits continued respectful attention independent of the overall rise or fall of suicide rates.

2. The hopelessness of the ego as a key suicide dynamic has been developed by, especially, Beck (e.g. Beck et al., 1975). The emphasis on hopelessness as a unipolar dynamic can be said to miss the counterpart – merciless violence and sadism which is found in the superego.

3. This is discussed by Campbell (2008) providing a place for the idea of self-preservative violence, as distinct from sado-masochistic excitement (see Perelberg, 1999, for a full discussion). Bion's idea of evacuation through massive projective identification also fits the idea of elimination.

9   Emerging into Adulthood

1. Erikson wrote about 'a new kind of identification, achieved in absorbing sociability and in competitive apprenticeship among his age mates. 'These new identifications are no longer characterised by the playfulness of child-hood and the experimental zest of youth; with dire urgency they force the young individual into choices and decisions which will with increasing immediacy lead to commitments for life. The task to be performed here by the young person and his society is formidable (Erikson, 1968, p. 155).

2. This may be already a piece of time expired social experience. The point was that she would be charged considerably more for phoning him.

3. The term 'intermediate household' is used in sociological approaches to leaving home (Jones, 1995). It has become an increasingly common form of transition, affecting both middle and working-class young people, though the type of accommodation may be different. Middle-class young adults live in shared student or post-student accommodation; working-class young adults live in hostels, board with relatives or in accommodation provided by employers (Furlong and Cartmel, 1997, p. 47).

BIBLIOGRAPHY

Achenbach, T (1998) 'Six-year predictors of problems in a national sample: IV. young adult signs of disturbance', *Journal of the American Academy of Child and Adolescent Psychiatry*, vol. 37, pp. 718–27.

Alexander, C (2000) '(Dis)entangling the 'Asian Gang': Ethnicity, identity, masculinity', ed. Hesse, B, *Un/settled Multiculturalisms*, London: Jed Books.

Allen, J and Land, P (1999) 'Attachment in adolescence', ed. Cassidy, J and Shaver, P, *Handbook of Attachment – Theory, Research and Clinical Implications*, New York: Guilford Press.

Ambrose, M (2001) 'The developmental and emotional implications behind the use young people make of family planning services', ed. Baruch, G, *Community Based Psychotherapy with Young People: Evidence and Innovation in Practice*, Hove: Brunner-Routledge.

Amiel, O (2001) 'Why come, why come back; developing and maintaining a long term therapeutic alliance with young people who have had a psychotic breakdown', ed. Baruch, G, *Community Based Psychotherapy with Young People: Evidence and Innovation in Practice*, Hove: Brunner-Routledge.

Anastopoulos, D (2006) 'The narcissism of depression or the depression of narcissism and adolescence', *Journal of Child Psychotherapy*, vol. 33, no. 3, pp. 345–62.

Anderson, R (1997) 'Putting the boot in: Violent defences against depressive anxiety', ed. Bell, D, *Reason and Passion: A Celebration of the Work of Hanna Segal*, London: Duckworths/Tavistock Clinic Series.

Anderson, R (1999) 'Introduction', in Anastasopoulos, D, Laylou-Lignos, E and Waddell M, *Psychoanalytic Psychotherapy of the Severely Disturbed Adolescent*, London: Karnac Books.

Anderson, R and Dartington, A (1998) *Facing It Out: Clinical Perspectives on Adolescent Disturbance*, London: Duckworths/Tavistock Clinic Series.

Arnett J (2000) 'Emerging adulthood: A theory of development from late teens through the twenties', *American Psychologist*, vol. 55, pp. 469–80.

Arnett J (2004) *Emerging Adulthood: The Winding Road from the Late Teens through the Twenties*, Oxford: Oxford University Press.

Back, L (1997) '"Pale Shadows": Racisms, masculinity and multiculture', in Roche, J and Tucker, S, *Youth in Society*, London: Sage Publications.

Bains, R (2001) 'Psychotherapy with young people from ethnic minority backgrounds in different community based settings', ed. Baruch, G, *Community Based Psychotherapy with Young People: Evidence and Innovation in Practice*, Hove: Brunner-Routledge.

Baruch, G (ed.) (2001) *Community Based Psychotherapy with Young People: Evidence and Innovation in Practice*, Hove: Brunner-Routledge.

Baumann, Z (2003) *Liquid Love*, Oxford: Polity Press.

Beck, A, Schuyler, D and Herman, A (1974) 'Development of suicidal intent scales' in Beck, A, Resnick, H and Lettieri, D (eds) *The Prediction of Suicide*. Bowie, Maryland: Charles Press.

Beck, U (1992) *Risk Society: Towards a New Modernity*, London: Sage Publications.

Beck-Gernsheim, E (1998) 'On the way to a post-familial family: From a community of need to elective affinities', *Theory, Culture and Society*, vol. 15, 3, pp. 53–70.

Bell, D (2000) 'Who is killing what or whom? Some notes on the Internal phenomenology of suicide', *Psychoanalytic Psychotherapy*, vol. 15, no. 1, pp. 21–37.

Bhabha, H (1990) *Nation and Narration*, London: Routledge.

Bhabha, H (1997) 'Culture's in between', ed. Bennett, D, *Multicultural States – Rethinking Difference and Identity*, London: Routledge.

Bhattacharyya, G and Gabriel, J (1997) 'Racial formations in youth in late twentieth century England', in Roche, J and Tucker, S, *Youth in Society*, London: Sage Publications.

Bick, E (1968) 'The experience of the skin in early object relationships', *International Journal of Psychoanalysis*, vol. 49, pp. 484–6.

Bick, E (1986) 'Further considerations of the function of the skin in early object relations: Findings from infant observation integrated into child and adult analysis.' *British Journal of Psychotherapy*, vol. 2, no. 4, pp. 292–301.

Bion, W (1962) *Learning from Experience*, London: Maresfield.

Bion, W (1963) *Elements of Psychoanalysis*, London: Maresfield.

Bion, W (1970) *Attention and Interpretation*, London: Maresfield.

Blos, P (1962) On *Adolescence: A Psychoanalytic Interpretation*, New York: Free Press of Glencoe.

Blos, P (1967) 'The second individuation process of adolescence', *Psychoanalytic Study of the Child*, vol. 22, pp. 162–86.

Blos P (1984) 'Son and father', *Journal of the American Psychoanalytic Association*, vol. 32, pp. 301–24.

Bollas, C (1991) *Forces of Destiny: Psychoanalysis and Human Idiom*, London: Free Association Books.

Bordo, S (1993) *Unbearable Weight*, Berkeley: University of California Press.

Bowlby, J (1988) *A Secure Base: Clinical Applications of Attachment Theory*, London: Routledge.

Bowley, J (1996) 'Survival at the front: A study of the work of the nursing staff in an adolescent psychiatric unit', MA Dissertation, Tavistock Clinic/University of East London.

Bowley, J and Bratley, M (2005) 'Making space for therapeutic work with adolescents and their families', *Journal of Social Work Practice*, vol. 19, no. 3, pp. 289–98.

Brah, A (1996) *Cartographies of Diaspora*, London: Routledge.

Brenman Pick, I (1988) 'Adolescence: Its impact on patient and analyst', *International Journal of Psychoanalysis*, vol. 15, p. 187.

Briggs, S (1995) 'Parallel process: Emotional and physical digestion in adolescents with eating disorders', *Journal of Social Work Practice*, vol. 9, no. 2, pp. 155–68.

Briggs, S (1997) *Growth and Risk in Infancy*, London: Jessica Kingsley.

Briggs, S (2005) Adolescents in distress: Britain on the slide? *Tavistock Policy Seminar Series*, June 2005, http://www.tavi-port.org.

Briggs S (2008) 'Postvention: The impact of suicide and suicidal behaviour on family members, professionals and organisations', ed. Briggs, S, Lemma, A and Crouch, W, *Relating to Self-harm and Suicide: Psychoanalytic perspectives on theory, practice and prevention*, London: Routledge.

Britton, R (1989) 'The missing link: Parental sexuality in the oedipus complex', ed. Steiner, J, *The Oedipus Complex Today*, London: Karnac Books.

Britton, R (1998) *Belief and Imagination: Explorations in Psychoanalysis*, London: Routledge.

Britton, R (2003) *Sex, Death and the Superego*, London: Karnac Books.

Brophy, M (2006) *Truth Hurts: Report of the National Inquiry into Self harm among Young People*, Camelot Foundation/Mental Health Foundation, http://www.selfharmuk.org.

Buttolph, A (2001) 'Homework, hip hop and hot pants' London Evening Standard, 09-07-01.

Buytendijk, F (1974) *Prolegomena to an Anthropological Physiology*, Pittsburgh: Duquesne University Press.

Bynner, J (2005) 'Rethinking the youth phase of the life-course: The case for emerging adulthood?' *Journal of Youth Studies*, vol. 8, no. 4, pp. 367–84.

Cahn, R (1998) 'The process of becoming-a-subject in adolescence', in Perret-Catipovic, M and Ladame, F, *Adolescence and Psychoanalyis: The Story and the History*, London: Karnac Books.

Campbell, D (2008) The father transference during a pre-suicide state, in Briggs, S, Lemma, A and Crouch, W, *Relating to Self-harm and Suicide: Psychoanalytic Perspectives on Theory, Practice and Prevention*, London: Routledge.

Campbell, D and Hale, R (1991) 'Suicidal acts', ed. Holmes, J, *Textbook of Psychotherapy in Psychiatric Practice*, London: Churchill Livingstone.

Chodorow, N (1995) 'Individuality and difference in how women and men love', ed. Elliott, A and Frosh, S, *Psychoanalysis in Contexts*, London: Routledge.

Cohen, S (2002) *Folk Devils and Moral Panics*, 3rd Edition, London: Routledge.

Coleman, J and Hendry, L (1999) *The Nature of Adolescence*, 3rd Edition, London: Routledge.

Collishaw, S, Maughan, B, Goodman, R and Pickles, A (2004) 'Time trends in adolescent mental health', *Journal of Child Psychology and Psychiatry*, vol. 45, no. 8, pp. 1350–62.

Cooper, A (2000) 'The state of mind we're in', *Soundings*, vol. 3, no. 1, pp. 118–38.

Cooper, A and Lousada, J (2005) *Borderline Welfare: Feeling and Fear of Feeling in Modern Welfare*, London: Karnac Books.

Dartington, A (1994) 'Some thoughts on the significance of the outsider in families and other social groups', ed. Box, S, *Crisis at Adolescence: Object Relations Therapy with the Family*, New York: Jason Aronson.

Dartington, A (1998) 'The intensity of adolescence in small families', ed. Anderson, R and Dartington, A, *Facing it Out: Clinical Perspectives on Adolescent Disturbance*, London: Duckworths/Tavistock Clinic Series.

Dartington, T, Miller, E and Gwynne, G (1981) *A Life Together*, London: Tavistock.

DoH (2004) The national service framework for children, young people and maternity services: The mental health and psychological well-being of children and young people, London: HMSO.

DoH (2006) Report on the Implementation of Standard 9 of the National Serrvice Framework for Children, Young People and Maternity Services. Annex: models of good practice, 17, London: HMSO.

Di Ceglie, D (2002) 'Castaway's corner', *Clinical Child Psychology and Psychiatry*, vol. 7, no. 3, pp. 487–91.

Di Ceglie, D and Freedman, D (eds) (1998) *A Stranger in My Own Body: Atypical Gender Identity Development and Mental Health* (pp. 185–97), London: Karnac Books.

Dubinsky, H (1999) 'Factors contributing to the psychotic breakdown of three adolescents', in Anastasopoulos, D, Laylou-Lignos, E and Waddell, M, *Psychoanalytic Psychotherapy of the Severely Disturbed Adolescent*, London: Karnac Books.

Edwards, T (1997) 'Sexuality', in Roche, J and Tucker, S, *Youth in Society*, London: Sage Publications.

Eisenbruch, M (1990) 'Cultural bereavement and homesickness', ed. Fisher, S and Cooper, CL, *On the Move: The Psychology of Change and Transition*, Chichester: John Wiley and Sons.

Emery, F and Trist, E (1969) 'The causal texture of organisational environments', in Emery, F, *Systems Thinking*, Harmondsworth: Penguin.

Erikson, E (1968) *Identity: Youth and Crisis*, London: Faber and Faber.

Flynn, D (2000) 'Adolescence', in Wise, I, *Adolescence*, London: Institute of Psychoanalysis.

Flynn, D and Skogstad, H (2006) 'Facing towards or away form destructive narcissism', *Journal of Child Psychotherapy*, vol. 32, no. 1, pp. 35–48.

Fonagy, P and Target, M (1999) 'Towards understanding violence: The use of the body and the role of the father', ed. Perelberg, R, *Psychoanalytic Understanding of Violence and Suicide*, London: Routledge.

Foucault, M (1977) *Discipline and Punish*, London: Peregrine.

Foucault, M (1979, 1984a, 1984b) *The History of Sexuality*, Volumes I–III, London: Penguin.

Foucault, M (1988) 'Technologies of the self', ed. Martin, L, Gutman, H and Hutton, P, *Technologies of the Self: A Seminar with Michel Foucault*, London: Tavistock.

France Diplomatie (2007) 'Young people and culture: The clichés die hard', http://www.diplomatie.gouv.fr/en/france_159/label-france_2554/label-france-issues_2555/label-france-no.-51_3594/feature-france-the-new-generation_3595/young-people-and-culture-the-cliches-die-hard_4722.html.

French, S and Swain, J (1997) 'Young disabled people', in Roche, J and Tucker, S, *Youth in Society*, London: Sage Publications.

Freud, S (1916) 'Some character types met with in psycho-analytic work', ed. Strachey, J, *The Standard Edition of the Complete Psychological Works of Sigmund Freud*, vol. 14, London: The Hogarth Press and the Institute of Psychoanalysis.

Freud, S (1917) 'Mourning and melancholia', ed. Strachey, J, *The Standard Edition of the Complete Psychological Works of Sigmund Freud*, vol. 14, London: The Hogarth Press and the Institute of Psychoanalysis.

Freud, S (1920) 'The psychogenesis of a case of female homosexuality', ed. Strachey, J, *The Standard Edition of the Complete Psychological Works of Sigmund Freud*, vol. 18, London: The Hogarth Press and the Institute of Psychoanalysis.

Freud, S (1923) 'The ego and the id', ed. Strachey, J, *The Standard Edition of the Complete Psychological Works of Sigmund Freud*, vol. 19, London: The Hogarth Press and the Institute of Psychoanalysis.

Freud, S (1924) 'The economic problem of masochism', *The Standard Edition of the Complete Psychological Works of Sigmund Freud*, vol. 19, London: The Hogarth Press and the Institute of Psychoanalysis.

Frosh, S, Phoeniz, A and Pattman, R (2002) *Young Masculinities*, Basingstoke: Palgrave Macmillan.

Frosh, S (1991) *Identity Crisis: Modernity, Psychoanalysis and the Self*, London: Macmillan.

Furlong, A and Cartmel, F (1997) *Young People and Social Change: Individualisation and Risk in Modern Society*, Buckingham: Open University Press.

Gardner, F (2001) *Self-Harm: A Psychotherapeutic Approach*, Hove: Routledge.

Garnett, L (1992) *Leaving Care and After*, London: National Children's Bureau.

Gay, P (1984) *The Bourgeois Experience: From Victoria to Freud; Volume 1 – Education of the Senses*, Oxford: Oxford University Press.

Ghuman, P (1999) 'Asian Adolescents in the West', Leicester: British Psychological Society Books.

Giddens, A (1991) *Modernity and Self-Identity*, Oxford: Polity Press.

Giedd, J, Blumenthal, J and Jeffries, N (1999) 'Brain development during childhood and adolescence: A longitudinal MRI study', *Nature Neuroscience*, vol. 2, pp. 861–3.

Gilligan, R (2008) 'Promoting resilience in young people in long term care – the relevance of roles and relationships in the domains of recreation and work', *Journal of Social Work Practice*, vol. 22, no. 1, pp. 37–50.

Gluckman, P and Hanson, M (2006) 'Evolution, development and timing of puberty', *Trends Endrocrin Metab*, vol. 17, pp. 7–12.

Graham, P (1986) 'Behavioural and intellectual development in childhood epidemiology', *British Medical Bulletin*, vol. 42, pp. 155–62.

Graham, P (2004) *The End of Adolescence*, Oxford: Oxford University Press.

Green, A (1992) 'A psychoanalyst's point of view concerning psychosis at adolescence', ed. Schwartzberg, A, *International Annals of Adolescent Psychiatry*, Chicago: University of Chicago Press.

Greenberg, H (1975) 'The widening gyre: Transformations of the omnipotent quest during adolescence', *International Review of Psychoanalysis*, pp. 231–44.

Griffin, C (1997) 'Representations of the young', in Roche, J and Tucker, S, *Youth in Society*, London: Sage Publications.

Habermas, J (1994) 'Struggle for recognition in the democratic constitutional state', ed. Gutman, A, *Multiculturalism*, Princeton, NJ: Princeton University Press.

Hale, R (2008) 'Psychoanalysis and suicide: Process and typology', ed. Briggs, S, Lemma, A and Crouch, W, *Relating to Self-harm and Suicide: Psychoanalytic Perspectives on Theory, Practice and Prevention*, London: Routledge.

Hall, S (1988) *Hard Road to Renewal*, London: Verso.

Hall, S (2000) 'Conclusion: The multi-cultural question', ed. Hesse, B, *Un/settled Multiculturalisms*, London: Jed Books.

Hawton, K and Rodham, K (2006) *By Their Own Young Hand: Deliberate Self-Harm and Suicidal Ideas on Adolescents*, London: Jessica Kingsley.

Heimann, P (1950) 'On Countertransference', *International Journal of Psychoanalysis*, vol. 31, pp. 81–4.

Hinshelwood, R (1989) *A Dictionary Of Kleinian Thought*, London: Free Association Books.

Hinshelwood, R (1999) 'Identity and some psychoanalytic implications', *Journal of Melanie Klein and Object Relations*, vol. 17, no. 1, pp. 149–60.

Hollway, W (1989) *Subjectivity and Method in Psychology*, London: Sage Publications.

Hollway, W and Jefferson, T (2000) *Doing Qualitative Research Differently: Free Association, Narrative and the Interview Method*, London: Sage Publications.

Horne, A (2004) '"Gonnae nae do that!" The internal and external worlds of the delinquent adolescent', *Journal of Child Psychotherapy*, vol. 30, no. 3, pp. 330–46.

Hoxter, S (1964) 'The experience of puberty', *Journal of Child Psychotherapy*, vol. 1, no. 2, pp. 13–26.

Irigaray, L (1991) 'This sex which is not one', ed. Gunew, S, *Feminist Knowledge: A Reader*, London: Routledge.

Jacobs, T (1990) 'The no age time: Early adolescence and its consequences', ed. Dowling, S, *Child and Adolescent Analysis: Its Significance for Clinical Work*, Madison, CT: International Universities Press.

Johannsson, T (2007) *The Transformation of Sexuality: Gender and Identity in Contemporary Youth Culture*, Aldershot: Ashgate.

Jones, E (1922) 'Some problems of adolescence', *British Journal of Psychology*, vol. 13, pp. 31–47.

Jones, G (1995) *Leaving Home*, Buckingham: Open University Press.

Jones G (2006) 'The thinking and behaviour of young adults' (pp. 16–25), Literature review for the social exclusion unit, ODPM, www.socialexclusion.gov.uk/downloaddoc.asp?id=786.

Joseph Rowntree Foundation (2001) 'Young men on the margins of work' Findings, York: Joseph Rowntree Foundation, http://www.jrf.org.uk/knowledge/findings/socialpolicy/441.asp.

Kennedy, R (1998) *The Elusive Human Subject: A Psychoanalytic Theory of Subject Relations*, London: Free Association Books.

Kennedy, R (2000) 'Becoming a subject: Some theoretical and clinical issues', *International Journal of Psychoanalysis*, vol. 81, pp. 875–92.

Klein, M (1922) 'On puberty', in Klein, M, *Love Guilt and Reparation and Other Works*, London: Hogarth, 1975 reprint.

Klein, M (1935) 'A contribution to the psychogenesis of manic-depressive states', in Klein, M, *Love Guilt and Reparation and Other Works*, London: Hogarth, 1975 reprint.

Klein, M (1946) 'Notes on some schizoid mechanisms', in Klein, M. *Envy and Gratitude and Other Works*, London: Hogarth, 1975 reprint.

Klein, M (1955) 'On identification', in Klein, M, *Envy and Gratitude and Other Works*, London: Hogarth, 1975 reprint.

Kleinert, S (2007) Adolescent health: An opportunity not to be missed, *The Lancet*, vol. 369, no. 9569, pp. 1057–8.

Kohut, H (1971) 'The analysis of the self. A systematic approach to the psychoanalytic treatment of narcissistic personality disorders', New York: New York International Universities Press.

Kristeva, J (1982) *Powers of Horror: An Essay on Abjection*, New York: Columbia University Press.

Ladame, F (2008) 'Treatment priorities after adolescent suicide attempts', ed. Briggs, S, Lemma, A and Crouch, W, *Relating to Self-Harm and Suicide: Psychoanalytic Perspectives on Theory, Practice and Prevention*, London: Routledge.

Ladame, F and Perret-Catipovic, M (2005) 'How to get young people into treatment: An old challenge – some new promising experiences', BCYP and ISAPP Conference, London, 29 October 2005.

Lash, S (1990) *Sociology of Post Modernism*, London: Routledge.

Laufer, M and Laufer, E (1984) *Adolescence and Developmental Breakdown* London: Karnac.

Laufer, E (1985) 'Loss of the sense of reality about death', ed. Laufer, M, *The Suicidal Adolescent*, London: Karnac.

Lawrence, M (2001) 'Loving them to death: The anorexic and her objects', *International Journal of Psychoanalysis*, vol. 82, pp. 43–55.

Lemma, A (2005) 'The many faces of lying', *International Journal of Psychoanalysis*, vol. 86, no. 3, pp. 737–53.

Lemma, A (2007) 'Being seen or being watched? A psychoanalytic perspective on body dysmorphic disorder', Conference paper, Tavistock Clinic, November 2007.

Lindsey, C (2005) 'Some implications of the children's national service framework for social work practice with regard to child mental health', *Journal of Social Work Practice*, vol. 19, no. 3, pp. 225–34.

Lowe, F (2001) Personal Communication

Lowe, F (2006) 'Containing persecutory anxiety: child and adolescent mental health services and black and minority ethnic communities', *Journal of Social Work Practice*, vol. 20, no. 1, pp. 5–26.

McDougall, J (1986) *Theatre of the Body*, London: Free Association Books.

McLean, G (2005) 'In the hood' The Guardian 13 05 2005 http://www.guardian.co.uk/politics/2005/may/13/fashion.fashionandstyle.

Magagna, J (2000) 'Severe eating difficulties: Attacks on life', ed. Rustin, ME and Quagliata, E, *Assessment in Child Psychotherapy*, London: Duckworths/Tavistock Clinic Series.

Mahler, M (1963) 'Thoughts about development and individuation', *Psychoanalytic Study of the Child*, vol. 8, pp. 307–24.

Mak-Pearce, G (2001) 'Engaging troubled adolescents in six session psychodynamic therapy', ed. Baruch, G, *Community Based Psychotherapy with Young People: Evidence and Innovation in Practice*, Hove: Brunner-Routledge.

Malik, R, Shaikh, A and Suleyman, M (2007) *Providing Faith and Culturally Sensitive Support Services to Young British Muslims*, Leicester: National Youth Agency.

Martin, B (1981) *A Sociology of Contemporary Popular Culture*, Oxford: Blackwell.

Mawson, C (1994) 'Containing anxiety in work with damaged children', ed. Obholzer, A and Roberts, V, *The Unconscious at Work*, London: Routledge.

Meltzer, D (1988) *The Apprehension of Beauty*, Perthshire: Clunie Press.

Menzies Lyth, I (1988) *The Dynamics of the Social: Selected Essays Vol. 2*, London: Free Association Books.

Miller, D (1969) *The Age Between: Adolescents in a Disturbed Society*, London: Cornmarket/Hutchinson.

Miller, L (1998) 'Psychotherapy with learning disabled adolescents', in Anderson, R and Dartington, A, *Facing It Out: Clinical Perspectives on Adolescent Disturbance*, London: Duckworths/Tavistock Clinic Series.

Morris, J (1991) 'Pride against Prejudice' London: Women's Press.

Musick, J (1993) *Young, Poor and Pregnant: The Psychology of Teenage Parenthood*, New Howen, CT: Yale University Press.

NICE (2004) 'The short term physical and psychological management and secondary prevention of self harm in primary and secondary care', NICE clinical guideline, http://www.nice.org.uk/guidance.

NICE (2005) 'Depression in children and young people: Identification and management in primary, community and secondary care', NICE clinical guideline, http://www.nice.org.uk/guidance.

NICE (2006) 'Guidance on the prevention, identification, assessment and management of overweight and obesity in adults and children', NICE clinical guideline, http://www.nice.org.uk/guidance.

Noam, G (1999) 'The psychology of belonging: Reformulating adolescent development', in Esman, A and Flaherty, L, *Adolescent Psychiatry; Development and Clinical Studies*, vol. 24, pp. 49–68.

O'Shaughnessy, E (1999) 'Relating to the Superego', *International Journal of Psychoanalysis*, vol. 80, pp. 861–70.

Papadopolous, R (2002) 'Refugees, home and trauma', ed. Papadopoulos, R, *Therapeutic Care for Refugees, No Place like Home*, London: Karnac Books.

Parekh, B (1991) 'British citizenship and cultural difference', ed. Andrews, G, *Citizenship*, London: Lawrence and Wishart.

Parker, D (2000) 'The Chinese takeaway and the diasporic habitus: Space, time and power geometrics', ed. Hesse, B, *Un/settled Multiculturalisms*, London: Jed Books.

Patel, V, Flissher, A, Hetrick, S and McGarry, P (2007) 'Mental health of young people: A global public-health challenge', *The Lancet*, vol. 369, no. 9569, pp. 1302–13.

Patton, G and Viner, R (2007) 'Pubertal transitions in health', *The Lancet*, vol. 369, no. 9567, pp. 1130–9.

Perelberg, R ed. (1999) *Psychoanalytic Understanding of Violence and Suicide*, London: Karnac Books.

Perret-Catipovic, M and Ladame, F (1998) *Adolescence and Psychoanalysis: The Story and the History*, London: Karnac Books.

Phoenix, A (1991) *Young Mothers*, Oxford: Polity Press.

Pini, M (1997) 'Technologies of the self', in Roche, J and Tucker, S, *Youth in Society*, London: Sage Publications.

Plaut, E and Hutchinson, F (1986) 'The role of puberty in female psychosexual development', *International Review of Psychoanalysis*, vol. 13, pp. 417–32.

Prendergast, S (1995) 'With gender on my mind: Menstruation and embodiment at adolescence', ed. Holland, J, Blair, M and Sheldon, S, *Debates and Issues in Feminist Research and Pedagogy*, Buckingham: Open University Press.

Prendergast, S and Forrest, S (1997) 'Hieroglymphs of the heterosexual: Learning about gender in school', ed. Segal, L *New Sexual Agendas*, Basingstoke: Palgrave Macmillan.

Radonic, Z. (2001) 'The clinician's experience of implementing Audit and its impact on the clinical process in the treatment of troubled young people', ed. Baruch, G, *Community Based Psychotherapy with Young People: Evidence and Innovation in Practice*, Hove: Brunner-Routledge.

Rhode, M (2004) 'Aspects of the body image and sense of identity in a boy with autism: Implications for eating disorders', ed. Williams, G, Williams, P, Desmarais, J and Ravenscroft, K, *Exploring Feeding Difficulties in Children: The Generosity of Acceptance*, vol. 1, London: Karnac Books.

Roberts, K (1995) *Youth and Employment in Modern Britain*, Oxford: Oxford University Press.

Roche, J and Tucker, S. (1997) *Youth in Society*, London: Sage Publications.

Rodriguez de la Sierra, L (2000) 'Working with addicts', in Wise, I, *Adolescence*, London: Institute of Psychoanalysis.

Rosenfeld, H (1987) 'Impasse and interpretation', London: Tavistock.

Ruggiero, I (2006) 'Consultation in adolescence: Hurried, terminable, interminable', *International Journal of Psychoanalysis*, vol. 2006, no. 87, pp. 537–54.

Rustin, ME (2000) 'What follows family breakdown? Assessing children who have experienced deprivation, trauma and multiple loss', ed. Rustin, ME and Quagliata, E, *Assessment in Child Psychotherapy*, London: Duckworths/Tavistock Clinic Series.

Rustin, MJ (1991) *The Good Society and the Inner World*, London: Verso.

Rustin, MJ (1995) 'Lacan, klein and politics: The positive and negative in psychoanalytic thought', ed. Elliott, A and Frosh, S, *Psychoanalysis in Contexts*, London: Routledge.

Sacks, O (1986) *The Man Who Mistook His Wife For a Hat*, London: Picador.

Sayers, J (1991) *Boy Crazy: Remembering Adolescence, Therapies and Dreams*, London: Routledge.

Segal, H (1995) 'From hiroshima to the gulf war and after', ed. Elliott, A and Frosh, S, *Psychoanalysis in Contexts*, London: Routledge.

Shakespeare, W (1611/1996) 'The Winter's Tale', Oxford: Oxford University Press.

Simpson, S (2005) 'Questions and hindsight: Work with Zara, an asylum seeking care leaver', *Journal of Social Work Practice*, vol. 19, no. 3, pp. 263–74.

SIRC (2004) 'Young people "talking not taking" drugs', http://www.sirc.org/publik/talking_not_taking.shtml.

Smith, D and Rutter, M (1995) *Psychosocial Disorders in Young People: Time Trends and Their Causes*, Chichester: John Wiley and Sons.

Sours, J (1981) *Starving to Death in a Sea of Objects*, New York: Aronson.

Souter, A and Kraemer, S (2004) '"Given up hope of dying": A child protection approach to deliberate self-harm in adolescents admitted to a paediatric ward", *Child and Family Social Work*, vol. 9, pp. 259–64.

Srinath, S (1998) 'Identificatory processes in trauma', ed. Garland, C, *Understanding Trauma: A Psychoanalytic Approach*, London: Duckworths/ Tavistock Clinic Series.

Steel, M (2001) 'The Older Person's Guide to Eminem' The Independent 28.08.01 http://www.independent.co.uk/arts-entertainment/music/ features/the-older-persons-guide-to-eminem-667182.html.

Steiner, J (1993) *Psychic Retreats*, London: Routledge.

Stern, D (1985) *The Interpersonal World of the Infant*, New York: Basic Books.

Tan, R (1993) 'Racism and similarity: Paranoid–schizoid structures', *British Journal of Psychotherapy*, vol. 10, no. 1, pp. 33–43.

Thomson, R, Holland, J, McGrellis, S, Bell, R, Henderson, S and Sharpe, S (2004) 'Inventing adulthoods: A biographical approach to understanding youth citizenship', *The Sociological Review*, vol. 52, no. 2, pp. 218–39.

Toumburou, J, Stockwell, T, Neighbors, C, Marlatt, G, Sturge, J and Rehrm, J (2007) 'Interventions to reduce harm associated with adolescent substance use', *The Lancet*, vol. 369, no. 9570, pp. 1391–401.

Tremain, R (1998) *The Way I Found Her*, London: Vintage.

Trevatt, D (2001) 'Working in a school for severely physically disabled children', ed. Baruch, G, *Community Based Psychotherapy with Young People: Evidence and Innovation in Practice*, Hove: Brunner-Routledge.

Turp, M (2008) 'Skin toughening and skin porosity: Addressing the issue of self-harm by omission', ed. Briggs, S, Lemma, A, Crouch, W, *Relating to Self-Harm and Suicide: Psychoanalytic Perspectives on Theory, Practice and Prevention*, London: Routledge.

Urwin, C (1998) 'Power relations and the emergence of language', ed. Henriques, J, Hollway, W and Urwin, C, *Changing the Subject: Psychology, Social Regulation and Subjectivity*, 3rd Edition, London: Routledge.

Van Heeswyk, P (1997) *Analysing Adolescence*, London: Sheldon Press.

Waddell, M (1998) *Inside Lives: Psychoanalysis and the Growth of the Personality*, London: Duckworths/Tavistock Clinic Series.

Waddell, M (2006) 'Narcissism – an adolescent disorder?' *Journal of Child Psychotherapy*, vol. 32, no. 1, pp. 21–34.

Wakelyn, J (2008) 'Transitional psychotherapy for looked – after children in "short-term" foster care', *Journal of Social Work Practice*, vol. 22, no. 1, pp. 27–36.

Walkerdine, V, Lucey, H and Melody, J (2001) *Growing Up Girl: Psychosocial Explorations of Gender and Class*, Basingstoke: Palgrave Macmillan.

Wallis, C (2004) 'What makes teens tick?', *Time*, Monday, 10 May 2004.

Warman, A and Jackson E (2006) 'Recruiting and retaining children and families' social workers: The potential of work discussion groups', *Journal of Social Work Practice*, vol. 21, no. 1, pp. 135–48.

Watson, D and West, J (2001) 'Managing change in residential child care', *Journal of Social Work Practice*, vol. 15, no. 1, pp. 91–101.

West, P and Sweeting, H (2004) 'Fifteen, female and stressed: Changing patterns of psychological distress over time', *Journal of Child Psychology and Psychiatry*, vol. 43, no. 3, pp. 399–411.

Wiener, J and Sher, M (1998) *Counselling and Psychotherapy in Primary Health Care: A Psychodynamic Approach*, Basingstoke: Palgrave Macmillan.

Williams, AH (1978) 'Depression, deviation and acting-out in adolescence', *Journal of Adolescence*, vol. 1, pp. 309–17.

Williams, AH (1998) *Cruelty, Violence and Murder: Understanding the Criminal Mind*, London: Karnac Books.

Williams, G (1997) *Internal Landscapes and Foreign Bodies*, London: Duckworths/Tavistock Clinic Series.

Williams, G (2001) 'Work with parents of psychotic children or adolescents', EFPP Conference, Caen.

Williams, G, Williams, P, Desmarais, J and Ravenscroft, K (2004) *Exploring Feeding Difficulties in Children: The Generosity of Acceptance*, vol. 1, London: Karnac Books.

Williams, S and Bendelow, G (1998) *The Lived Body: Sociological Themes, Embodied Issues*, London: Routledge.

Wilson, P (1996) 'The anti-social tendency', *Journal of Child Psychotherapy*, vol. 22, no. 3, pp. 394–8.

Winnicott, D (1971) *Playing and Reality*, Harmondsworth: Pelican.

Wise, I (2000) *Adolescence*, London: Institute of Psychoanalysis.

Wittenberg, I (1970) *Psycho-Analtyic Insight and Relationships: A Kleinian approach*, London: Routledge & Kegan Paul.

Wren, B (2002) '"I can accept my child is transsexual but if I ever see him in a dress I'll hit him": Dilemmas in parenting a transgendered adolescent', *Clinical Child Psychology and Psychiatry*, vol. 7, no. 3 , pp. 377–97.

Wright, J, Briggs, S and Behringer, J (2005) 'Attachment and the body in suicidal adolescents', *Clinical Child Psychology and Psychiatry*, vol. 10, no. 4, pp. 477–91.

Young, L and Gibb, E (1998) 'Trauma and grievance', ed. Garland, C, *Understanding Trauma: A Psychoanalytic Approach*, London: Duckworths/Tavistock Clinic Series.

Name Index

Subject Index